# My Wound is Deep

### A History of the Later
### Anglo-Scots Wars 1380–1560

My wound is deep; I fain would sleep;
Take thou the vanguard of the three,
And hide me by yon braken bush,
That grows on yonder lilye lee.

*The Battle of Otterburn*

*This book is for Stephanie and Edward,
and in memory of Charlotte.*

# My Wound is Deep

## A History of the Later Anglo-Scots Wars 1380–1560

RAYMOND CAMPBELL PATERSON

JOHN DONALD PUBLISHERS LTD
EDINBURGH

ISBN 0 85976 465 6

*British Library Cataloguing in Publication Data.*

A catalogue record for this book is available
from the British Library.

PostScript Typesetting & Origination by Brinnoven, Livingston.
Printed & bound in Great Britain by J W Arrowsmith Ltd, Bristol.

# Contents

# List of Maps

# Preface

As Edward III neared the end of his life in the early summer of 1377 the war with Scotland had been over for twenty years. But the peace on the Border was a fragile, artificial creation. None of the issues which led to the outbreak of the Wars of Independence in 1296 had been addressed and settled. Edward and his successors continued to claim, when the occasion suited them, to be the feudal overlords of Scotland. There was no final treaty, only an uncertain truce, continually renewed and continually broken. England still held substantial amounts of Scottish territory. On both sides of the Border the marcher lords waited, fully armed, ready to seize any occasion to pursue their bitter personal quarrels.

From the late 1370's a new kind of conflict began to take shape on the Borders, which was to last, on and off, for almost two hundred years. For Scotland the central issue was no longer that of national self preservation, as it had been during the Wars of Independence, but rather an attempt to shake off the legacy of these wars and emerge out of the shadow of England. Even so, there was no certainty that Scotland's political independence was indeed secure. Although, for much of the period this book covers, England was preoccupied with her French wars, and then with a serious dynastic struggle, there were four major invasions of Scotland, as well as countless minor ones. Finally, the emergence of a new aggressive strain in English foreign policy under Henry VIII saw the last phase of the struggle for Scotland's freedom in the years after 1542.

The problem for both countries was that the conflict of the late thirteenth and early fourteenth centuries had created a deep and lasting mutual mistrust. Scotland could never be sure of England's true intentions; England saw Scotland's French alliance as a permanent threat to her national security. Peace proposals failed because Scotland would not end the Auld Alliance. The Treaty of Perpetual Peace in 1502, the first full agreement between the two countries since 1328, was flawed for this very reason, and ended on a cold, wet hillside in Northumberland in 1513.

For Scotland the alliance with France was essential for her national security. James IV took the road to Flodden not in pursuit of conquest or glory, but for the preservation of France. However, the course of the fifteenth century saw a dramatic transformation in the character of the Auld Alliance. The French connection had been particularly valuable to Scotland in the 1330's, when the kingdom's political independence was close to extinction. In the years following the disaster of Agincourt, with England and France locked in a life or death struggle, Scotland had performed an equally valuable service by providing the French with military aid against the almost overwhelming force of Henry V. But with the end of the Hundred Years War France emerged as one of the great European powers, and the alliance was no longer one of equals. As time passed France began to use her partner as a counter to England in a game of European power politics. This became obvious in the late fifteenth and the early sixteenth centuries, when a dangerous struggle emerged between the French royal house of Valois and the Habsburgs of Austria and Spain, into which Scotland was drawn, often against her own national interests. In the end, by one of history's strangest ironies, Scotland was seeking, in alliance with England, to defend its liberty against France.

Flodden was the greatest of all the Border battles. It was also the last great infantry battle of the middle ages. Both armies fought more or less in the same way as their predecessors had at Halidon Hill in 1333 and Neville's Cross in 1346. Although the English longbow was less significant than in the past, it was still used to considerable effect. The Scots had a powerful artillery train, but almost no skill in its use. After Flodden the art of warfare underwent a profound change. In continental Europe the French led the way in the use of artillery. New techniques in fortification began to replace the old medieval castles, which were vulnerable to concentrated gun fire. Heavy cavalry, long considered to be obsolescent, acquired a new significance after the French defeated the Swiss pikemen at the Battle of Margiano in 1515. Although the English were slow to change from their traditional reliance on the longbow, by the end of the reign of Henry VIII they had learned much from their experience on the Continent. Scotland was simply too backward economically to keep up with these changes. The host that was called out to face the English invasion of 1547 was little different from that summoned by Robert Bruce in 1314.

Yet despite the advances in military thinking England was no nearer conquering Scotland in the sixteenth century than she had been in the fourteenth. English generals could win battles against Scotland, often with considerable ease, but they could not hold the country. Protector Somerset, acting for the underage Edward VI, won a resounding victory at the Battle of Pinkie near Musselburgh in 1547, but he faced the same problems of transport and supply that had frustrated Edward I in the 1300's. The garrisons he established throughout south east Scotland in the late 1540's were well equipped and fortified; but the soldiers were isolated for months on end, starved of even the most basic necessities. The problem of maintaining garrisons in hostile territory was not to be solved until the days of the great German general Wallenstein during the Thirty Years War in the first half of the seventeenth century. Learning from his example, Oliver Cromwell was the first Englishman in history to complete a successful and lasting conquest of Scotland.

After Henry IV's invasion of 1400 no other English king came in arms to Scotland, preferring to leave matters to wardens, lieutenants and other appointees. Successive English sovereigns neglected the north because of economic problems, civil disturbances and involvement in continental war. One way of achieving their ends in Scotland without the expense and risk of full scale invasion was to make use of rebel or disaffected factions within the country. From the time of Henry IV the MacDonald Lords of the Isles, anxious to secure their independence from Scotland, were often to seek alliance with England. From time to time other rebel noblemen looked for English assistance against their lawful sovereign. The problem became particularly acute in the sixteenth century, especially after the humiliating debacle of Solway Moss in 1542, when a number of important Scots noblemen were released from captivity after agreeing to serve the English King. The fact that Scotland preserved its independence despite the best efforts of a portion of the governing class says much for the determination of the ordinary people of the realm to resist the English, whatever the cost.

It was, of course, always the ordinary people who bore the brunt of the perennial Anglo-Scots conflicts, particularly on the Borders where the long wars forged a unique frontier community. To begin with it was the local nobility, the Percies of Northumberland and the Douglases of southern Scotland, who guided these nascent warrior societies; but when their power was broken by central government smaller family groups or 'clans' emerged into the foreground of the Border struggle: an asset in times of war; a liability in times of peace. Invasion and the threat of invasion precluded the development of normal commercial life and a settled agrarian economy. It made cross Border raiding or reiving virtually a daily occurrence, regardless of the political relations between the two countries.

The reiver, whether Scots or English, was rarely concerned with issues of national politics, but his activities would often provide the pretext for the renewal of full scale war. Unsettled conditions on the Borders led to the creation of special march or Border laws and the appointment of wardens on both sides of the divide who were charged with enforcing them. These men, often drawn from local families, were expected to combine the role of soldier, diplomat, lawman and spymaster all in one. But it proved to be a virtually impossible task to preserve the peace, even when the will was present. With the final end of the Auld Alliance in 1560, and the obsolescence of the old claim of feudal superiority, all of the main political issues between England and Scotland were largely settled; but forays by the Armstrongs, Grahams and the other warrior clans got steadily worse. It wasn't until King James VI, the greatest reiver of all, crossed the Border in 1603 to claim the English throne as his prize that a final peace began to settle on the old frontier.

The story I am now setting out to tell begins where my previous book *For The Lion. A History of the Scottish Wars of Independence* left off. For her help and assistance my thanks are due, once again, to my wife, Fiona Spencer Paterson.

Edinburgh, 1997                                                            *R C P*

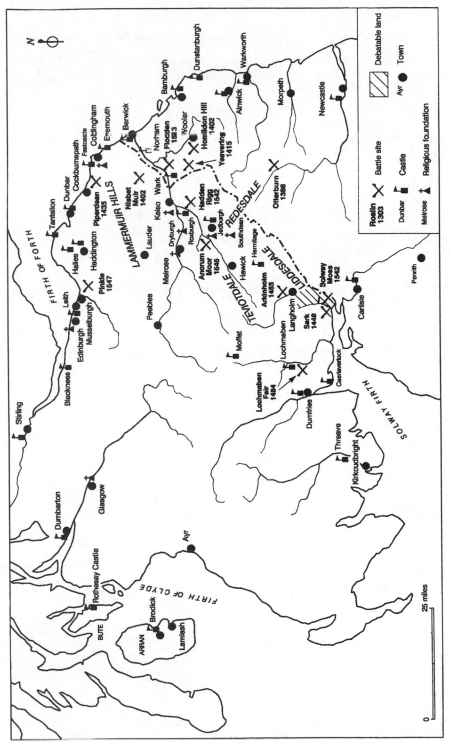

Map 1. *The Border Wars, 1380–1560.*

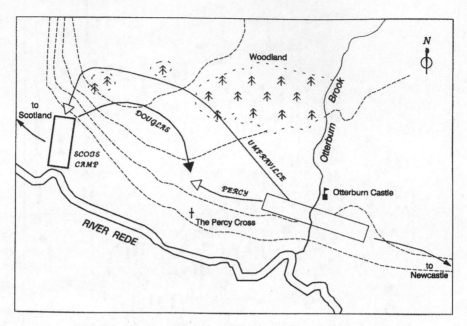

Map 2. *The Battle of Otterburn, 19–20 August 1388.*

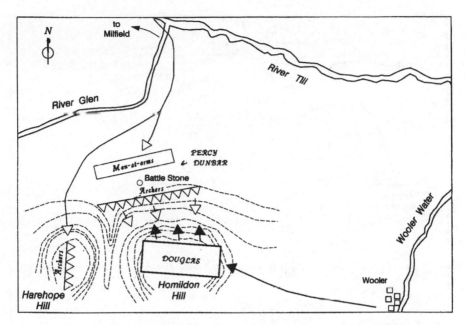

Map 3. *The Battle of Homildon Hill, 14 September 1402.*

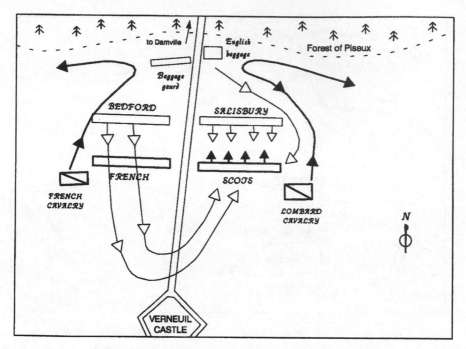

Map 4. *The Battle of Verneuil, 17 August 1424.*

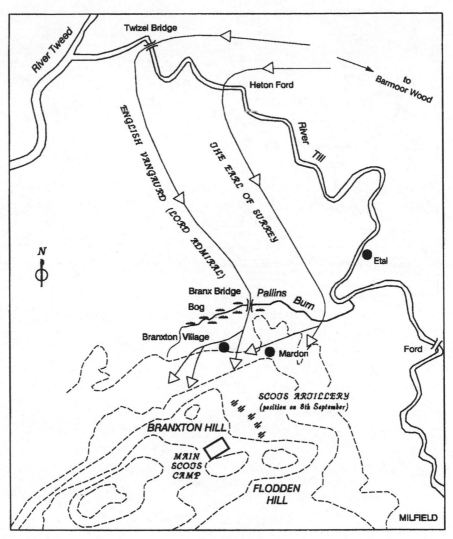

Map 5. *Surrey's March to Flodden, 8/9 September 1513.*

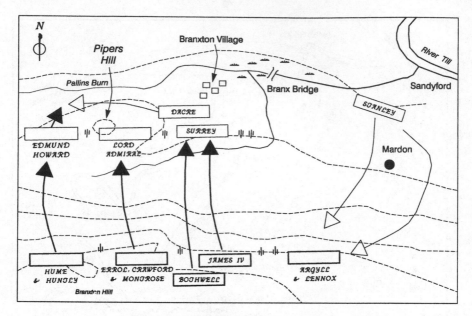

Map 6. *The Battle of Flodden, 9 September 1513.*

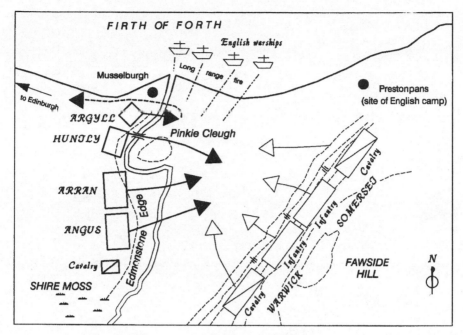

FIRTH OF FORTH

English warships

Musselburgh

Long range fire

to Edinburgh

ARGYLL

Prestonpans
(site of English camp)

HUNTLY

Pinkie Cleugh

ARRAN

Edmonstone Edge

Cavalry

ANGUS

Cavalry

SOMERSET

Infantry

Infantry

Infantry

WARWICK

FAWSIDE
HILL

N

Cavalry

SHIRE MOSS

Map 7. *The Battle of Pinkie, 10 September 1547.*

# CHAPTER 1
# Ill Met by Moonlight

I never heard the old song of Percy and Douglas that I found my heart more moved than with a trumpet.

*Sir Philip Sydney*

When Edward III died in June 1377 his legacy to his ten year old successor, King Richard II, was an unfinished war with France and an uncertain peace with Scotland. The problem on the northern frontier was particularly acute. While England recognised that the attempts to conquer Scotland between 1296 and 1356 had all been expensive failures, she was reluctant to abandon either her imperial pretence or the remaining territory she still held in the south of the country. In the west English troops controlled Annandale from the old Bruce stronghold of Lochmaben Castle; and in the east they still held much of Roxburghshire and Berwickshire, with strong garrisons at Jedburgh, Roxburgh and the town of Berwick itself, the headquarters of the occupation regime. The security of these territories was delegated to the northern families of Neville, Dacre and, above all, the Percies of Alnwick, whose chief, Henry Percy, was created Earl of Northumberland shortly after Richard's succession.

For the Scots the political demarcations in the south were a constant reminder of English aggression during the Wars of Independence. While they had been obliged to recognise the English presence as part of past truce agreements, the occupation had not been accepted in any definitive peace treaty. It was particularly aggravating to the Earls of Douglas and March, both of whom had traditional claims to lands in the area. The bitter feud between the Percies and Douglases over Jedworth Forest dominated the Borders for many years. For these men national politics and personal prestige became closely linked, creating a volatile, dangerous atmosphere. The ragged Border was set to become the nursery for a new war.

Robert II, the first of the Stewart Kings of Scotland, who came to the throne in 1371, was concerned by the possibility of fresh English aggression. Although the truce of 1370 was not due

1

expire until February 1384, Robert's anxieties about national security led to a renewal of the French alliance shortly after he was crowned, the first of many such renewals over the next two hundred years. Fearful of the mighty Edward III he was not, however, prepared to take the risk of going to war in the short term, despite French inducements to do so.

After the death of Edward the political situation underwent a dramatic change. England was now ruled by a minor, and her government divided by the rivalries of his uncles, headed by John of Gaunt, Duke of Lancaster. This was too good an opportunity to let pass. Regardless of the truce, and the feelings of King Robert, the Border lords began an unofficial war against their English counterparts. George Dunbar of March nibbled away at English outposts in the Merse and attacked Annandale, while William, the first Earl of Douglas, began operations in Teviotdale. Before long the general situation became too dangerous for English tax gatherers to go about their business. Worse was too follow. In August 1377 the English gathered for the annual fair at Roxburgh, a town they controlled from the nearby castle. March, angered by the murder of one of his retainers, arrived at the burgh early in the morning with a large body of armed followers. What happened is described by the chronicler Pluscarden:

> He then surrounded and hemmed in the town of Roxburgh where the crowd of people was thickest, and made such slaughter and pillage of the English at the same fair, that not a single one of those who were there escaped out of his hands; nor did he give quarter to any male, but massacred them all and delivered them to the edge of the sword; and even such as retreated into the houses and defended themselves he burnt to death.

Military action was not confined to land. In the North Channel Scottish privateers attacked English shipping, raided northern Ireland and carried their activities as far south as Wales. In 1378 Andrew Mercer, the son of a prominent Perth merchant, headed a Franco Scottish squadron against English merchantmen in the North Sea, and sacked Scarborough, a town which had given particular offence to his family.

In London the deteriorating condition of the marches was so alarming that King Richard ordered the Bishop of Durham, to go north with his household to assist in repelling Scots attacks. But despite the best efforts of both the Bishop and the Earl of

2

Northumberland, the situation did not improve. The following year a party of Scots adventurers even managed to capture Berwick Castle. Although it was quickly retaken by the Earl of Northumberland, this attack on English power on the frontier was clearly a serious blow to national prestige. A reprisal raid by Northumberland and his son, the famous Harry 'Hotspur', met with mixed success. Although the English devastated parts of southern Scotland, one of their columns under Sir Thomas Musgrave, the warden of Berwick, was intercepted near Melrose and defeated in a fierce engagement with the Earl of Douglas. Musgrave, his son and many other Englishmen were taken prisoner. The marches became so dangerous that Northumberland was obliged to report to the Royal Council that the warden of Lochmaben Castle had refused to remain in his post any longer, and had taken to his heels.

Inevitably the growing violence spilled over from the occupied regions of southern Scotland into the northern counties of England. In retaliation for Northumberland's raids the Earl of Douglas led the most serious incursion into England since the Wars of Independence. In 1380 he crossed the western march with a large force and fanned out across Cumberland and Westmorland. From the Forest of Inglewood the Scots drove off a huge booty in livestock. Penrith was sacked on its fair day and many smaller settlements were destroyed. The chronicler Walsingham claims that these raids turned northern England into a desert, and that the Scots were so savage that they even played football with the heads of their dead enemies. But the ardour of the invaders was cooled by an outbreak of plague, which they carried with them back north, where the spread of the disease led to the following prayer:

> Gode and Saint Mungo, Saint Romayn and Saint Andrew,
> schield us this day fro Goddis grace, and the foule death that
> the Englishmen dien upon.

Clearly, if this smouldering conflict were allowed to continue, the two countries would, once again, descend into full scale war. But the English government, headed by John of Gaunt, was anxious to preserve the tattered peace. Gaunt, who had a claim in right of his second wife to the throne of the Spanish kingdom of Castile, was particularly keen to avoid complications with Scotland. There was even some suspicion in London that the English marcher lords,

3

charged with preserving the truce, were more interested in pursuing their feud with the Scots. It was certainly true that the Percies, who, as wardens of the march, were allowed to maintain private armies at public expense, had more to gain by war than by peace. Believing it was possible to improve relations with the Scots the government appointed Gaunt in 1379 and again in 1381 as lieutenant on the marches, a serious blow to the power of the local nobility, especially Northumberland.

Using the fourteen year truce of 1370 as a basis for discussions Gaunt did his best to secure a peace within a peace. He also made it plain to his Scottish counterparts in the negotiations what the implications of failure would be. In an attempt to arrest further Scots encroachments on the frontier, he appeared at a March or truce day in October 1380 with a grand retinue of no less than 14 bannerets, 162 knights, 1492 squires, and 1670 archers: an impressive display of 'peaceful' force which cost the government some £5,000. This worked — up to a point. The truce was renewed and it appeared that King Robert was genuine in his desire for better relations. But he depended on the goodwill of his powerful Border barons, who, like the Percies, were not keen to accept restraint. There seems also to have been a growing distrust of Gaunt in the English Royal Council, where it was felt that in order to pursue his ambitions in Spain, he may have been prepared to surrender too much to the Scots. To prevent this he was told to make no territorial concessions in his continuing negotiations. Ultimately Gaunt failed because neither side was willing to agree terms which might have formed the basis of a permanent peace.

The truce was due to expire on 2 February 1384, and nobody appeared willing to extend it. In the spring of 1383 the English negotiating position began to harden, demonstrating, perhaps, that Gaunt's influence was beginning to decline. In May they demanded that all of the lands captured by the Scots since 1376 should be returned. In the following January they followed this up by threatening to invade the country if the balance of David II's ransom was not paid — 24,000 merks was still outstanding — and if Robert did not agree to pay homage to Richard. Alarmed by this new aggressive note, the Scots turned to France. In August 1383 Robert entered into a new agreement with Charles VI, promising to renew the war in return for 40,000 gold francs, 1000 suits of armour, and the assistance of 1000 men-at-arms.

Even before the truce expired the Scots Borderers launched an unusually large raid into Northumberland. The government apologised and blamed 'irresponsible' elements on the Borders, even offering to renew the truce. But soon after Lochmaben Castle in Annandale, held by the English since 1333, was attacked by a force led by the Earls of March and Douglas, and by Douglas's kinsman, Archibald the Grim, Lord of Galloway. The English, despite the warnings, were unprepared for this. All attempts to relieve the castle from Carlisle were successfully parried, and the commander, Sir William Featherston, surrendered on 4 February, after a siege of only two days. To prevent it being retaken it was razed to the ground in accordance with the military teachings of Robert Bruce. Fearing that this success would be followed up by an attack on Roxburgh, Ralph, Baron of Graystoke was sent with a body of troops to reinforce the garrison; but he was ambushed by the Earl of March at Benrig seven miles to the west of the castle and taken prisoner.

All of this was too much for Richard, now close to manhood. Gaunt was given a special commission to invade Scotland and avenge the loss of Annandale. Scotland was now faced with the most serious English invasion since Edward III's Burnt Candelmas of 1356; yet, when it came, it was a surprisingly mild affair. The Duke crossed the Border on 4 April with a large army and advanced up the east coast rout towards Edinburgh, supported by a fleet. He clearly hoped to trap the Scots in battle, but they had not yet forgotten the dangers of facing the English longbowmen, and simply withdrew before the invader, drawing him ever deeper into a hostile country in the time honoured manner, finally slipping out of reach beyond the Forth. The English navy landed on Inchcolm Island in the Forth and ravaged the abbey. But Lancaster himself, however frustrated he may have been by his elusive enemy, was mindful of the hospitality he had received in Scotland when he had taken refuge there during the Peasants Revolt in 1381, and refused to allow his troops to destroy Edinburgh. A party of English soldiers managed to land in Fife and set fire to a few villages, but had to flee back to their ships after being attacked by a Scots force. Running short of supplies and with weather conditions beginning to deteriorate, Lancaster had no choice but to withdraw to Berwick. By April 23 he was back in Durham. His campaign had been so devoid of large scale destruction that the English monastic chroniclers complained that he did not even bother to burn the Border abbeys, an oversight to be made good by his nephew in the following year.

Lancaster's invasion was a clear strategic failure and marks the beginning of the end of his involvement with Scotland. Unable to force the Scots into battle or to get them to accept peace terms, he was forced to conclude that matters were best left to the northern nobility, well used to the traditional tactics of raid and counter raid. The government simply could not afford to maintain a large standing army on the march, and had to rely on the Percies, Nevilles, Graysokes and Dacres to raise the necessary force, as and when it was needed. The danger in this, of course, was that the initiative passed once again to the northern magnates whose aims did not always coincide with those of the King. Their resentment of any kind of outside interference was one of the factors that led to the fall of Richard II in 1399.

After the withdrawal of Lancaster the Scots took the offensive. Earl William of Douglas began the systematic reconquest of Teviotdale, a campaign so successful that in the words of Andrew of Wyntoun:

> ...nouwir fur na fut of lande
> Was at thar pessse than of Inglande,
> Outtane Berwik and castellis twa,
> Roxburgh and Jedworde war
> Bot al that war withe out ye wall
> War at Scottis mennys saye all.

William died shortly after the conclusion of the Teviotdale operation and was succeeded as Earl by his son James, soon to acquire immortal fame.

The new Earl joined with the King's son John of Carrick in his determination to pursue an aggressive policy on the Borders, even against the wishes of the more pacific Robert. Shortly after John of Gaunt's departure a body of French envoys arrived at the court of Robert II announcing that at Leulighen earlier in the year King Charles had concluded a truce with England in which Scotland was included, if she wished. Clearly aware of the dangers of facing England on his own Robert was keen to accept this break in hostilities. But in the wake of the diplomats a party of French knights, led by Geoffrey de Charny, also came to Scotland looking for trouble. Their appeal for action was simply too much for the group of young noblemen around Douglas and Carrick to ignore, and the King, a man well advanced in years and of no great authority, was effectively overruled. Douglas and Carrick led the Frenchmen south in June in a raid into Northumberland, where the lands of Percy and Mowbray were ravaged.

During this season a party of Scots managed once again to take Berwick Castle, which was held briefly while Henry Percy was attending parliament. Censured by his fellow peers for negligence, the humiliated Earl hurried back north, keen to take revenge. But the Scots resisted all of his best efforts to retake the castle by assault, and he was reduced to bribing them to leave. Thereafter Northumberland, assisted by the Earl of Nottingham, launched his own counter raid into southern Scotland. Honour then seems to have been satisfied on both sides and Scotland accepted incorporation in the Truce of Leulighen, destined to last until 1 May 1385.

Despite this there was no real desire for peace. In both Scotland and France the truce simply provided a breathing space to allow them to regroup and plan fresh hostilities against the old enemy. In November the government of Scotland was taken from the feeble Robert and given to his eldest son John, the ally of the Earl of Douglas, signalling the adoption of a more warlike policy. In Paris, King Charles and his council formulated plans for a two pronged attack on England when the truce expired in May. At the port of Sluys in the Low Countries a fleet and army was assembled to invade southern England. This was to be supported by a cross Border invasion by the Scots. To encourage his allies Charles sent the subsidy and military support promised in the treaty of 1383. During the winter an expeditionary force of 2000 men-at-arms, knights, esquires, cross-bowmen and other infantrymen was fitted out, ready to sail to Scotland in the spring. It was commanded by Jean de Vienne, Comte de Valentinois and Admiral of France, who also came with 1400 spare suits of armour and the agreed financial subsidy, to be divided amongst the King and the leading nobles.

The French fleet set sail and landed at Leith and Dunbar at the beginning of May. This was to date the largest party of Frenchmen ever to set foot in Scotland. Trouble began almost at once. There was simply nowhere to billet such a large body of men with their attendants and equipment. They had to be split up and sent to various places, including Dunbar, Dalkeith, Dunfermline and even as far away as Kelso. Scotland's backwardness and poverty was a shock to the French, used to much greater comfort than the country could provide. The chronicler Froissart describes their reaction;

> ...it is a poore countre...and whan that provisyon falyeth, there is none to gette in the countre. Whan the barownes and knightes of Fraunce who were wonte to fynde fayre hostryes, halles hanged, and goodly castelles, and softe beddes to rest in, sawe themselves in that necessitie, they began to smyle, and said to the admyrall, Sir, what pleasure hath brought us hynder? We never knewe what povertie meant tyll nowe.

The Scots themselves found the French uncomfortable and arrogant allies. In their own land the knights were used to commandeering whatever they wanted, regardless of the feelings of the common people. But when they sent out foragers into the Scots countryside over 100 of them were killed by the outraged peasantry. Poverty had created a kind of rough democracy which the French found intolerable, describing Scotland as a second Prussia for desolation and savagery. After a few weeks they were obliged to enter into a formal agreement with the government, which, amongst other things, forced them to accept the necessity of paying for all they received.

Only in making war on the English did the French and Scots find a common purpose. The Scots host was assembled on the orders of the King, and the allies, all wearing the cross of Saint Andrew, advanced to the Border in July. Roxburgh, too strong to be taken by assault, was bypassed. The Franco Scots crossed the eastern march and successfully attacked the smaller fortresses of Wark, Ford and Cornhill, before ravaging the countryside between Berwick and Newcastle. But the wet weather had a bad effect on morale. Hearing of the approach of a powerful English army the decision was taken to fall back over the Border. By this time it was also clear that the grand strategy of crushing England between a northern hammer and a southern anvil had failed to materialise. De Vienne and the Scots were now dangerously exposed.

For Richard in London the military situation in the early summer was alarming: the French were in the north and a large force was also known to be gathering in Flanders. But as time passed it was clear that the projected invasion of southern England was not going to come. The town dwellers of the Low Countries, traditional allies of the English, were creating difficulties for the French, whose expedition finally had to be aborted. Richard and his council therefore decided to gather a grand army and invade Scotland, the campaign to be headed by the King himself, in what was to be his first — and last — taste of war. A summons was sent out commanding the host to meet Richard at Newcastle on 14 July. Altogether 13,734 troops were assembled — 4,590 men-at-arms and 9,144 archers — the largest contingent being supplied by John of Gaunt. The whole force crossed the eastern Border on 6 August, the largest enemy army to enter Scotland since Edward III's invasion of 1335. With it came a Welshman called Owen Glendower, destined to acquire fame in another field of war altogether.

Richard was also accompanied by a rather more sinister figure — Henry le Despenser, Bishop of Norwich. At this time western Christendom was divided between rival popes, with England following Pope Urban in Rome and Scotland Pope Clement in Avignon. In 1383 Despenser, a cold blooded fanatic, had led a murderous 'crusade' against the supporters of Clement in Flanders, and his presence on Scottish soil was to justify the coming destruction of the Border abbeys. The author of the *Westminster Chronicle* describes the army's progress:

> That night the king encamped with his army in the forest of Ettrick, causing to be put to death all the Scots and Frenchmen he was able to take prisoner...From this point they moved on for about a week towards Melrose Abbey, giving free and uninter-rupted play to slaughter, rapine, and fire raising all along a six mile front and leaving the entire countryside in ruins behind them; and Melrose Abbey itself, since it provided harbour to our enemies, was swallowed up in devouring flame. From there as far as the Scottish Sea (the Firth of Forth) they laid waste to the whole territory of Lothian, driving their adversaries, French and Scots alike, before them, burning down every place and castle... in which their enemy had refreshed themselves, and reducing Newbattle Abbey to dust.

The situation, however, was not quite as the chronicler says. Richard was faced with the same scorched earth policy that had often frustrated his ancestors. What could be moved from his path was moved. The country people took refuge in the hills with their livestock and goods. Douglas and the other Scots commanders declined to give battle, simply falling away before the English, preferring to allow them to flounder in the mud. The countryside was said to be so empty that even the birds had taken wing, with the single exception of owls. By the time Richard reached Edinburgh many of his soldiers were falling sick and some were beginning to die of hunger.

Leaving a small force to shadow Richard and pick off stragglers, the Earl of Douglas with Archibald the Grim and Jean de Vienne slipped over the west march and began a major raid in Cumberland and Westmorland. An attack on Carlisle failed, but the undefended countryside was put to fire and sword, the raiders carrying the destruction as far south as Penrith.

At Edinburgh Richard was faced with a dilemma. His provision fleet had failed to arrive and the army was seriously short of supplies. He had been no more successful than his uncle had been the previous year in bringing his elusive enemy to battle. He had no siege equipment with him and the Scots still held the castle. A council of war was held and Gaunt recommended that the army either continue the advance into the north of Scotland or push across the country and intercept Douglas and de Vienne on their way back from England. But Richard declined to move further, using the occasion to heap petulant insults on his uncle, reminding him of his disastrous campaign in France during the twilight years of the previous reign, when he had lost half his army to hunger and disease. Stung by this rebuke Gaunt agreed to accompany his nephew back to Berwick. Before the end of August the army had returned to Newcastle, their only battle honours being the smouldering ruins of Melrose, Dryburgh, Newbattle and Saint Giles in Edinburgh. The great campaign had been another expensive fiasco, crashing to ruin against a Scottish policy of non resistance.

With the departure of the English there was no more reason for the French to remain. The country did not have the capacity or resources to feed and house them over the winter season, and they had proved themselves of limited value when it came to the cut and thrust of Border warfare. The French themselves, finding little glory in Scotland, were anxious to return home; but they were not allowed to do so until they had paid for the damage they caused and the goods they had received. The allies, rarely comfortable with each other at close quarters, parted on very poor terms. It is even suggested by Froissart that the French expressed the wish that England and France make peace so that their Kings could join together and come to Scotland '...utterly to destroy that realm for ever.'

In essence the whole episode was ill conceived, with no thought given to the logistical difficulties of maintaining such a large force. It is best summarised by the nineteenth century historian Patrick Fraser Tytler who said:

> ...the great causes of failure are to be traced to the impossibility of reconciling two systems of military operations so perfectly distinct as those of the Scots and French, and of supporting, for any length of time, in so poor a country as Scotland, such a force as was able to offer battle to the English with any fair prospect of success.

With their inconvenient allies out of the way the Scots closed the campaigning season by embarking on a fresh attack on England. Douglas, accompanied by Robert, Earl of Fife, the younger brother of John of Carrick, crossed the Solway sands and raided Cockermouth, a part of England apparently untouched since the time of Robert Bruce. The country was such a rich source of plunder that they remained for three days collecting booty. Thereafter conditions on the Border settled down, and the Scots agreed to a truce on 24 October, which was successively extended to June 1388.

In England few of the senior nobility were impressed with Richard either as a soldier or a king. His campaign in Scotland had been wasteful and unproductive. He was surrounded, moreover, by a clique of unpopular favourites, in much the same manner as his great grandfather Edward II. The nobles also looked back wistfully to the vanished glory of Edward III. Richard was altogether too pacific for their taste. With the support of parliament a group of noblemen, known as the Lords Appellant, took control of the government in the spring of 1388. But they proved themselves to be no more competent than the discredited King. Their mismanagement of the nation's affairs was directly responsible for the greatest military disaster of Richard's reign.

The truce with Scotland was due to expire on 19 June. No steps were taken either to extend it or to strengthen the defences of the north. To make matters worse, a serious quarrel had arisen between the Percies and Nevilles, who carried the responsibility for the defence of the Border. For the Scots this opportunity was too good to miss.

The storm broke in late June when the Scots launched raids across both the east and west march. Following the success of this 'reconnaissance in strength' their tactics became bolder. Sir William Douglas of Nithsdale, an illegitimate son of Archibald the Grim, crossed the Irish sea, sacked Carlingford in the north of Ireland, and ravaged the Isle of Man before returning to his base in Galloway. But the worst blow came later in the summer. By the end of July a large concentration of Scots troops had built up in Jedworth Forest. The leaders held a council of war at the church of Southdean, about ten miles south west of Jedburgh. Here it was decided to launch a two pronged attack into England: the main spearhead was to cross the west march into Cumberland, and in support of this a diversionary attack was to be made across the Reidswire into north east England. The western thrust was to be led by the Earl of Fife, and that in the east by the Earl of Douglas, supported by the Earls of Dunbar and Moray. It was important for this smaller force — some 6,000 men — to be as hard hitting and as mobile as possible to deceive the English into believing that it was the vanguard of a larger invasion army.

In England the Earl of Northumberland, locked in the fastness of Alnwick Castle, realised that he was faced with something more alarming than the usual hit and run raid. With no help coming from the south, and with insufficient force available to him to meet the Scots in the field, he sent his sons Henry and Ralph to see to the defence of Newcastle. Beyond that there was nothing more he could do other than continue the build up of local levies. With his troops concentrating at Alnwick and Newcastle it was clear that he believed that the main blow would fall in the east.

In early August Fife's force — said to have been 20,000 strong — began operations in Cumberland. At the same time Douglas ascended the Cheviots by Reidswire, crossing the Border at Carter Bar, and then past Ottercrops Hill and Rothley Crags. The Tyne was forded above Newcastle, the advance continuing as far as Branspeth in County Durham. So far the speed of his attack had enabled him to evade detection; but once into Durham the smoke rising from the outlying homesteads announced the presence of the Scots to the whole countryside. Douglas continued his destructive swathe through the county, collecting much booty in the process, before recrossing the Tyne and advancing on Newcastle. Here the Percy brothers, expecting a major siege, made ready to defend the recently constructed town walls.

In the west, aside from the garrison at Carlisle, there appear to have been no troops capable of resisting Fife. Lacking siege engines he tried to take the city by assault, but the defences were too strong. He lost 540 men who were either killed or captured, although he managed to capture the sheriff, Peter de Tilliol and 300 other prisoners. The countryside was at his mercy. Taking advantage of this he fanned out across the area as far as Brough in Westmorland. Appleby was seized and destroyed as were most of the villages in the Eden Valley. But news from the east forced him to draw his operations to a premature halt and return to Scotland.

Behaving with considerable boldness Douglas led repeated attacks on the defences of Newcastle between 15 and 17 August. This was a risky move: he was not equipped to carry out a siege; Newcastle was one of the main muster points for English troops in the north; it is likely there were more soldiers inside defending the town than were outside attacking; and with Northumberland at Alnwick there was always a danger that his retreat would be cut off. But the very audacity of Douglas's actions had the effect of convincing the English that his force was indeed only the vanguard of a much larger army close by. Frequent skirmishes took place at the outer defences of the western wall. In Froissart's account Douglas is said to have captured Harry Hotspur's own pennon, although this story reads as if it has been added to provide some romantic colour, a technique in which the chronicler excels.

When Hotspur awoke on the morning of the 18th it was to find that the Scots had vanished during the night. By now the deception was clear and he determined to set off in pursuit with all haste, before his enemy slipped back across the Border. Hotspur had at his disposal some 8,000 troops, and true to his impetuous nature he decided to set off once his force was organised, rather than wait for reinforcements promised by John de Fordham, the Bishop of Durham.

After leaving Newcastle, Douglas moved in a north westerly direction, making for the valley of the River Rede, intending to take the same route back to Scotland by which he had entered England. He was in no particular hurry despite the obvious danger of his situation. His force was, of course, weighed down with plundered livestock and other booty; but when he reached the tower of Ponteland a few miles to the north west of Newcastle he paused to attack this unimportant obstacle, thus alerting Hotspur to the direction of his retreat. The tower was defended by Amyer de Atholl, a descendant of the Scottish Earls of Atholl who had gone over to the English during the Wars of Independence. Ponteland fell and Atholl was taken prisoner.

By the evening of the same day the Scots reached the valley of the River Rede at a place called Otterburn. Here Douglas set up camp astride the road, with his right flank close to the river and his left stretching out on the slope leading up to the moors, approximately one mile beyond Otterburn Tower. Most of the following day, Wednesday 19 August, was spent on an unsuccessful assault on the tower. With his men tired by their exertions Douglas prepared to settle down for another night by the banks of the Rede. Believing himself to be safe from attack he did not even take the precaution of posting sentries, an action suggesting a dangerous degree of overconfidence. But for the outcome of what was to follow history is likely to have passed a very different verdict on the second Earl of Douglas.

Hotspur made good progress in his march from Newcastle, but it is likely that he believed his enemy to be further ahead. When he entered the valley of the Rede in the dying summer light of the 19th he was simply looking for a place to camp: his men were tired and stretched out in a long column reaching back to Ponteland. But there, a short distance to his front, were the Scots. Two choices were open to him: to wait for the morning, allowing his men to rest and regroup before beginning the battle, thus allowing the usual English superiority in the longbow to have its full effect; or to take the high risk strategy of beginning an immediate attack, hoping to gain the advantage of surprise. Hotspur would not wait for dawn: battle would be joined at once. To prevent the Scots slipping away he detached part of his force under Sir Thomas Umfraville and his brother Robert with Sir Thomas Grey, Sir Robert Ogle and Sir Matthew Redmayn on a wide sweep to the north, past the Scottish left flank and then, in the words of John Hardyng's chronicle, to 'holde them in that they fled not away' while the main body of the army launched a frontal attack.

With the sudden approach of the English in the fading light there was considerable confusion in the Scottish camp, which was taken completely by surprise. Pluscarden describes the scene:

> They rose at once and rushed to arms, but scarcely could a bare half of them arm themselves. The earl of Douglas also rose, and in his haste could hardly put on his armour or fasten it with the

14

buckles, owing to the confusion of the sudden onslaught of the enemy; so he rushed forward with uncovered face to marshal the line of battle...

Gathering as many of his men as he could Douglas began a daring counter attack that was to win him a battle and immortality. He approached Percy's right flank to the north, racing swiftly along a wooded hillside, with a slight depression covering his approach for the last 200 yards, before falling on the astonished Englishmen in the silver light of the summer moon with loud cries of A Douglas! A Douglas! The ensuing battle was one of the strangest in all the Anglo Scottish wars. Because of the poor visibility Percy was unable to make effective use of his archers. Each man fought in a grim hand to hand contest with only enough light to see for a short distance around him. The spectral combat paused whenever clouds flitted across the face of the Moon, allowing all a welcome rest in the brief darkness, only to begin again with renewed vigour when the wind carried them past. In these conditions the struggle continued for several hours amidst the shrieks of the wounded and dying, over ground slippery with blood. At some point during the night Earl James was mortally wounded, but by whom and in what manner is not known, despite Froissart's theatrical account. Andrew of Wyntoun simply says:

> Bot ye Erll James thar was slane
> That na man wist on quhat manere.

His body was found the following morning stripped of his armour and with a great wound in his neck. Unaware of his death his comrades fought on, steadily pushing the English downhill. After plundering the Scots camp Umfraville's unit returned to aid the main force; but this did not affect the outcome of the battle. As dawn broke Harry Hotspur's army began to crumble, with men fleeing the battlefield in increasing numbers. Hotspur was taken prisoner, as was his brother Ralph, who had been badly wounded. They were joined in captivity by Sir Ralph Langley, Sir Robert Ogle, Sir John Lilburn, Sir Thomas Walsingham, Sir John Felton, Sir John Coupland, Sir Thomas Abingdon and many others. Altogether over 1800 men were slain or captured. A number of Scots were also taken prisoner in their over hasty pursuit of the English, including Sir James Lindsay of Crawford who set off after Sir Matthew Redmayn, only to be taken by the Bishop of Durham's men.

When the Battle of Otterburn was being fought the Bishop was on his way from Newcastle with 2000 cavalry and 5000 infantry. They arrived at Ponteland on the morning of the 20th, where they were met by groups of men fleeing from the field, which had such a demoralising effect that the whole force retired back to Newcastle.

The principal cause of the English defeat at Otterburn is simply stated — Hotspur was a brave soldier but a bad commander, a truth succinctly summarised by the *Westminster Chronicle*:

> The calamity that befell our countrymen on this occasion at Otterburn was due in the first place to the heady spirit and excessive boldness of Sir Henry Percy, which caused our troops to go into battle in the disorder induced by haste; and in the second place because the darkness played such tricks on the English that when they aimed a careless blow at a Scotsman, owing to the chorus of voices speaking a single language it was an Englishman that they cut down...

For the Scots the mood of triumph was darkened by the discovery of the dead Douglas. He was carried back to Scotland and buried with honours beside his father in Melrose Abbey.

> My friends you ask me how I do?
> My soul is now prepared to go,
> Where many wounds have made their way.
> Conceal it, till you have won the day;
> Pursue your hopes: thus he dy'd
> Then the whole ranks 'A Douglas' cry'd
> And charg'd afresh, that thou might'st have
> Revenge and honour in the grave.

In London the government of King Richard reacted far too slowly to the crisis in the north. All too late, the Earl of Arundel, who had been engaged in naval operations against the French in the Channel, was ordered to take the fleet to assist the northern lords. On August 13, with Fife already at Carlisle and Douglas approaching Newcastle, Richard wrote to John of Gaunt in Gascony in alarming terms, telling him that the Scots were '...slaying men, women and children in the cradle...'and that they had advanced almost to the gates of York. Lancaster was also told of the King's intentions to take to the field in person, and ordered to raise the

Gascon lieges to join Richard before the end of the month, hardly a realistic prospect given the distance involved.

When news of the defeat at Otterburn finally arrived the search for scapegoats began immediately. The obvious candidate was the Bishop of Durham, who was criticised by the Royal Council for arriving too late to help Harry Hotspur. Curiously, no official blame seems to have been attached to Hotspur himself for his military incompetence. He was generally perceived as a rather heroic figure, with both King and parliament contributing towards his ransom. The real villains, of course, were not priests or soldiers but politicians — the Lords Appellant, whose obsession with France, and neglect of Scotland, had led to the worst English military reverse since the days of Robert Bruce. Their mismanagement of the nation's affairs did much to restore the credibility of Richard, who was able to ease them from power by the following spring.

The first task was to deal with the immediate crisis. Towards the end of August a council meeting was held in Northampton, where the King expressed his willingness to lead an army against the Scots. But as they showed no sign of following up their victory, and it was already late in the campaigning season, it was decided to postpone further action until the new year. The council met again at Westminster on 20 January 1389 and decided that Richard would invade Scotland on 1 August. The frontier was strengthened by the appointment of the Earl of Nottingham, the earl marshal of England, as warden of the east march, and the Earl of Northumberland and two others as wardens of the west. They were to have a force of 600 lances and 2000 archers, all provided at the King's expense, until he arrived at the Border in person.

In Scotland the death of Douglas led to a minor political revolution. The Earl of Carrick, long associated with the dead hero, had been disabled by the kick of a horse, which seems to have induced a life long depression. With Douglas gone the decision was taken by a general council meeting in Edinburgh on 1 December to replace Carrick, who was considered incapable of dealing with the expected English reaction to Otterburn, in the role of the King's lieutenant with his younger brother Robert, Earl of Fife, thus beginning one of the most enduring political careers in Scottish history.

Douglas's death also created another set of problems in southern Scotland. He left no heir and was succeeded to the title by his kinsman Archibald the Grim, an illegitimate son of the great Sir

James Douglas, the companion in arms of Robert Bruce. There was some dispute over the legality of this. Sir Malcolm Drummond, the brother-in-law of the second Earl, believed that he had a better claim. Angry at the success of Archibald, he and other supporters of the Douglas party, including the brothers John and William Haliburton and Sir James Sandilands sought the support of Richard II. Safe conducts were issued in their favour, and they made ready to cross the Border, intent on becoming the nucleus of a new 'disinherited' party, which had caused such trouble for Scotland during the Wars of Independence. However, their designs were frustrated when, against all expectations, the war ended almost as suddenly as it had begun.

With both England and Scotland keen to pursue hostilities it looked as if 1389 was going to be just as violent as 1388. The Scots were determined to keep the military initiative. Both Berwick and Carlisle were attacked in the October following Otterburn. These assaults were repulsed; but in February of the following year another force crossed the western march and plundered the barony of Gilsland. John Beaumont, one of the wardens of the east march, retaliated by raiding as far north as Falkirk. An even bigger invasion followed on 25 June led by Thomas Mowbray, Earl of Nottingham, and Ralph, Lord Neville, in which Peebles was destroyed. But the English were forced to retreat after a serious dispute broke out amongst a number of the northern nobility and after they encountered a larger army led by Fife and the new Earl of Douglas. A section of the Scots force bypassed the English, crossed the Border on 29 June and raided Northumberland as far as Tynemouth. On their return to Scotland the rearguard was badly mauled when it was attacked by Sir Matthew Redmayn and Sir Robert Ogle. This was to be the last action of the Otterburn war.

Richard had begun his year determined to reverse the policy of the Appellants by making peace with France in order to pursue the war in Scotland. Negotiations took place at Leulighen. Despite the best efforts of Richard's envoys the French refused to abandon the Scots. But, in any case, the English were beginning to run seriously short of cash, so the King's military plans were looking unrealistic. Against this background a formal truce between England and France was concluded on 18 June. Scotland was to have the option of inclusion.

When news of the peace terms reached Scotland some of the

younger nobles wanted to continue with the war at a time when the country still held the military advantage over the enemy. However, they were overruled by Douglas and Fife, both of whom were keen to accept peace for their own reasons: Douglas wanted to build up his power base on the Border free from the threat of English intervention on behalf of Drummond; and Fife had to be free to deal with political problems north of the Forth, where the third of King Robert's sons, Alexander, the Wolf of Badenoch, was causing trouble. The English and French envoys were, therefore, received by Robert II at Dunfermline, and Scotland ratified the new treaty. With successive extensions it was to last until the end of Richard's reign.

Seen against this international background Otterburn, although it settled none of the outstanding political issues between England and Scotland, had more than local significance: it contributed directly towards the end of the first phase of the Hundred Years War. The following year Robert II died peacefully at Dundonald Castle after a reign of mixed fortunes, but on balance not completely unsuccessful. He was succeeded by his eldest son John, who because his name was so ill omened in both the history of Scotland and England, took the title of Robert III. Sadly for him, fate was not so easily deceived. Robert's succession made no difference to the government of the country, which continued in the hands of the Earl of Fife.

As the years passed Richard became more attached to a policy of peace. His efforts to interfere with Scots independence were restricted to the arena of diplomacy, and give the appearance of political posturing rather than indicating any serious aggressive intention on his part. In the truce negotiations of 1394 his ambassadors were instructed to put forward a 'maximum programme' as an opening gambit. The King of Scotland was to do homage to Richard as his feudal superior; the magnates and prelates were to recognise the English King as their sovereign lord; and all the lands ceded to England by Edward Balliol in 1334 were to be handed back. Recognising that these demands were likely to be rejected the envoys were allowed to fall back on a 'minimum programme', asking only for the Border lands the English held in 1369. Richard's only 'concession' was to drop the demand for the remainder of David II's ransom. To put additional pressure on the Scots Richard opened negotiations with the Lord of the Isles, whom he professed to recognise as an independent prince. He also attempted to induce the Earls of Douglas and March into accepting English allegiance. But the Scots refused to accept any of his terms. With French help Scotland was able to counter all of Richard's diplomatic coercion, and was included in the twenty eight year truce of 1396. By this time Richard had come to see that the real risk to peace and security came less from the Scots than sections of his own nobility.

In the north the Percies had become 'Princes of the March', who thrived in war and withered in peace. Resentful of the interference of outsiders, the King included, they were happy to take government money to pursue their private quarrels. The peace of the 1390's left them with outstanding territorial claims against the Scots and threatened to reduce their military importance. They found a large degree of support amongst many in the north, for whom war had become a way of life. With the King no longer prepared to support their private armies and ready to appoint outsiders to the post of warden the Percies became part of a general conspiracy against him headed by his cousin Henry Bolingbroke, the son and successor of John of Gaunt, and a former Appellant. On 30 September 1399 Richard II, abandoned by all, was forced to abdicate, and thus passed the last King of England to succeed to the throne by undisputed hereditary right. Shortly after he disappeared behind the walls of Pontefract Castle; by February 1400 he was dead. Meanwhile, Bolingbroke was crowned King Henry IV. A crown, won by force, was to be held by war. The seeds of a great fifteenth century tragedy had been sown.

# CHAPTER 2
## Death Comes to Homildon

*My friends, why stand we here to be slain like deer?*

*Sir John Swinton*

Henry's first task was to consolidate his hold on England. He had, therefore, no desire for any complications on his northern frontier. One of his earliest acts was to write to Robert III offering to renew the truce. Robert was in no hurry to agree to this request. The chance of exploiting the political uncertainty in England was too good to miss, and more aggressive counsels began to prevail. Robert even took the provocative step in his letter of 2 November 1399 of addressing Henry as Duke of Lancaster, although he had been crowned on 13 October, a deliberate breach of protocol which caused the new King considerable annoyance.

He was even more annoyed when a raiding party crossed the Tweed in a surprise attack on Wark Castle, which was captured and destroyed in the absence of its keeper, Sir Thomas Gray. When parliament met on 10 November Henry announced that he intended to punish the Scots personally for this major breach of the peace. But it was far too late in the season for any significant counter action to be taken.

When the Great Council gathered at Westminster on February 9 1400 it was announced that the Scots were still ravaging the northern march. Henry believed that this aggression was preliminary to a major Scots invasion assisted by the King of France, a conclusion which Robert's failure to reply to renewed peace proposals helped to confirm. At this dangerous time Henry was to receive assistance from an unexpected quarter.

The heir to the Scottish throne, David Stewart, Duke of Rothesay, was betrothed to Elizabeth Dunbar, the Earl of March's daughter. To secure this marriage March paid a large sum of dowry money to the King; but the Earl of Douglas, fearing an extension of Dunbar's power in southern Scotland, paid an even larger amount to allow his daughter Marjory to marry Rothesay instead. With the aid of Robert of Fife, now Duke of Albany, Douglas was able to obtain the consent of parliament to have the betrothal to

Elizabeth set aside. Dunbar was outraged. Neither able to have his daughter married nor to have his dowry money returned, he wrote to Henry IV in February invoking their common kinship through the old Anglo Scottish house of Comyn, and pleaded for assistance:

> Of the quhilk wrang and defowle to me and my dochter in swilk manner done, I, as ane of yhour poer kyn...requere yhow of holp and suppowal fore swilk honest service as I may do efter my power to yhour noble lordship, and to yhour lande...

Henry was delighted by this. March, who fought with the second Earl of Douglas at Otterburn, was the most skilled soldier of his generation on either side of the Border. Moreover, a political arrangement with Dunbar offered Henry the prospect of an easy entry into Scotland across the eastern frontier, guarded by the Earl's powerful castle at Dunbar. A safe conduct was issued allowing March to enter England. He entrusted the safekeeping of Dunbar Castle to his nephew, Sir Robert Maitland, who betrayed this trust by handing it over to Archibald, Master of Douglas, the eldest son and namesake of Archibald the Grim. Stung by this treachery March wrote to Robert III protesting at the unjustified seizure of his castle, saying that he was only on England in business and that he had not forsworn his allegiance to the King; but his appeal was denied. It is not absolutely certain that the Earl was intending to switch allegiance at this stage. By the precipitate action of Archibald Douglas a doubt changed into a certainty. Walter Bower, author of the *Scotichronicon*, reports:

> The earl of March was very angry over these matters and sent for his sons and his following. These were men strong in vigour and fierce in spirit as they gathered round him in large numbers. By joining in every military expedition of the English they more than any others tyrannised the lands near the marches of Scotland...

On 25 July 1400 March took the final step when he entered into an agreement with Henry IV, withdrawing his allegiance from Robert, the 'pretended' King of Scotland. The loss of so skilled a soldier was to have a serious outcome for the Scots, and one cannot help feeling that the treatment he received at the hands of King Robert, Douglas and Albany was shabby and ill advised. The later Scots historian John Major summarises the position well:

> Hence let kings take a lesson not to trifle with men of fierce
> temper...nor yet with their daughters. Rather than this woman
> had been scorned, it were better that the Scots had given her a
> dower of two hundred thousand pieces of gold.

This was an ideal opportunity for Henry. Where one senior
Scottish noblemen led, others may follow. Negotiations were
opened up with Donald, Lord of the Isles, and his brother John
of Islay, and a defensive alliance was entered into, as if between
independent princes. Instructions were issued to the Border lords
to seduce as many Scots as possible away from their allegiance to
Robert III. For Henry war came as something of a relief from
domestic problems, offering a way of cementing his as yet uncertain
authority at home.

Henry sent summonses to all his leading noblemen to meet him
in arms at York on 24 June. At the end of May permission was
given for privateers to operate against the Scots at sea, and these
enjoyed some notable successes, capturing Sir Robert Logan, the
Admiral of Scotland, and David Seaton, Archdeacon of Ross, who
was intercepted carrying letters to the King of France. Both men
were sent to the Tower of London.

When he came to York, Henry received defiant messages from
King Robert offering to renew the peace on the basis of the Treaty
of Northampton of 1328 — a full recognition by England of
Scottish independence and the abandonment of the claim to
sovereignty. This only served to provoke Henry still further. But
he was delayed for several weeks at York because of shortage of
money and supplies, finally setting off from Newcastle at the end
of July with a large army of over 13,000 men, of whom 11,000
were archers. The Royal Council in London had been active in
organising a supply fleet, which was sent to meet the King at
Newcastle.

Unfortunately for Henry the omens were not good. The Scots
were no more intimidated by the approach of his host than they
had been by Richard's in 1385. Continuing wet weather had a
bad effect on the morale of his troops; the garrisons of Roxburgh
and Berwick both threatened to desert; disease had broken out,
and food continued to be in short supply. Despite these difficulties
the King was not to be deflected from his purpose. Up to the point
he reached Newcastle the pretext for the invasion was to punish
Scots raids on the marches. But with the example of March

before him he now switched tactics, reviving the old claim of overlordship. On 6 August he wrote to Robert in the form of an 'invitation', calling on him to be at Edinburgh on the 23rd of the month, ready to pay homage to his feudal superior. A supplementary declaration was also sent to the leading magnates and prelates, requiring them, in terms of the allegiance they owed to the crown of England, to ensure that Robert obeyed his summons. Henry now moved forward. The garrisons at Roxburgh, Carlisle, Harbottle, Jedburgh and Norham were all strengthened before he crossed the Border on 14 August, on what was to be the last invasion of Scotland by a reigning English king.

The following day the English entered Haddington. Three days later they were at Leith, where yet another summons was issued to Robert. Henry's invasion was a curious affair, and gives all the appearance of being one of history's great bluffs. His control over his troops was admirable, the path of his advance being no more destructive than that of his father in 1384. His progress to Edinburgh took him through the lands of the Earl of March, so it's likely that he would be anxious to avoid alienating potential support for his cause. However, the chronicler Walter Bower maintains that Henry acted as he did because he was himself 'half a Scot', a descendent on his mother's side of the Comyn Earls of Buchan. A more likely explanation for his moderation would seem to be that he was trying to build on Dunbar's defection by exploiting the perceived weakness of the Scottish crown to attract others disaffected by the domination of Douglas, Albany and Rothesay. If so, it was a serious and expensive miscalculation.

While he was at Leith, Henry's political gamble, if such it was, began to fail. There was no sign of a political revolution, and no sign of Robert. Rothesay and Douglas defied the English from the stronghold of Edinburgh Castle. Albany with the rest of the army was at Calder Wood, fifteen miles away from the powerful enemy host, which he wisely decided not to engage in battle, but well situated to threaten the English lines of communication. Small parties of guerrillas operated under the cover of the woods to pick off stragglers. Henry's supply situation, moreover, was becoming particularly bad, as the fleet had not yet arrived. After making a perfunctory attempt to take Dalhousie Castle in Mid-Lothian he decided the time had come to withdraw. Some fragment of honour was saved after the Scots promised to 'consider' Henry's claim to superiority. Thereafter the army made its way back to the Border in haste, crossing into England on 29 August. The campaign, like that of 1385, had been an expensive fiasco. It had achieved none of Henry's expressed aims, rekindled the Border war and, what is worse, made England look vulnerable. It was to be the last major invasion of Scotland for eighty two years.

Henry's inglorious retreat was, as so often in the past, a signal for a major Scottish onslaught. But the King had sensibly taken the precaution of ensuring that the garrisons on the Border were left strong enough to provide an effective first line of defence. On 29 September 1400 the commander of Harbottle Castle, Sir Robert Umfraville, inflicted a serious reverse on a party of Scots raiders at Fullhopelaw — Philip Law — near Reidswire, killing 200 and taking many prisoners. The captives included Sir Robert Rutherford and his five sons, Sir William Stewart, Sir Simon Carter and John Turnbull, a particularly notorious captain known by the aggressive nickname of 'Out wyth Swerd.' All were sent to the Tower or the Fleet Prison in London. This setback cooled some of the martial ardour in Scotland and both sides entered into negotiations for a truce, which was concluded on 9 November to last for six weeks in the hope that this would lead to a more permanent settlement.

Conditions remained quiet over the winter. Both sides seemed anxious to come to an agreement. After his experience of the summer Henry was keen to avoid antagonising the Scots. In Scotland a peace party emerged headed by the King, Rothesay and Albany. But this was opposed by a new and dangerous faction in Scottish politics. In December Archibald the Grim died. He was succeeded as fourth Earl of Douglas by his son Archibald, the brother-in-law of the Duke of Rothesay, fated to be known to history by the unfortunate title of Tyneman — the Loser.

Douglas headed a body of young lords opposed to any permanent settlement with England. As far as he was concerned his fortunes were born in war, and would be maintained by war. A successful peace is likely to have involved concessions to the house of Percy in the disputed area of Jedworth Forest; and it would certainly have meant the restoration of George Dunbar, Earl of March. Douglas' aims were simple: to consolidate his hold on the lordship of Dunbar and to pursue his cross Border feud with the former Earl and his Percy allies. He would use any means to achieve these ends, including participation in a conspiracy which led to the downfall and death of his brother-in-law, David, Duke of Rothesay.

The tensions within Scotland were evident in the early months of 1401 when Rothesay wrote to Henry suggesting that the proposed peace talks be moved from the west march, where the war party was dominant, to Melrose in the east. In response to this it was agreed that Rothesay and the Earl of Northumberland meet at Melrose on 25 April. But before these talks took place the political atmosphere changed, and Douglas had had his first taste of blood.

In February Dunbar, accompanied by Harry Hotspur and Lord Thomas Talbot, crossed the eastern march with a large raiding force, intent on attacking Patrick Hepburn of Hailes, one of Dunbar's former retainers who had incurred his particular displeasure by refusing to defect with him the previous year. They advanced to the neighbourhood of Haddington. Two assaults on Hailes Castle were repulsed by a vigorous defence; but the nearby villages of Hailes, Traprain, and Markle were destroyed by fire. The raiders camped at Linton, where they were surprised by the country levies led by Douglas, and forced to retreat in some disorder back to Berwick by way of Cockburnspath.

When the English commissioners came north to attend the peace talks they were met by a Scottish delegation headed not by David of Rothesay but by the Earl of Douglas, signalling a major change of direction in Scotland. Although the temporary truce was extended, nothing more definite was decided, and the meeting was abandoned. When full talks were finally reconvened at Yetholm in Roxburghshire on 17 October the signs were not good. Once again the Scots were headed by Douglas and the English delegation was led by Northumberland with Harry Hotspur, as warden of Berwick, and others. Their principal negotiating position was little different from that pursued by Richard II in the 1390's: in return for a final peace Robert was to recognise English overlordship and accept summonses to attend the English parliament. To try to ensure some 'fairness' the English offered to put these claims to arbitration by 'sage and discreet persons'; to which the Bishop of Glasgow suggested that Henry's questionable right to the crown of England be put to a similar process of arbitration. As an alternative, and in place of the elusive final peace, the English suggested a thirty year truce, provided that the Scots agreed to leave Berwick, Jedburgh and Roxburgh in English hands with arrangements for secure communications. As part of this package Dunbar was to be restored to his lands in Scotland. Failing this a further short truce was to be arranged, in which Dunbar was to be included as an ally of the English, and the three aforementioned castles left unmolested. Douglas was intransigent. He refused to consider the restoration of the Earl of March or to guarantee English security in the Border castles. Northumberland requested that the truce be extended to Christmas, to allow him to receive further instructions from London; but Douglas refused to consider even this moderate request. The talks broke up on 20 October. No sooner had Northumberland and his colleagues returned to England than Douglas came charging across the Border, burning the town of Bamburgh. The message he sent to Henry could not be clearer.

For many in Scotland the time appeared to be right for a new aggressive posture towards England. Henry was in considerable military and political difficulty. In Wales the remarkable Owen Glendower, a man of the stature of William Wallace, was enjoying astonishing success in the greatest rising against the English since 1295. Some limited Scots help had already been sent to Wales. In June, Scottish cruisers had arrived at the English held stronghold of Caernarfon, but were driven off by some ships flying the flag of Harry Percy. Another Scots vessel with 35 armed men on board was captured at Milford Haven. The news that the Scots and English were once more on the verge of war was greeted enthusiastically by Glendower's camp at Glyn Dyfrdwy. In November 1401 he wrote to Robert III invoking a common Celtic ancestry and telling of a prophecy that Wales would be delivered with Scottish help from the tyranny of their mutual enemy the Saxons — 'Sassenachs.' He asked Robert to send men-at-arms which:

> ...may aid me and may withstand, with God's help, mine and your foes...to the chastisement and mischief and of all the past mischiefs which I and my ancestors of Wales have suffered at the hands of mine and your mortal foes.

The French government also tried to interest Robert in Owen's cause, sending to his court the Welsh knight Davit ap Jevan Coz; but any projected Scots assistance for Wales was effectively ended by the major defeat at Homildon Hill in 1402 and the capture of Prince James in 1406.

In Scotland the final triumph of Douglas and the war party was secured by a palace revolution. Since 1399 the Scots government had been headed by David of Rothesay, who replaced his uncle

27

Robert of Albany as lieutenant general. Albany, an ambitious man, did not settle easily to a subordinate position. Alleging misconduct he had Rothesay arrested in January 1402 and imprisoned in Falkland Castle, one of his own properties. This was a dangerous move and much depended on the attitude of the Earl of Douglas. After the arrest the two men met at Culross. Although Albany himself had been linked with the peace party, he seems to have offered Douglas a free hand on the Border and state support for his war policy in return for the Earl's acceptance of the fall of Rothesay. The opinion of the King mattered to no one. Douglas concurred with Albany's coup, and for a time Scotland's foreign policy was dictated by the cross Border feud. Albany, an indifferent soldier but a skilful politician, was restored to the post of lieutenant general, and went on to dominate the government of Scotland until his death in 1420. David, Duke of Rothesay, never emerged from his prison in Falkland Castle. Two months after his arrest he was dead, in circumstances which have never been clear; but it seems likely that he was murdered by neglect. The heir to the Scottish throne was now the seven year old Prince James.

War came ever closer in 1402. In Skye a half crazed English vagrant was discovered who bore a passing resemblance to Richard II. He was brought over to the mainland and housed by Albany at Stirling. Although the man himself denied he was Richard — a truth confirmed by a visiting French envoy who knew the former King — Albany and Douglas determined to gain the maximum propaganda value from his presence in Scotland. It was openly declared that Richard had escaped from Pontefract, and he was now about to return to take possession of what was rightfully his with the support of a large Scottish army. This early form of psychological warfare had an unsettling effect on Henry and his realm. The pseudo Richard — sometimes known as the Mammet — was declared to be one Thomas Warde of Trumpington; but the story that the old King was still alive spread throughout England, acting like a magnet to all those disaffected from the government of the usurper, especially among certain religious orders. Throughout England county sheriffs were ordered to arrest all those who were spreading the rumour that Richard was in Scotland. Similar orders were also sent to the Earl of Northumberland and the Bishop of Carlisle. At the same time instructions were sent out to the northern counties to be ready to resist the expected Scots invasion.

The Scots had made full preparations for the coming conflict. In January 1402 the Earl of Crawford, Admiral of Scotland, arrived in Paris to appeal for help against the English. At the end of the month he entered into a personal alliance with the Duke of Orleans. A small fleet was fitted out at Harfleur in Normandy, and Crawford was joined by a group of knights led by Jacques de Heilly and Pierre des Essarts. The flotilla left port in March, spending some time attacking English shipping in the Channel, before arriving in Scotland at the end of July, ready to join Douglas' invasion of England.

The campaigning season had opened deceptively well for the Scots. John Haliburton of Dirleton had had undertaken a particularly lucrative raid into Northumberland, returning with much booty. Encouraged by this success, Patrick Hepburn the younger of Hailes organised his own expedition. He crossed the Border in June 1402 with 400 mounted men, advancing far deeper into Northumberland than Haliburton had, and remaining longer than was prudent. Loaded down with plunder he was intercepted on his return by the Earl of March and Harry Hotspur at Nisbit Muir in Berwickshire on the 22nd of the month. A fierce engagement ensued, with the outcome in the balance for some time. But the English were reinforced by March's son, Gavin Dunbar, riding hard from Berwick with an additional 200 men. Hepburn was killed, as were many of the gentry of Lothian. The prisoners included Sir John Haliburton of Dirleton, Sir Thomas Haliburton, Sir Robert Lawder of the Bass and John and William Cockburn. The place at which the Battle of Nisbit Muir was fought was for long after known as Slaughterhill, an illustration of the intensity of this small fight. March followed up this success by taking possession of Fast Castle on the Berwickshire coast. The news of this welcome victory was warmly received by the beleaguered Henry at Harebourgh on 30 June, on his way to campaign in Wales. He wrote to the Council announcing the good news, and advising of a further success against Scots raiders at Carlisle. For Scotland Nisbit Muir was a sad blow; but far worse was to follow.

Anxious to revenge this defeat Douglas appealed to Albany for aid. Troops began to concentrate in large numbers on the east march. The French knights came, apparently having forgotten the hard days of 1385. Douglas was also joined by forces led by Murdoch Stewart, Albany's eldest son, his kinsman, George

Douglas, the Red Earl of Angus, Thomas Dunbar, the Earl of Moray, and a party of Gallwegians, led by Fergus Macdouall. Other contingents were headed by the heads of the houses of Erskine, Grahame, Montgomery, Seton, Sinclair, Lesley and the Stewarts of Angus, Lorn and Durisdeer. This was a national rather than a Border army, comprising some 10,000 men in all.

By early August Henry was already aware of the build up of troops on the Border. He ordered the sheriff of Lincoln, who had intended to accompany him to Wales, to hold his troops in readiness to assist Northumberland if necessary; but beyond that he was content to leave matters to the northern levies.

The storm finally broke at harvest time. Dense columns of Scots crossed the Border, in all probability following the same route that the second Earl of Douglas had in 1388; but this was no surprise attack: the whole of the northern countryside was alerted to the presence of the enemy. The motive for the campaign was quite simply one of revenge: there was absolutely no pretence that the Scots came in support of the Mammet, even though one of his keepers, Lord Montgomery, was present with the army. Moving south eastwards without interruption Douglas marched through Northumberland onwards into County Durham, ravaging and plundering all the way. On the advice of the Earl of March the Percies decided to let them come on, with the intention of intercepting them on their return, when their progress would be slowed by plundered livestock. The whole countryside gave way before the invaders. It is estimated that over 1000 people left Northumberland, fleeing south in the pursuit of refuge. Panic spread to Newcastle, where 100 armed men were detailed to watch the walls every night for the duration of the emergency, and armed vessels stood ready on the Tyne.

Archibald Douglas, who clearly was attempting to cast himself in the role of the heroic second Earl, appears to have been blind to the danger into which the army was being drawn. The English troops were concentrating at Alnwick and Dunstanburgh Castles to the north of his position, poised to cut off his retreat. Douglas also seems to have been blinded to reality by the comforting illusion that the victory at Otterburn had given the Scots a decisive edge over their opponents — failing to appreciate how close they had been to disaster on that occasion. He also appears to have taken comfort from the strength of his force, perhaps believing that most of the English army was far away with Henry on the Welsh marches. Loaded down with booty he began a leisurely retreat through the valley of the River Till back towards the Border at Coldstream, ready to reacquaint his countrymen with the power of the longbow.

When he reached Wooler on 14 September Douglas learned that the enemy were ranged right across his line of retreat at Milfield, just over five miles to the north west. Appreciating the extreme danger of his situation he ordered the army, booty and all, to deploy in a dense phalanx on the nearby height of Homildon — now Humbelton — Hill. This was a good position, rising in successive tiers to an elevation of nearly 1000 feet above sea level, with a flat top upon which there were some ancient fortifications; but it was also twined with another eminence, the nearby Harehope Hill, separated from Homildon by a ravine, although within arrow range. Douglas was well situated to repel a charge by English cavalry; but the very densness of his army and his failure to secure Harehope Hill made him extremely vulnerable to archery; and it was archers who made up the bulk of the approaching English army.

From Milfield the English army advanced down the Till valley, under the leadership of Northumberland, Hotspur and March, accompanied by Sir Hugh Fitzhugh, Sir Ralph Eure and a Cumbrian contingent led by the Lord of Graystoke. On finding their enemy at Homildon they took up their own battle positions. The exact distribution of the English troops is not altogether clear from the sources, so a recreation of the Battle of Homildon Hill inevitably has to involve a degree of guess work. It would certainly appear that a body of longbowmen was allowed to occupy Harehope Hill, without interruption from Douglas. Here they were comfortably out of the range of the Scottish short bow, and protected by the deep ravine which runs between Harehope and Homildon. The rest of the army, including the remaining archers and the men-at-arms, seems to have been deployed on the lower ground, slightly towards the north west of the Scots in a field, subsequently known as Red Riggs, where a stone still stands that is said to commemorate the battle.

Hotspur, true to his nature, wanted to begin the battle by ordering an immediate charge on the Scots. He was restrained by March whose knowledge of the fighting strengths of both sides was invaluable: as a Scot he was well aware that his own people fought best at close quarters, whereas the English had the greatest advantage in dealing death from a distance with the mighty longbow. Each of the longbowmen was armed with twenty-four arrows, and it was said of old that they carried twenty-four Scots under their belt. Never was this truer than at Homildon Hill, perhaps the most complete victory for the longbow in English history.

From Harehope and the lower reaches of Homildon the arrows began to whistle into the packed Scottish ranks. The archers moved slowly forward, firing at repeated intervals with devastating effect. The lightly protected Gallwegians suffered most; but even the latest plate armour failed to deflect the punch of the arrows, which broke through helmets with ease. The Scots were so badly deployed that they had scarcely any room to manoeuvre or use their weapons. The horror of the situation was made worse by the screams of the horses and the plundered livestock, maddened by the whisteling missiles. Still Douglas stood fixed on the hillside, as if waiting for divine intervention. Walter Bower depicts the scene thus:

> ...the English bowmen, advancing towards the Scots, smothered them with arrows and made them bristle like hedgehogs, transfixing the hands and arms of the Scots to their own lances. By means of this very harsh rain of arrows, they wounded others and they killed many.

Even the bravest soldiers could only take so much of this. It was not, as a later historian was to say, a question of fighting: the only test of courage was to stand and die without turning their backs upon an enemy they could not reach. The advancing English archers were unsupported by other infantrymen and could conceivably have been dispersed by a cavalry charge, as their ancestors had been by Robert Keith at Bannockburn. But no such attack was ordered by Douglas, who appears to have been frozen by indecision. Finally two knights, Sir John Swinton and Sir Adam Gordon, could take no more, and ordered their own retainers, some 100 men in all, to follow them on a downhill charge. Unsupported by the main army, both men were killed, and their attack was quickly destroyed. Only then did Douglas order a general advance. The survivors of Swinton and Gordon's men were streaming back only to be met by their comrades coming down from the heights, which caused some confusion, made worse when the whole army came upon a sudden precipice.

The English archers remained calm, simply giving way, more rapidly in the centre than on the flanks, firing all the time. Before reaching the enemy the Scottish army finally broke, fleeing in all directions, with riderless horses charging wildly across the valley of the River Till. The English men-at-arms, who had not been engaged at all till now, joined in the pursuit, which continued all the way to the Tweed, thirteen miles to the north, where a further 500 Scots were drowned in a desperate attempt to escape, their bodies borne rapidly downstream by the strong current.

An unknown number of men died on the slopes of Homildon Hill; perhaps thousands. Apart from Swinton and Gordon the recorded dead include Sir John Swinton of Callander, Sir Alexander Ramsay of Dalhousie, Sir Roger Gordon, Sir Walter Scott and Sir Walter Sinclair. There was also a rich hoard in prisoners, numbering amongst them Murdoch of Fife, the Earls of Moray, Angus and Orkney; the Barons of Montgomery, Erskine, Seton, and Abernethy; Sir Robert Logan, Sir William Graham, Sir Adam Forster, Sir David Fleming and Pierre des Essarts with a number of the French knights. The chief captive was Archibald, Earl of Douglas, who, despite his costly armour, had been wounded in five places, losing one of his eyes. Two of the prisoners, Sir William Stewart of Teviotdale and Thomas Kerr, were subsequently executed as traitors by Hotspur on the grounds that they had formerly been in the allegiance of the English King. Only five Englishmen are said to have been killed; and while one is normally suspicious of claims of this kind, in the circumstances of the battle this is, perhaps, not improbable.

Homildon Hill was a serious blow to Scottish morale, showing what Otterburn might have been if Percy had kept his head. It was a reminder of the massed power of the longbow, which prevailed against the Scots in the previous century at Dupplin Moor, Halidon Hill and Neville's Cross, but which appears to have been forgotten in the intervening years. It was also Archibald Douglas' first major battle, and he never did more to deserve the title of Tyneman. Many years passed before Scotland forgot the Battle of Homildon Hill. Douglas's ill fated raid was the last major invasion of England until another Scots army campaigned in the valley of the Till in the late summer of 1513.

Homildon Hill also had unforeseen short term consequences in England, leading directly to the greatest challenge Henry ever faced to his right to hold the crown. The matter began with the fate of the prisoners taken at the battle, who had since been distributed to various strongholds, including the castles of Graystoke, Dunstanburgh and Roxburgh. On 22 September Henry wrote to his victorious northern magnates forbidding them to ransom any of their captives. There was nothing unusual in this. Some of these men were important state prisoners. Edward III had issued similar orders after the Battle of Neville's Cross in 1346; as had Henry on the occasion of the more recent engagement at Fulhopelaw in September 1400. But Homildon Hill had added greatly to the prestige of the Percies, and contrasted sharply with Henry's poor performance against Glendower. Their success had, so says the chronicler Adam of Usk, left them 'too much puffed up', Harry Percy especially. While Northumberland came to London on 20 October to hand over his own prisoners, chief amongst whom was Murdoch, Earl of Fife, Hotspur absolutely refused to hand over Douglas. This quarrel was patched up, but it left a smouldering sense of discontent, erupting into full scale rebellion in the summer of 1403. Henry doubtlessly intended to use the prisoners as a lever to obtain a lasting settlement with Scotland; but the quarrel with the Percies, and growing concern over their ambitions, deprived him of this opportunity.

After Homildon Scotland was in a critical situation. She was now as open to invasion as she had been in the aftermath of Neville's Cross, when the English had re-established their control over much of the south in the country. The quarrel over the Homildon prisoners and the lateness of the season had offered a temporary relief; but by the spring of 1403 a major threat appeared to be taking shape. Henry declared that the whole county of Douglas, with the valleys of Teviotdale, Eskdale, Liddesdale, Lauderdale, Selkirk and Ettrick Forest and Galloway to be conquered and annexed to England. There is some suggestion that his ultimate aim was to push the Border as far north as the Forth; to reclaim, in other words, all those territories granted by Edward Balliol to Edward III in 1334.

Claiming these lands was one thing; holding them quite another. On 2 March 1403 a further proclamation was issued awarding most of the forfeited territory to the Percies, exempting some areas that were claimed by the Earl of Westmorland, the lands of the Earl of March and the towns of Roxburgh and Annan, which were to be held by the King, who was also to have a general overlordship over the whole. This was the 'reward' the Percies were promised for Homildon; but considering that the Scots were still in possession of the 'conquered' lands it might conceivably be likened to parcelling out the Moon: it cost the King nothing; it was likely to cost Northumberland a great deal. The Percies raised their retainers; but they were shortly to be used for a very different purpose from the one Henry intended.

Hotspur crossed the Border in May 1403 to begin a rather half hearted campaign of conquest. There was no attempt to co-ordinate his activities with the Earl of Westmorland, who had quarrelled with the Percies over the division of the spoils. One of Percy's columns advanced as far north as Innerwick in East Lothian, taking possession of the castle. However, the whole operation came to a halt at the small tower of Cocklaws in Teviotdale, just north east of Ormiston, near Hawick. The castle was held by John Grymslow, who refused to surrender, offering Percy a courageous defence instead. At this point an air of unreality enters the proceedings. Hotspur had not the time, resources or patience to reduce the first and least of all the obstacles he is likely to have faced in southern Scotland. There is a possibility that the Percies were simply using their operations in Scotland as a cover for a projected rebellion against Henry. Walter Bower certainly thinks so:

> But it is more true to say...that he (Hotspur) caused an army to be collected not to attack a castle but to confound — little by little — his lord, Henry King of England...

With his mind on greater matters, Hotspur entered into an agreement with Grymslow, who promised to surrender the castle if not relieved by 1 August. Northumberland and Hotspur petitioned Henry for more money: instead he announced that he was ready to come in person with the royal army to assist them in the conquest. The prospect of the King in arms in their own country was too much for the Percies to bear. Walter Bower explains what happened:

> For that war which was expected and dreaded by the Scots in many ways and which was to begin on this side of the Border of the kingdom of England at Cocklaws in the north he transferred happily at the appointed time by diverting our bondage like a rushing river to the south to be fought at Shrewsbury on the borders of Wales.

Hotspur left Scotland on his way to join up with the army of Owen Glendower, with a view to replacing Henry as King with 'Richard' or with Edmund Mortimer, the former King's one time heir. Prior to this he made an agreement with Archibald Douglas, who had recovered from the wounds he had received at Homildon, to join him with a party of his retainers. In return the Tyneman was promised Berwick and his liberty free of ransom. This accommodation with his enemy was too much for Dunbar, who came to offer his valuable advice to the King. By 16 July 1403 Henry was aware of Hotspur's rebellion. A summons was issued for troops to join him to resist Percy 'who has joined our Welsh rebels and has some of the King's Scotch enemies with him.' On Dunbar's advice the King advanced rapidly to intercept Hotspur and his allies before they were able to join with Glendower. On 21 July 1403 Hotspur was defeated and killed at the Battle of Shrewsbury. The dead also included the Scottish knight Robert Stewart of Hartshaw. Douglas, no more lucky in battle, was wounded and captured, having lost one of his testicles in the fight.

While the Shrewsbury campaign was under way Albany raised an army in Scotland to come to the relief of Cocklaws, doubtless already in possession of information that Hotspur was far away to the south. Innerwick was retaken, and the Lieutenant advanced safely into Teviotdale to conduct a vainglorious march around Cocklaws, although he made no attempt to exploit the confusion in England by attacking Jedburgh, Roxburgh or Berwick.

The Percy rebellion effectively removed all pressure from the Scottish march and allowed Albany the leisure to reflect on his situation. Douglas's policy of aggression had been a clear failure. With Henry preoccupied with the aftermath of Hotspur's rising the time had come to pursue a more peaceful line in foreign policy. By the early summer of 1404 official relations between the two realms were beginning to return as near to normal as possible, although the Borders were still very unsettled. Norham Castle was repaired and a state of alert maintained at Newcastle, where the obligation to maintain a nightly watch caused the citizens considerable strain. A new truce was arranged, although the high seas remained very dangerous, with English and Scottish privateers operating at will. In May 1405 a Scottish buccaneer, Thomas Macculloch, attacked English ports in Ulster before being run down in Dublin Bay. A retaliatory raid was mounted by parties of Anglo Irish merchants from Dublin and Drogheda in June, with attacks being made on Whithorn and Arran, where Lamlash was ravaged and Brodick Castle seized. The captain of the castle was held to ransom and his son killed.

Albany's truce was at best a fragile creation. In 1405 it broke down altogether when Northumberland, who had made his peace with Henry after Hotspur's death, rose in rebellion, and opened negotiations with the Scots government. A force under Henry Sinclair, Earl of Orkney and Lord of Roslin, advanced to his support, attracted by the prospect of gaining Berwick as a reward. Sinclair entered Berwick in the company of James Douglas, brother of the captured Earl, and John Stewart, Albany's second son and the future Earl of Buchan. By the time they arrived in early June Northumberland's rebellion was already in a state of collapse, with Henry rapidly approaching Berwick from the south. They remained just long enough to extract what they could from the unfortunate town, sparing only the religious foundations, before returning to Scotland accompanied by Northumberland, his young grandson, Henry Percy, Hotspur's son and heir, and his ally Lord Bardolph.

Angry at the Scots breach of the truce and their support for the rebels, the English launched a raid into southern Scotland under the leadership of Henry of Monmouth, Prince of Wales, the future King Henry V. Lauderdale, Teviotdale and the Ettrick Forest were all plundered. With the truce now openly disregarded on both sides the Scots made their own forays across the Border. The neighbourhoods of Roxburgh and Berwick were attacked repeatedly, and all the winter stores for the castle garrisons destroyed. Outside the walls the situation was so dangerous that none dared attend the cattle or work in the fields. Provisions could only be taken to Berwick and Fast Castle with difficulty because of Scots vessels operating in the area between the Tweed and the Tyne under the command of Alexander Stewart, Earl of Mar.

Northumberland soon found that his stay in Scotland was to be far from comfortable. Some of the Scottish nobility, headed by the Douglases, with the possible help of Albany, were plotting to arrest him and exchange him for Earl Archibald. Northumberland was warned of this by one of King Robert's closest advisers, Sir David Fleming. He and Bardolph fled from Scotland, taking refuge with Glendower in Wales. His grandson was left in the custody of Bishop Wardlaw of St Andrews.

Although the Border war had settled down by early 1406 the political situation in Scotland was highly volatile. Albany and the Douglases, led by James Douglas of Balvenie, were distrusted by that shadow King, the wretched Robert III, and his associates David Fleming and the Earl of Orkney. There was considerable concern about the safety of the eleven year old Prince James, the second Duke of Rothesay, who, with the ailing King Robert, was all that stood between Albany and the throne.

The decision to send the prince to France for his safety appears to have been precipitated by an incident in the south east of Scotland when James and a party led by Sir David Fleming and the Earl of Orkney were in danger of being ambushed by Sir James Douglas and troops coming from Edinburgh Castle. James, with Orkney and a small retinue, took refuge in the castle on the Bass Rock off the East Lothian coast. Fleming attempted to evade the Douglas pursuit, but was intercepted and killed at Long Hermiston Moor near Haddington on 14 February. News of his death was brought to Orkney and Prince James by Alexander Seton. It was clearly too dangerous for the Prince to return to his father's court. James therefore waited for some time before a ship could be found to carry him to France. No attempt was made to obtain a safe conduct from Henry, suggesting the importance of speed and secrecy. He finally obtained a passage on the *Maryenknecht*, a merchantman out of Danzig; but on the 22 March 1406 his ship was boarded by a group of English pirates from Great Yarmouth operating off Flamborough Head. Realising the importance of their captive their leader, one Hugh atte Fen, immediately sent him to the King. It was said that he was wrongfully taken at a time of truce; but it was *only* a truce; the two countries were, after all, officially at war, and James had set foot in England, willingly or otherwise, without a safe conduct from Henry. Such an important prize was not to be surrendered easily.

On 4 April Robert III died at his favourite residence of Rothesay Castle, leaving his own epitaph as 'The worst of kings and the most wretched of men in the whole realm.' His captive son was now James I, *de jure* King of Scots. He was to spend the next eighteen years as a 'guest' of three successive English monarchs. In Scotland Albany ruled supreme.

# CHAPTER 3
# A King in Captivity

Bewailing in my chamber thus allone,
Despeired of all joys and remedye,
Fortirit of my thoght and wo begone...

*King James I*

The Scots government reacted with remarkable calmness to the capture and imprisonment of James. Although he was declared to be King at a General Council held in Perth in June 1406, almost nothing was done to obtain his release. Half hearted and perfunctory protests were made to the English government; but this did not stop the truce being renewed for a further year. King Henry soon had the measure of Albany and his all too obvious ambitions. Anxious to consolidate his position in Scotland, Albany, who was soon to refer to the Scots as 'his subjects', was keen to avoid upsetting Henry; keen, in other words, to avoid anything which might lead to the premature return of the inconvenient James. For Henry, James was a useful tool with which to influence the political situation in Scotland. Albany ruled Scotland less by the 'Grace of God' — a style he adopted in official documents — than by the gift of England. His true desire is revealed in a bond he entered into with the Earl of Douglas in June 1409 against 'all deadly persons', in which the possibility is raised that Albany might 'grow in time to come to the estate of King.'

While peace was more convenient for Albany's political purposes, he was a great survivor; and when the occasion demanded he was prepared to be carried along by events, rather than controlling them. The Borders were always difficult to control, a position not made easier by the absence of the Earl of Douglas. Northern England still remained unsettled in the wake of the Percy rebellion. Northumberland and Bardolph were confident enough to return to Scotland in 1408, presumably in the expectation of receiving support from at least some of the nobility against Henry. Although they received no encouragement from Albany the two men crossed the Border in February to raise the Percy retainers in rebellion, only to go down in defeat and death at the Battle of Bramham Moor.

Northumberland's final adventure had the effect of destabilising the Border once more. The position was so bad that the King's son, John of Lancaster, who had replaced the rebel Earl as warden of the march, wrote to the council in London at the end of July that there was so much lawlessness on the frontier that he feared that this would lead to the renewal of full scale war. Although the truce was renewed in April 1409, reiving and pillaging continued, with central government lacking the will or the resources to deal with the problem.

Sometime in 1408 or 1409 Archibald Douglas, tiring of his imprisonment, returned to Scotland, apparently having broken the terms of his parole. The restoration of Douglas to his old power base in southern Scotland was too much for George Dunbar, Earl of March. His valuable service to the English crown had not brought the restoration of his lost earldom; and with Scotland and England at 'peace' this objective seemed further off than ever. His situation in the north of England, moreover, was far from comfortable. Many remained fiercely loyal to the Percies, and March was blamed for their downfall. One contemporary chronicler went so far as to say that he had deliberately influenced Henry IV against them, claiming that he '...desired the death of Henry Percy so that he might dominate more easily in the parts of Northumberland.' The Countess of March was even driven to writing to the King, complaining that she and her husband could not retire to their castle at Cockburnspath because they had incurred the hatred of the Percy faction. But March the soldier was really of no more value to Henry, so he began to consider other ways to restore his fortunes. He approached Albany, who, recognising that this was the kind of man that it was better to have on his side, agreed to restore him to his old estates, with the exception of Lochmaben and Annandale, which remained in Douglas hands as the price of reconciliation. March's previous treason was excused on the rather unlikely grounds that it was all part of a plan to ruin the Earl of Northumberland, whom he regarded as Scotland's greatest enemy, thereby making skilled use of the current prejudice against him in northern England.

After the capture of Prince James Henry began to neglect his northern march, as the letters of his son John of Lancaster testify. He was seriously short of money, and could simply not afford to maintain the northern frontier and be ready to react to the situation in France. After 1409 Henry's government was more and more preoccupied with events across the Channel. The King, Charles VI, had for some time been lost in the hopeless night of madness, and a dangerous rivalry had developed between the powerful houses of Orleans and Burgundy, offering Henry the opportunity for intervention.

Against this background Lancaster was left to manage as best he could. Garrisons were left unpaid; castle walls began to crumble for lack of repair. The outposts like Jedburgh, Roxburgh and Fast Castle were especially vulnerable. Despite the truce the walls had to be watched day and night. Those who wandered outside were liable to be murdered. The situation was particularly bad at Jedburgh Castle, which, like Roxburgh, had been in English hands since the Scots defeat at Neville's Cross. Isolated in Teviotdale the garrison was close to cracking. The captain, Robert Hoppen, was reduced to making the dangerous journey to Berwick to beg for wages and to warn that the castle was so dilapidated that it was likely to fall to the Scots. Still nothing was done; and on 7 May 1409 Hoppen's prophecy came true when the castle was taken, apparently with some ease, by the country people of Teviotdale, for whom the English garrison had long been a burden. Albany reacted immediately to this unexpected success, ordering that the castle be completely destroyed to prevent it falling back into English hands. But this proved to be more difficult than its capture, forcing the government to provide some financial assistance for the labour required. James Douglas stood by with an armed force to protect the workers as they took the castle apart stone by stone.

The negligent government in London took fright at this shift of power on the Borders and immediately made arrangements to provision and reinforce Roxburgh and Fast Castle. From Fast Castle the warden, Thomas Holden, began some limited counter attacks against Scots guerrilla bands in his neighbourhood. But his position continued to be vulnerable; and in 1410 the castle was taken in a surprise attack by Patrick Dunbar, fourth son of the Earl of March. Holden, whose men had been responsible for considerable damage in the Lothians, was taken prisoner.

The limited war on land was accompanied by one at sea. Alexander Stewart, Earl of Mar, continuing to act in the role of chief Scottish buccaneer, captured the *Thomas*, a ship belonging to Richard Whittington of London, the Dick Wittingdon of fairy tale fame. A powerful riposte to the Scots attacks on land and sea came when Sir Robert Umfraville, vice admiral of England, led a squadron of ten ships into the Forth, ravaging the countryside on both sides of the estuary. Blackness and Leith were attacked, and fourteen Scottish merchantmen were taken as prizes. Umfraville remained in the area for fourteen days, finally retiring with such a rich booty that he was nicknamed Robin Mend-market in northern England. He followed this up with a cross Border raid, accompanied by his young nephew Gilbert, the titular Earl of Angus, ravaging the countryside about Kailwater, Rulewater, Jedworth Forest, and setting fire to the town of Peebles during the market day. As a reward for his endeavours he was appointed as constable of Roxburgh Castle. But Umfraville's exploits, gratifing as they were, did nothing to restore the serious contraction of English power represented by the fall of Jedburgh and Fast Castle.

Despite these provocations Henry and Albany attempted to shore up the crumbling peace. In 1411 a seven year truce was concluded, which expressly stated that no prisoner taken before Michaelmas 1410 was to be released. For Albany this inconveniently included his son Murdoch, taken at Homildon Hill; but at least it ensured that James remained secure in his English prison. Freed for the time being from any threat from the south the Governor now had to face a new danger on his northern flank.

Going back to the days of Somerled, the founder Clan Donald, the great MacDonald lordship of the Isles had enjoyed an ambiguous relationship with the crown of Scotland. Only formerly part of the kingdom since 1266 the Isles nurtured their own independent tradition. They were inhabited by people who were fiercely loyal to chiefs and traditions, but who had little sympathy with the more abstract concepts of patriotism. For them the kings of Scotland were remote and unsympathetic figures, often alien to a native Celtic tradition, and they rarely considered themselves bound by formal feudal oaths. Their loyalty was not automatic: it had to be earned. But once it was, it was hard to break. It was not the king, as such, that they followed to Bannockburn and Flodden, but Robert Bruce and James IV. But when central government was weak, or the monarch was a child, these attachments broke down, allowing them to revert to their own native traditions. By the late fourteenth century the semi independent Lordship had taken definite shape, when the chiefs of Clan Donald were recognised by their followers as *Ri Innse Gall* — the King of the Hebrides. In the treaties between France and

England and their allies in 1392, 1394 and 1398, Donald, Lord of the Isles, appears as an ally of the English, although he was the nephew of Robert III. Andrew Lang highlights the thinking behind Donald's political associations:

> Just as Scotland naturally turned towards France and the French alliance, so the Celtic prince, the Lord of the Isles, turned towards England and the English alliance. It would be childish to call this conduct 'unpatriotic'; the Celt recognised no common part in lowland patriotism...

Donald negotiated with Richard II in 1388 as an independent prince; and again with Henry IV in 1405 and 1408, when a treaty of peace and alliance was concluded. When the occasion was necessary Donald was quite prepared to make war on the 'foreigners in Alba' (Scotland). In 1411 he found the occasion in a dispute over the huge earldom of Ross, which comprised not only the island of Skye, but Ross and Cromarty, parts of Argyll and Invernesshire on the mainland.

When William, the fifth Earl of Ross, died he left as his sole heir his daughter Euphemia. Euphemia had two children by her marriage to Sir Walter Leslie — Alexander, who inherited the earldom in 1398, and Margaret, who married Donald of the Isles. Alexander Leslie died in 1402, leaving as his sole heiress another Euphemia. A weak and sickly woman, Euphemia decided to enter a nunnery, which meant, by the conventions of the day, that she was legally 'dead', and the earldom of Ross vacant. In terms of feudal law it should then have passed to the Lord of the Isles in right of his wife Margaret Leslie. But this would have meant a huge extension in Donald's power; the power, in other words, of an ally of England. In the circumstances Albany, with Euphemia's agreement, simply decided to ignore the rights of inheritance and proposed to award the earldom to his second son John Stewart, Earl of Buchan. So simple family greed could be cloaked in concerns about national security. Donald was outraged, inevitably deciding to press his claim by force of arms.

At the call of the Lord of the Isles, most probably in the traditional form of the fiery cross, a huge force of MacDonalds and their allies assembled; supposedly 10,000 in all. The army advanced rapidly over Ross, meeting no resistance until it came to Dingwall, where it was confronted by a force commanded by Angus Dhu, which was rapidly overcome, after Dhu's brother,

Roderic Gald, and the greater part of his men had been killed. From Dingwall, Donald marched into Moray by way of Inverness, plundering over a wide area. The Highland army continued into Strathbogie, devastating lands belonging to Alexander Stewart, Earl of Mar. There was no doubt that Donald had now won the earldom of Ross by the sheer power of his military might; but his campaign now took on a more sinister hue when he proposed to destroy Aberdeen and the lowland counties south to the Tay.

Reacting with great haste to the emergency, a small army was gathered in Aberdeen and the north east under the Earl of Mar. In the city an anxious look out was kept for Donald's host, and panic spread when his camp fires could be seen at night not many miles to the west on the banks of the River Don. Not a moment too soon Mar arrived with the levies of Angus and the Mearns. With him came Sir Alexander Ogilvy, sheriff of Angus; Sir James Scrymgeour, constable of Dundee and the hereditary standard bearer of Scotland; Sir Alexander Irvine; Sir Robert Melville; Sir William de Abernethy, a nephew of Albany; and many other barons with their retinues. They were met by Sir Robert Davidson, the provost of Aberdeen, with a body of citizen soldiers, who guessed what lay ahead if the Highlanders reached the town. Mar left Aberdeen behind, riding to the west, before coming across Donald's men on 24 July 1411 at the village of Harlaw, on the water of Ury, close to its junction with the River Don.

> And thus the martial earl of Mar
> Marcht with his men in richt array,
> Before the enemy was aware,
> His banner bauldly did display,
> For weel eneuch they knew the way,
> And all their semblance weel they saw,
> Without all danger or delay,
> Come hastily to the Harlaw.

Mar's army was heavily outnumbered by the host from the Highlands and Islands; but he had with him a high proportion of experienced men-at-arms, and his troops were generally better armed and disciplined. Scrymgeour and Ogilvy were in charge of the vanguard, while Mar commanded the rear with the bulk of the troops, including the Irvings, the Maulers, the Morays, the Straitons, the Lesleys, the Stirlings and the Lovels, all under their various chiefs.

44

Taking up position Mar's men braced themselves to receive the mighty Highland charge with level spears and raised battle axes. Scrymgeour and the men-at-arms managed to hold the onslaught, cutting their way through their more lightly armed opponents. Many fell dead; but still more came on. The Constable of Dundee was killed, overwhelmed by the weight of his opponents, as was the Provost of Aberdeen, surrounded in death by his fellow townsmen. One baron by the name of Lesley was cut down with all six of his sons. But still Mar and his men cut, hacked and thrust. Donald's men fought with equal determination, suffering casualties twice as heavy as their opponents. Over 1000 of his men are said to have fallen, the chiefs of the MacLeans and MacKintoshes amongst them. There was no subtlety to the Battle of Harlaw, no great technical skill in military matters: it was simply a grim and bloody slog, where naked courage and determination for once played a greater part than tactics and disposition. In the end it was a battle that was neither lost nor won. It continued until nightfall, when the two sides disengaged, Donald's army left for the north west, while Mar's, too exhausted to move, fell asleep where they lay, surrounded by the silence of death. The slaughter had been savage in a contest long remembered as 'The Reid Harlaw'.

The bloodiness of Harlaw took the heart out of Donald's war; and although the struggle with Albany continued to the following year, he eventually submitted, agreeing to become a vassal of the crown and surrendering his claim to Ross and his English alliance. Thus ended the first and greatest attempt to establish an independent kingdom in the north. In a sense Harlaw can be viewed also as episode in the continuing struggle against England. Although there is absolutely no evidence to suggest that Donald received any direct aid from Henry, one of his chaplains, John Lyon, went to negotiate with the English King before the campaign started. But the government at the time certainly placed the battle in the same class as those fought against England, extending the same feudal privileges to the families of those slain 'for the defence of the realm.' It is certainly true that if the Lord of the Isles had won Albany, squeezed between Henry of England and a resurgent Celtic power, would have been in considerable difficulty. No sooner had this war in the north finished than a truce was concluded between England and Scotland on 17 May 1412. It was declared that from the River Spey to Mont St Michael in Cornwall the two countries would cease all hostilities for a period of six years.

In England James had grown to manhood, ready to become a king, but with no prospect of release in sight. In obvious frustration he wrote to the Scottish nobility in January 1412 blaming Albany for the delay in obtaining his freedom. It is true that the Governor continued to be more concerned about the ransom of his son Murdoch than he did about that of his nephew and sovereign. But all discussions ended when Henry IV died on 20 March 1413. He was succeeded by the warrior King, Henry V, anxious to kick over the traces of his father's usurpation, uniting the nation behind him by reliving past glories in a major new phase of the Hundred Years War. As the first sign of his reign the conditions in which James and Murdoch were kept became temporarily more severe. Hoping to further the release of his son, Albany continued to adhere to a peaceful policy on the march during Henry's accession.

Over the next two years Henry continued with his preparations for the French war, although he was mindful of the need to attend to security in the north. Not willing to be taken in by Albany's good intentions he attempted to make good some of the neglect that the Border defences had suffered during his father's reign. In 1414 the warden of the east march, Henry's brother John of Lancaster, newly created Duke of Bedford, warned him that Berwick's walls were close to ruins. Extensive repairs were carried out on the King's orders here and at Roxburgh. However, the King was alarmed by a petition delivered to parliament in the same year outlining the general effect of the Border wars on life in the north. Robbery, it was reported, had become a way of life for many; the districts of Hexham, Tynedale and Redesdale were said to harbour renegade Scots and other outlaws; and the men of Redesdale were so lawless that the sheriff of Northumberland dared not enter the area to carry out his duties without the support of a small army. Above all, the predatory instincts of the peoples of the Border were so pronounced that they represented a real danger to peace and security. Bedford had done his best in difficult circumstances, but it clearly appeared to Henry that the best way of controlling the march was to have a man in place who could command the loyalties of local people; and the obvious candidate was Henry Percy, the son of Hotspur, who had long been living in Scotland, a semi hostage, since his grandfather's rebellion. In the ensuing negotiations the release of Murdoch Stewart was tied to a prisoner exchange for Percy. Nothing was done for James; for it suited both men that the Scots King should remain in captivity.

In the spring and summer of 1415 Henry's army and navy were concentrating at Southampton preparing for the invasion of France. His brother John was to be left in England to attend to the security of the realm, especially the northern Border. But the King had no desire to fight a war on two fronts, and was ready to reach agreement with Albany on the ransom of Murdoch and the return of Henry Percy. In mid May John Stewart, Earl of Buchan, Murdoch's brother, and Walter Stewart, his son, came to London to make the final arrangements for the proposed exchange. Things went well; and on 21 May Henry issued instructions for Murdoch to be taken closer to Scotland. Shortly afterwards, however, the agreement was aborted by an unexpected development, the circumstances of which are not at all clear from the records. All that is certain is that, while on his way to the Border, Murdoch was freed from his escort by a group of Englishmen, who held him for a week before he was retaken by one Ralph Pudsey.

While the return of Murdoch Stewart was generally considered to be a desirable objective in Scotland, the restoration of the house of Percy was of obvious concern to many on the Borders, especially the Earl of Douglas. Henry V was not yet the hero King of Agincourt, and there were many in England who saw him as no more than the son of a usurper. Opposition was both secret and open. Some like Richard, Earl of Cambridge, wanted to replace Henry with Edmund Mortimer, the English Earl of March, who had a stronger legal claim to the crown; while others persisted in holding to the belief that Richard was still alive in Scotland. Most prominent amongst the latter were a group of early Protestant reformers known as the Lollards, of whom Sir John Oldcastle, Lord Cobham, was the chief. The English government later asserted that the attempted abduction of Murdoch was part of a Lollard conspiracy. It seems highly unlikely that Albany was involved in these shadowy proceedings, although there may have been some connection between the Lollards and the Border lords, for whom the return of Murdoch and the retention of Percy would have been a desirable outcome. Two years later Thomas Payne, a confidential agent of Cobham, was arrested and charged with a similar plot to free James I.

Frustrated by the failure to have his son released Albany was prepared for a time to listen to more militant advice. As so often throughout history there were people in Scotland deluded into believing that English preoccupation with Continental adventures meant that the northern counties were vulnerable to attack. Now, with Henry poised to sail for Normandy, a large raiding force, said to be some 4,000 strong, entered Northumberland in July 1415. On the 22nd of the month they were encountered by Sir Robert Umfraville in the valley of the River Glen at the foot of Yeavering Bell, part of the Cheviot range only two or three miles to the north west of Homildon Hill. Umfraville's force was heavily outnumbered by the Scots; but he had 300 longbowmen who made good use of the restricted ground. The encounter was brief and sharp: sixty of the marauders fell dead and 360 were taken prisoner, with the remainder being pursued some twelve miles back to the Border.

The Battle of Yeavering Bell marked a premature end to the truce of 1412. When he heard of it Henry ordered the northern sheriffs to be ready to resist further Scots incursions. But Archibald Douglas managed to slip through their defences, riding as far south as Penrith, which was put to the flames. In retaliation the English crossed the western march and destroyed Dumfries. However, Henry, other than ordering some limited counter measures, was prepared to overlook Scots aggression, pre-occupied as he was with his coming war in France. Before he sailed from Southampton he empowered Richard, Lord Grey and others to negotiate with Albany for a renewal of the truce. Although there is no evidence that Grey's mission was successful the Border appears to have remained quiet while Henry completed the capture of Harfleur in Normandy and marched to immortality at Agincourt.

Henry's great victory on Saint Crispian's day — 25 October 1415 — opened for England a prospect not seen since the days of Edward III and the Black Prince. A major campaign of conquest was now possible. First the issue of Border security had to be addressed. For Henry the release of Percy was now imperative. As Agincourt had also helped to weaken Scots aggression for the time being, and the freedom of Murdoch was equally important for Albany, the two men were finally exchanged at Berwick on 28 February 1416. Percy was restored to his grandfather's lands, created second Earl of Northumberland and appointed warden of the east march. In Scotland Murdoch was soon closely involved in Albany's government, and was recognised in official documents as a kind of 'heir apparent.' With James left to seethe in impotent frustration in the Tower the Albany Stewarts were, for all practical purposes, the uncrowned kings of Scotland.

Henry made use of James as a political pawn, exploiting the divisions in Scotland between those who did and those who did not wish to see him return. In the spring of 1416 he decided to increase the political temperature in the north by reviving the claim of suzerainty, proposing to release the captured King in return for a formal recognition of English overlordship. Not surprisingly, the claim was rejected by the Scottish Estates, who supported their action by ordering that the Treaty of Northampton of 1328, in which Edward III had renounced the claim of overlordship, be published in all the main towns.

So far Henry had done no more than play into Albany's hands; but he proceeded to undermine him by proposing to release James on parole in return for hostages of the first rank, to include the long suffering Murdoch of Fife, and the Governor's second son, John of Buchan. This placed Albany in a difficult political situation: refusal would have meant that he was putting his own family interests before those of the King; acceptance would end his hold on power and all that he had worked for over the previous few years. In anticipation of agreement Henry allowed James to be taken to Pontefract, and then on to Raby Castle, even closer to the Border.

For Albany war offered the only 'patriotic' way out of his dilemma. This had the twin advantage of gaining him the support of the ever militant house of Douglas and ending peaceful negotiations for the foreseeable future. He also coupled his war plans with a half baked plot to free James, offering a convenient and insincere way of proving his 'loyalty.' Towards the end of 1416 and again in early 1417, feelers were put out to the Lollard underground in England. On behalf of the Governor, Archibald Douglas made contact with Sir John Oldcastle. Discussions were held about the possibility of a rising in the north of England on behalf of the Mammet, still living in Scotland, to coincide with a Scots invasion. Oldcastle and his men were also to break James out of Pontefract.

Needless to say, James had no knowledge of these plots. Anxious for the proposed parole agreement to go ahead, and worried by the delays, he sent John Lyon, the chaplain who had formerly acted for the Lord of the Isles, to appeal to the Scottish Council meeting at Perth in June 1417. But the intrigues of Albany and Douglas effectively destroyed any hopes he had. In July Henry was once again in France, ready to begin the conquest of Normandy. On the day that he left, the Earl of Northumberland learned that Albany was planning to attack Berwick by land and sea. Similar information had been received by Umfraville at Roxburgh, who also expected to be attacked. The anticipated invasion looked like being the biggest for some years. By mid August the Scots began a two pronged attack — Albany against Berwick and Douglas against Roxburgh. This was no raid, but a campaign of conquest, and both forces came supplied with siege equipment, artillery included. For Albany this was the most serious military operation he had been involved in since he crossed into Cumberland in 1388.

John, Duke of Bedford, acting as Regent in the absence of the King, was quick to respond to the emergency. From his base at Leicester he gave orders for the raising of troops. In the north Thomas Beaufort, Duke of Exeter, Henry Bowet, the Archbishop of York, and the Earl of Northumberland were assembling the local militia. All England north of the Trent responded to the crisis.

While these preparations were underway Albany's guns were battering the walls of Berwick, after which an unsuccessful attempt was made to take the town by assault. At Roxburgh, Douglas had begun mining operations against the castle and was predicting that he would take the stronghold within a fortnight. He was not given the time. At Barmoor near Lowick, a few miles south of Berwick, Bedford and Exeter met up with the northern levies under the earls of Westmorland and Northumberland. Exeter is said to have remarked that a high proportion of the troops were as good as any that were serving in France, demonstrating once again the military capacity of the English medieval state. On hearing of their approach Albany, not willing to face seasoned troops in open battle, retreated in haste leaving all his siege equipment. Not bothering overmuch about the fate of Douglas, he paused only long enough to set fire to the town of Norham just over the Tweed. Learning of the debacle to the east, Douglas made good his own escape. Thus ended what Albany's critics in Scotland soon called the 'Foul Raid' (foolish raid). As a military operation it was a dismal failure, reflecting badly on the Governor's prestige; but in political terms it served his purpose: the release of James was now further away than ever. Not surprisingly, the Lollard rising in England was also a failure. Oldcastle was captured and martyred in December by being suspended in chains over a slow fire.

The Foul Raid unsettled the Borders for the next two years. Reacting to the Scottish provocation Umfraville was given orders to carry out extensive reprisals. He crossed the Border time and again, destroying Hawick, Selkirk, Jedburgh, Lauder and Dunbar, and ravaging Ettrickdale, Lauderdale and Teviotdale. In the summer of 1418 a small English flotilla of six ships carrying 120 men-at-arms and 240 archers put to sea with instructions to attack all Scots shipping. The repeated blows forced Scotland on the defensive. Albany was keen to reach agreement, but Henry, who had enough of the Governor's vacillations, was after blood. In the summer of 1419 Sir William Douglas of Nithsdale, a kinsman of Earl Archibald, was captured on the west march and sent to the Tower. The sole Scots success came in the same year when Sir William Haliburton crossed the Tweed and took Wark Castle in a surprise attack, massacring the entire garrison. He only managed to hold it for a short time before it was retaken by Sir Robert Ogle. Haliburton and all twenty-three of his surviving men were then beheaded and their bodies thrown over the battlements. Atrocities were commonplace. Walter Bower reports the case of William Drax, the English prior of Coldingham, who set fire to his own church, burning to death some Scottish refugees who had taken shelter there to escape from Umfravilles's raiders.

As can be imagined, against the background of this ruthless war, espionage and intrigue were commonplace. Perhaps the most curious case is that of John Hardyng, soldier, chronicler, forger and spy. An employee of the Percies, Hardyng had fought with them at Homildon Hill and elsewhere on the marches. He came to the attention of Henry V and was sent on a spying mission into Scotland in 1418, to discover the best way of invading the country, and to collect evidence on the English claim to overlordship. He stayed in Scotland until 1421. During his mission he was badly beaten up, and developed a pathological hatred of the country, which he liked to compare to Hades, ruled over by Pluto in a 'palace of pride.' Hardyng left Scotland to spend the next fifty years of his life trying to persuade successive English Kings to enforce their feudal rights over the country, so convinced of the justice of his case that he even set about forging the necessary documents. In his dedication to Edward IV in 1463 he makes plain his feeling that Scottish independence was an insolent presumption:

Englande and Wales as to their soveraygne
To you obey, whiche shuld thinks share of ryght,
To see Scotlande thus proudly disobeye
Ayenst them two which bene of gretter myght,
It is a shame to every mannes syght...

While Hardyng was busy gathering or creating the materials for his chronicle, another visitor came to Scotland. The war in southern Scotland was of minor account compared with the great life and death struggle in northern France. Running short of both money and soldiers the Dauphin Charles sent the Duke of Vendôme to appeal to Albany for military assistance. With the consent of parliament the Governor agreed to send an auxiliary force to France under his son Buchan and Douglas's eldest son, the Earl of Wigtoun. Albany was enthusiastic about the planned expedition: it was popular with many of the barons, offering an outlet for their aggressive energies; it would help to take pressure off the marches; and with an increasing number of Scots going to France James was likely to remain a prisoner of Henry for some time to come. But the presence of the Scots in France was destined to have an effect quite different from that conceived by Albany.

When Albany died in September 1420 an uneasy equilibrium had returned to the Borders. By general agreement he was succeeded in the post of Governor by his son Murdoch, the second Duke of Albany. Murdoch was a disaster in the post, occupying a role in Scottish history similar to that of Oliver Cromwell's son, Richard, during the history of the Protectorate. Soon the pressures for the return of James began to mount. Aware of the effectiveness of the Scots troops in France Henry considered releasing James in 1421 in return for a ransom, hostages and the withdrawal of military aid for the Dauphin Charles; but he was still a prisoner when the English King died in August 1422.

Henry was succeeded to the throne of England by his infant son, now Henry VI. The new regency council, dominated by the little King's uncles, was faced with enormous tasks. Henry's death had been a serious blow to morale; the country was virtually bankrupt; and the French war was nowhere near an end. England could not afford the burden of maintaining a permanent state of readiness on the marches; and the flow of Scots mercenaries to

Charles was causing difficulties in France. The release of James, tied to an English alliance and an agreement to withdraw the Scots from the French service, appeared to offer a political solution to these problems. Almost immediately the new government adopted a more conciliatory position, associated with Cardinal Henry Beaufort, more than any other individual.

Beaufort, a skilled financier, politician and diplomat, was one of the first to appreciate the dangerous limitations of English war policy. With the country fully committed to Henry V's French adventure for the foreseeable future, Beaufort realised that peace with Scotland was imperative. James appeared to offer a route to peace. The Cardinal and other members of the council enjoyed good relations with the Scottish King, who had now spent most of his formative years in England. Happily, James had also fallen in love with the Cardinal's niece Joan, the daughter of the Earl of Somerset, which appeared to offer another way of increasing English and Beaufort influence in Scotland.

Negotiations for James' release continued throughout 1423. On 19 August the Scottish parliament meeting at Inverkeithing appointed William Lauder, the Bishop of Glasgow, George Dunbar, the Earl of March, and James Douglas of Balveny to agree the final terms. They travelled to York, where they met with the English commissioners. The principal English demand was for £40,000 '...for the maintenance and expenses of the lord King James during the time of his stay in England...' to be paid in six annual instalments of 10,000 merks, hostages to be given to ensure compliance. If possible this financial settlement was to be tied to a final peace treaty; but if this could not be obtained then a truce should be agreed. The English negotiators also made attempts to have the Scots troops removed from France. The Scots negotiators evaded this question, declaring that this was beyond their remit. In subsequent negotiations James also refused to be drawn on this matter, saying that these men were beyond his control, only committing himself to sending no further reinforcements. The York discussions also allowed for the marriage of James to some unspecified high born English lady, the details to be settled by a further embassy. The draft agreement was concluded on 10 September. It took on its final form in London on 4 December. Early in the new year James married Joan Beaufort. As a wedding gift 10,000 merks of his 'expenses' were remitted. In February he came north to Durham to complete the arrangements for his return to Scotland; the hostages came to England; and in early April 1424 the King was home, his long exile at an end.

The Treaty of London is a curious document, guaranteeing virtually nothing. James had been in England for eighteen years, seven years longer than David II. But in the end, the English, in their haste to do a deal, had obtained very little indeed. There was no final peace and the Scots expeditionary force with Charles was not recalled. A seven year truce was agreed; but something more lasting was needed. Even James' promise to send no more troops to France was to have no lasting value. Joan Beaufort, however much the King loved her, was to have very little influence in Scottish politics. There was, of course, the money; but even here less than 10,000 merks was ever paid, and James was to show himself to be singularly unconcerned over the fate of the hostages, one of whom, Malise Graham, Earl of Mentieth, was to spend twenty-six years in England. As the military situation in France went from bad to disastrous the English were never to be in a position to collect the balance.

The Treaty of London was Cardinal Beaufort's big political gamble; and it failed. Ultimately, James owed his liberty not to the goodwill of Beaufort or the Royal Council but to continuing English concerns about the impact of the Scots soldiers in France; and it is to an account of these men that our story now turns.

# CHAPTER 4
# A Foreign Field

Ye shall hear of wars and rumours of wars: see that ye
be not troubled: for all these things must come to pass
but the end is not yet.

*The Gospel according to St Matthew*

In the autumn of 1419 the French state was beginning to come
apart. The King, Charles VI, was insane. From early in the century
the country had been torn between the houses of Burgundy and
Orleans, the latter more generally known as the Armagnacs. In
1407 John the Fearless, Duke of Burgundy, had his bitter rival
Louis, Duke of Orleans, murdered in the streets of Paris. In the
civil war which followed both sides sought the friendship of Henry
IV. In response, English troops came to France in 1411 and again
in 1412, causing much destruction. The two parties managed to
settle enough of their differences prior to Henry V's invasion of
1415, suffering equally in the disastrous defeat at Agincourt; but
the quarrel re-emerged in the aftermath, becoming even more
bitter. When Henry landed for a second time in Normandy in
August 1417 ready to begin a systematic campaign of conquest,
the resistance he faced tended to be local rather than national.

Henry's war was an ugly affair, pursued with a single minded
determination by a man who was convinced that he had every
right to the throne of France. He was a good soldier, but a man of
little patience or mercy. There was no room for chivalry. The King
was intolerant of any kind of resistance, which was met with terror.
In 1417 Thomas Basin, the future Bishop of Lisieux, recorded
the effect of the campaign in Normandy on the local people:

It is not easy to convey what terror was inspired among the
inhabitants by the name of Englishmen alone — fear so sudden
that nobody, or almost nobody, thought there was any safety
other than in flight. If in most of the towns and fortresses those
captains who had garrisons had not shut the gates, and if the
inhabitants had not been restrained by force as well as by fear, it
is beyond question that many would have been left totally deserted
as certainly happened in some places. Indeed the people,

55

unnerved by a long period of peace and order, simple as they were, generally thought that the English were not men like everyone else but wild beasts, gigantic and ferocious, who were going to throw themselves on them and then devour them.

Their fears were not without foundation. When Caen fell in early September 1417 men, women and children were herded into the market place and massacred on Henry's orders. Some 2,000 had been killed when the King finally ordered a halt, after he saw an infant still sucking at the breast of a headless woman. Thereafter, in his mercy, he allowed his troops to rape and plunder throughout the town at will, deaf to the entreaties of the kneeling crowds. At the siege of Rouen in 1418 the garrison, close to starvation, opened the gates to allow some 12,000 civilians out in the hope that they would be allowed to pass through the English lines. These people were mostly old men, women and children. Instead of letting them go Henry ordered his troops to herd them into the ditches beneath the city walls to die slowly of hunger and exposure. Children were seen to wander amongst the crowds begging for food, saying that their parents were dead. Mindful of his Christian duty the King allowed new born babies to be taken out for baptism, before being lowered back down to their mothers.

The first pleas for Scots military aid were sent to Albany by the Dauphin Charles, the head of the Armagnac party, towards the end of 1418. Parliament was assembled and it was decided to send a force of volunteers, some 6,000 men in all, to be commanded by John Stewart, Earl of Buchan, Archibald Douglas, Earl of Wigtoun, and Sir John Stewart of Darnley. Transport was provided by the Dauphin's allies Castile and Aragon, who carried the Scots to France in a small fleet of forty ships. Henry, learning of their approach, sent his brother Bedford, to intercept them; but he arrived too late. Buchan and his troops landed safely at the port of La Rochelle in September 1419, a particularly fateful month for France.

Worried by English progress through Normandy John the Fearless of Burgundy tried to reach an understanding with his Armagnac enemies. Several meetings were held. At first things seemed to go well. But the hatred against John was deep. His supporters in Paris had been responsible for an appalling massacre of the Armagnac faction in 1418. When John came to

56

met Charles at the Bridge of Montereau on 10 September 1419 he was assassinated.

The new Duke of Burgundy, Philip the Good, was outraged at this breach of faith; and on Christmas Day 1419 he signed a treaty of alliance with Henry V. In this he had the support of the Queen of France, the unpleasant and notorious Isabeau of Bavaria, whose hatred of her son Charles extended to denying his legitimacy. The following March, Henry met with Philip, Queen Isabeau and the mad King Charles at Troyes in Champagne. Here it was agreed that Henry would give up his immediate claim to the throne of France, and would instead become the heir and regent of Charles in place of the Dauphin. The Treaty of Troyes was cemented by a marriage between Henry and Isabeau's daughter Catherine. Henry also bound himself to reduce those areas in the south of the kingdom which still acknowledged the authority of the disinherited Dauphin Charles.

From his refuge at Bourges in the province of Berry Charles could do nothing to stop these developments. Almost all of northern France was in the hands of his enemies. Mocked as the 'King of Bourges', he was short of both troops and money, so the entry of Buchan and the Scots into his capital was a considerable relief. Before long the Scots formed a high proportion of the Dauphinist forces; and by the summer of 1420 the 'Army of Scotland' was a distinct force in the French royal service.

The French war was no longer one of mobility but of garrisons and sieges. Rather than keeping Buchan's force as a compact whole it was split up to help defend the various strongholds in the Seine valley upstream of Paris, and further to the west in Maine and Anjou. Some of the troops were sent to Languedoc in the south of France to help reduce the remaining pockets of Burgundian support. The first action they saw against the English was at the siege of Melun, on the River Seine to the south east of Paris, in July 1420. Aware of the presence of Scots, Henry brought the captive King James I to the walls of the town, calling on his countrymen to surrender. They refused. The siege continued month after month, the garrison defying the best efforts of Henry's big guns. It wasn't until November, when the defenders were close to starvation, that Melun finally capitulated. As a condition of surrender the town authorities were compelled to hand over all of the Scots in the garrison, twenty of whom were subsequently hanged as 'traitors' to their King. But this did nothing to discourage the others, and fresh troops arrived from Scotland in early 1421.

When Henry returned to England in February 1421, after an absence of over three years, he had good reason to be pleased with the progress he had made: the long struggle begun by Edward III in 1337 seemed close to completion; he and his allies controlled a huge proportion of France; and he was the legally acknowledged heir of Charles VI. Still there were a number of worrying concerns. For one thing, his troops, even with Burgundian support, were seriously overstretched; and for another, parliament was to show itself to be increasingly reluctant to provide further finance for the apparently endless war. Most worrying of all was the growing presence of Scots in the Dauphin's forces. His mind began to turn to the possibility that the release of James might help to stop these reinforcements. For the time being, however, he was content to leave matters in France to Thomas, Duke of Clarence, his eldest brother and heir presumptive to the throne of England.

In February Clarence, with a force of 4,000 men-at-arms and archers, began a punitive raid in Maine and Anjou. Buchan and the Scottish field army were at Tours on the Loire, where they were joined by some local French levies, commanded by the Constable de Lafayette. The normal practice since Agincourt had been to avoid English armies in the field; but this was Clarence, not Henry V. Hearing that the English were near Bauge to the north west of Tours the allies decided to advance in that direction in an attempt to cut Clarence off before he could withdraw back into Normandy. After a rapid march the combined Franco Scots force arriving at Bauge in the evening of Good Friday 21 March 1421. There was no sign of the English, so the troops made camp at the little village of Vieil Bauge, just over a mile to the south west of the town. Clarence was reported to be some distance away at Beaufort. Between the two armies ran the Couosnon, a deep, rapid river with only the narrow bridge at Bauge by which it might be crossed. Buchan took the precaution of guarding the bridge with a picked force of thirty men under Sir Robert Stewart of Railston. He was backed up by a slightly larger force stationed at the nearby church with Sir Hugh Kennedy.

From his headquarters at Beaufort, Clarence had sent his men on raiding parties throughout the adjacent countryside. On approaching Bauge on the morning of Saturday 22 March one of these parties, thought to have been under the command of Sir Gilbert Umfraville, came across some Scots foragers, who were captured and taken back to Clarence for questioning. Up to that point Clarence had been completely unaware that there was such a large enemy force in the neighbourhood. He also appears to have been pleasantly surprised. Since Agincourt the French and their allies had taken to fighting behind the walls of castles and fortified towns. This was an inglorious form of war, which clearly did not altogether suit Clarence, a hot headed and impetuous man, with something of the character of Harry Hotspur. Jealous of his older brother's great victory at Agincourt, at which he had not been present, he now decided that his own chance for glory had come. Ignoring the fact that his troops were dangerously dispersed, and that the all important archers were not in camp, he decided on an immediate attack. Both John Holland, the Earl of Huntingdon and Gilbert Umfraville failed to dissuade him from this purpose. Even King Henry's instructions that no English army should go into battle without the support of the longbow, did not deflect him. Despite the closeness of Easter, Clarence set out at once with all the troops at his disposal, around 1500 men, accompanied by the Earls of Huntingdon and Somerset, Sir Gilbert Umfraville, Sir John Grey and Lord Roos. The Earl of Salisbury was left behind to gather up the archers and follow on as quickly as he could.

Clarence's approach to the bridge at Bauge was spotted by some of La Fayette's scouts, who rode off as quickly as they could, shouting in alarm. No sooner had the Scots stood to arms than the spearhead of Clarence's column was upon them. The fight for the bridge was fierce, Stewart's men giving a good account of themselves before they were joined by Kennedy. The main Franco Scots army was still some way off at Viel Bauge, so it was imperative that this small body of soldiers hold out as long as possible to allow their comrades to organise. Unable to force his way across the bridge Clarence resorted to fording the river, which he only managed to do with some difficulty. With their flank turned, the Scots retreated, allowing the mounted English force to advance as fast as they could across the bottleneck of Bauge Bridge, and then charge up a slope towards Viel Bauge, situated on a ridge some 300 yards from the banks of the river. Once in the village the fighting continued through the streets. With his troops strung out across the ridge back down to the bridge Clarence, all too late, began to appreciate the extreme danger of his position. He halted as many troops as he could and attempted to reorganise them beneath Viel Bauge. But at this point Buchan and his men began to pour over the ridge in alarmingly large numbers, soon enveloping the English and forcing them back downhill. The Scottish chronicler Pluscarden describes the scene:

> (The Scots) are most mighty men at a sudden chase and very good with the spear; and they came pouring in at the word with great shouting...and with so impetuous an onset did they assail and bear down on the English chiefly with spears and maces of iron and lead and keen edged swords, that they bore down and felled to the earth both the chiefs and their comrades...

Clarence was one of the first to die, to be followed soon after by Umfraville, John Grey and Lord Roos. The survivors were pushed back to the boggy ground around Bauge Bridge by sheer weight of numbers. Over 1000 Englishmen were killed. Many were taken prisoner, including the Earls of Huntingdon and Somerset. Salisbury arrived late in the day after the action was over, managing to retrieve Clarence's body before retreating back to Normandy.

Set against the other great contests of the Hundred Years War, the Battle of Bauge was a relatively minor affair; but it had a huge impact, at least in the short term. For the first time in the war the English had been defeated in battle, and what is worse, Clarence was the first heir presumptive in the country's history to have met death in this manner. At midnight on the day of the battle the earls of Buchan and Wigtoun wrote to the Dauphin with news of the victory:

> ...all the power of your enemy's army is either taken or killed. And for that reason, most high and mighty prince, we pray you ardently that it will please you to come into Anjou so as to go forth into Normandy, for with the help of God everything is yours...

As a token of the triumph the banner of the dead Clarence was sent along with the letter. Charles was jubilant. The Scots in France were no more popular with the country people than the French had been in Scotland in 1385. Many at Charles' court had criticised them as only good for drinking wine and eating mutton. Now they had fully repaid his confidence:

> Ye who were wont to say that the Scots were of no use to the
> kingdom, and were worth nothing save as mutton eaters and
> wine bibbers, see now who has deserved to have the honour and
> the victory and the glory of the battle.

News of the victory spread across Europe, destroying the myth of English invincibility. In Rome Pope Martin V remarked that the Scots were the antidote to the English; and in London Charles, Duke of Orleans, a prisoner of the English since Agincourt, expressed the hope that he could obtain his liberty in return for some of the captives taken by Buchan and Wigtoun. Buchan was rewarded by being created Constable of France, the highest military office in the land, and a particularly distinguished honour for a foreigner.

For a brief period it looked as if Lancastrian France was about to unravel. Charles, a man with few soldierly qualities, took to the field in person, advancing with a combined Franco-Scottish force into Perche, taking the towns of Montmirail, Boisrufin, Beaumont-le-Cletif and Gaillardon. The army advanced to Chartres, dangerously close to Paris, and Scots raiding parties are said to have penetrated as far north as the capital. Alencon, close to the frontier of Normandy, was attacked, and the garrison so hard pressed that it had to appeal to the Earl of Salisbury for aid. Salisbury, now the senior military commander in France, managed to gather together a scratch force by taking troops from all the garrisons in Normandy; but he still had insufficient strength to face his enemies in battle, and had to retreat to the north, losing 300 men in his rearguard to the advancing dauphinist army. Even so, the Dauphin's campaign was badly managed: rather than concentrating his strength it was dispersed over too wide an area to make a decisive impact on his weaker foe.

In England Henry reacted to the news from France with his usual calmness. It was clear to him that Clarence had been routed because he had offered battle without archers, and it is said that if he had survived he would have been court marshalled for disobeying orders. It was imperative to restore the situation as quickly as possible. Henry set about organising the troops and money for a fresh campaign. By now the first flush of glory had passed from the King's French war, and many were becoming aware of its ruinous financial consequences. The chronicler Adam of Usk recorded his own feelings:

Our Lord the King, after rendering every man throughout the kingdom who has money, now returns to France. Woe is me! mighty men and the treasure of the realm will be foredone about this business. And indeed the grievous exactions of the people are accompanied by murmurs and smothered curses.

Despite Henry's best efforts he was only able to collect enough money for 900 men-at-arms and 3,300 archers. He sailed from Dover at the end of May, destined never to see England again. With him came James I, whom Henry intended to use to try to persuade the Scots to lay down their arms. Henry's presence in the field was enough on its own to effect an English recovery before a blow had been struck. Unwilling to face the King in battle Charles abandoned the siege of Chartres. Shortly afterwards Henry took Dreux, fifty miles to the west of Paris, and a whole host of lesser garrisons surrendered to him without a fight. After driving most of the Dauphinist forces back over the River Loire, he settled down with his small army before the walls of Meaux, the largest enemy stronghold near the capital, defended by a mixed force of French and Scots. The siege of Meaux continued throughout the winter season. It was a bitter, hard affair, fought out in deteriorating weather conditions. Dysentery began to spread in the cold, wet English trenches. Henry himself took ill. Meaux finally surrendered in May 1422. Most of the garrison were spared in the agreement entered into, with the exception of those of 'Wales or Scotland, if any such there be.'

Henry could not shake off the illness contracted at Meaux. He got steadily weaker, and finally died at the castle of Bois-de-Vincennes near Paris at the end of August. Shortly before his death he was confronted by some invisible presence, which appears to have warned him of the fate of his soul, for he suddenly said 'You lie, you lie; my portion is with the Lord Jesus.' The long suffering Charles VI survived him for some weeks, dying on 21 October. In terms of the Treaty of Troyes the new King of England and France was the infant Henry VI. In the south the Dauphin was recognised as King Charles VII, although he was to remain uncrowned for some years. The fate of Lancastrian France was in the hands of the Duke of Bedford.

With the war in temporary hibernation the weakness of Charles' military command became more apparent. As well as the Army of Scotland he was dependent on other foreign units, principally mercenaries from Lombardy in Italy and some Spanish contingents, as well as the French forces he was able to gather. This polyglot army made co-ordination difficult. Moreover, many of the French officers resented Buchan as the supreme commander, and there was widespread resentment of the Scots in general, which, in part, explains the coming military disasters.

The campaign of 1423 got off to a reasonable start despite these difficulties. Salisbury was driven out of Vendome; and later in the season a Scots unit under John Stewart of Darnley, the Constable of Scotland, helped to repel an English column making for Bourges. Looking for more decisive action Charles concentrated his army in the summer, with the intention of attacking the important Burgundian fortress at Cravant on the River Yonne. With Buchan back in Scotland seeking fresh reinforcements, command was entrusted to Darnley, who was accompanied by contingents from Lombardy and Aragon. Aware of the danger Bedford sent reinforcements to his field commander Thomas Montague, the Earl of Salisbury, who was also joined by some Burgundian units.

On 31 July 1423 Salisbury and his army approached Darnley at Cravant. The two armies were separated by the Yonne, over which there was a single bridge, a situation reminiscent of Bauge. This time, however, there were no deficiencies in the English command. Stewart deployed his men to hold the bridge and the river banks on either side. Leaving Lord Willoughby de Broke to force the bridge, Salisbury looked for a crossing point further upstream. With a covering fire provided by the English archers and cannons the Burgundian infantry attacked the bridge, held by the Scots with Lombard and Spanish support. The first assault was held; but a second was more successful, and the fighting was now taking place in the narrow strip of land between the river and the town. With arrows now flying into their ranks at close range the Lombards and Spaniards broke and fled, leaving their Scots and French comrades to defend themselves as best they could. A sortie by the Burgundian garrison from the town into the rear of Charles' forces added to the confusion; and when Salisbury's archers appeared on the flank the position was hopeless. The Scots continued to fight on with desperate courage; but the French troops withdrew from the field and, according to one account, 'left the brave men to perish.' Casualties were high, amounting to as many as 4,000 killed and wounded.

Darnley was taken prisoner, having lost an eye in the struggle. He was joined in captivity by Sir William Forster, Sir Alexander Meldrum, Sir Thomas Seton, Sir William Hamilton and his son and Sir Thomas Coleville. Amongst the lesser prisoners was one seventeen year old Peter Forest, who, unable to raise a ransom and fearing he would die in prison, agreed to take service with the English.

The Battle of Cravant was a serious blow for Charles, and made Buchan's mission in Scotland all the more vital. At the beginning of 1424 he arrived back in France with another 6,500 men. In place of Wigtoun, who remained in Scotland, he brought that bird of ill omen, Archibald the Tyneman. With James set to be released the English had seen to it that this was the last Scots army to enter the French service. On 24 April 1424 the army — 2,500 men-at-arms and 4,000 archers — entered Bourges, helping to raise Charles' spirits. He rewarded Douglas by creating him Duke of Touraine. Douglas thereupon travelled to Tours, the capital of his new duchy, where the Scots were well received. The bad behaviour of his men soon caused the citizens to regret their generosity: several weeks later he was asked to move them out of town. In general the Scots allies behaved little better than the English enemies when it came to helping themselves to other people's property. A contemporary poem laments the difficulties experienced by the French civilians:

> Behold us through the frosty air, begging, in
> rags, the scanty dole.
> For all is gone. The hungry Scot, and haughty
> Spaniard, in their turn,
> Have stripped us to the skin, God wot! and left
> us to lament and moan.

In August the new army made ready to march into action to relieve the castle of Ivry near Le Mans, under siege by the Duke of Bedford. Douglas and Buchan left Tours on 4 August to link up with the French commanders, the Duke of Alencon and the viscounts of Narbonne and Aumâle. But before the army could arrive Ivry surrendered to the English. Uncertain what to do the allied commanders held a council of war. The Scots and some of the younger French officers were eager for battle; but Narbonne and the senior nobility had not forgotten Agincourt, and were reluctant to take the risk. As a compromise it was agreed to attack the English strongholds on the Norman border, beginning with Verneuil in the west. The town was taken by a simple trick: a group of Scots, leading some of their fellow countrymen as prisoners, pretended to be English, and claimed that Bedford had defeated the allies in battle, whereupon the gates were opened.

On 15 August Bedford received news that Verneuil was in French hands and resolved to make his way there as quickly as he could. As he neared the town two days later the Scots persuaded their French comrades to make a stand, Douglas apparently having forgotten the lessons of Homildon. He is said to have received a message from Bedford that he had come to drink with him and prayed for an early meeting. Douglas replied that having failed to find the Duke in England he had come to seek him in France. The army then deployed a mile north of Verneuil on an open plain astride the road leading out of the Forest of Piseux. Narbonne and the French division was situated on the left of the road, supported by a wing of French cavalry, while Douglas and Buchan were on the right supported by a similar wing of Lombard cavalry. Aumâle was given the overall command; but the heterogeneous army defied all attempts at co-ordinated direction. On emerging from the Forest Bedford drew up his army in two divisions to match the allies, with the usual distribution of men-at-arms in the centre and archers on the wings. He also took the precaution of posting a strong reserve of 2,000 archers to the rear to guard the baggage. Bedford commanded the division facing the French, and Salisbury that facing the Scots.

At 4 o' clock in the afternoon, as if by some prearranged signal, the two hosts advanced simultaneously. Once Bedford had taken his troops within arrow range he ordered a halt and the archers started to drive their stakes into the ground, a simple but effective device for snaring cavalry. The ground had been baked hard by the summer sun, and the stakes could only be forced in with difficulty. Seeing an opportunity the French began an immediate attack out of synchronisation with the Scots division. The archers on Bedford's extreme right were caught off balance, allowing the French cavalry to break through their ranks, leaving that flank of the English army dangerously exposed. This opportunity was lost when the cavalry failed to wheel round. They continued their charge away towards the baggage train to the north, while the men-at-arms in Bedford's division began a spirited attack on the French infantry to their front. Unable to withstand this pressure

65

Narbonne's division broke and was chased back to Verneuil, where many, including Aumâle, were drowned in the moat.

Having disposed of the French, Bedford called a halt to the pursuit and returned to the battlefield, where Salisbury was closely engaged with the Scots, now standing alone. The Lombard cavalry, anxious that their French counterparts were poised to take all the spoils, charged round the English left flank towards the baggage. By the time they arrived the French had been driven off by Bedford's reserve, which then turned on the Lombards and chased them from the field. Having tasted blood the reserve decided on their own initiative to enter the main battle, advancing on the unsupported Scottish right wing. The Battle of Verneuil reached its closing stages when Bedford returned from the south to take the Scots in the rear. Now almost completely surrounded the Scots made a ferocious last stand, falling and dying with shouts of 'A Clarence! A Clarence!' ringing in their ears. A contemporary French account describes the horror of the scene:

> It was a frightful spectacle to behold the hills of slain heaped up in the field of battle, especially where the strife had been with the Scots, for not one of them received quarter. The cause of this implacable slaughter without mercy was the pride of the Scots. Before the engagement, the Duke of Bedford having sent to know what were the conditions of the combat, they replied that they were not on that day either giving quarter to the English nor receiving it from them. This reply kindled the fury of the enemy against them, and caused their extermination.

Verneuil was one of the bloodiest battles of the Hundred Years War, and was likened by the English to a second Agincourt. Some of the Scots escaped, but not many. Altogether 6,000 allied troops were killed, including some 4,000 Scots. The English lost approximately 1,600 men, an unusually high figure for them, and far greater than the losses at Agincourt, indicating the ferocity of the fight. The Tyneman fought on the losing side for the last time. He was joined in death by the Earl of Buchan. The Army of Scotland had been severely mauled; but it was not yet ready to march out of history. Greatly saddened by the catastrophe at Verneuil Charles continued to honour the survivors, one of whom, John Carmichael of Douglasdale, the chaplain of the dead Earl of Douglas, was created Bishop of Orleans.

After Verneuil the remaining Scots regrouped under the leadership of John Stewart, ransomed after his defeat at Cravant. Over the next few years they took part in some limited operations against the English. At the end of 1426 they helped Arthur de Richemont defeat the English at Mont St Michel, forcing them back into Normandy, after which Darnley was given the singular honour of being allowed to quarter his own coat-of-arms with the *fleur de lys*, the royal arms of France. The Scots also saw action at the relief of Montargis in 1427, where the infantry were ably commanded by Hugh Kennedy. However, these operations were of a limited nature. Without substantially more troops Charles could not hope to defeat the main English and Burgundian armies. Indeed, the general picture was so bad that Charles is said to have contemplated giving up his hopeless struggle and taking refuge amongst the Scots. In the end he applied not for asylum but for soldiers.

In July 1428 a distinguished embassy came to Scotland to appeal to King James. It was headed by the Archbishop of Reims, and the poet Alain Chartier. They were accompanied by Darnley, resplendent with his French titles of Sire d' Aubigny et de Concressault and Comte d' Evereux. In meeting with the King and his court Chartier described the Auld Alliance as:

> ...inscribed not upon sheepskin parchment but engraved upon the flesh of men; written not in ink but in blood.

After this poetic flourish the embassy proceeded to ask for a fresh agreement based on a marriage between James' daughter Margaret and Charles' son Louis. Margaret's dowry was to be paid not in cash, but in troops — 6,000 of them. Recognising that this request was in conflict with the English truce agreement of 1424, and was likely to involve James in war, Charles offered the Scottish King, as an additional inducement, the rich French county of Saintonge, a cause of much future friction between the two realms. While James was reluctant to conclude a firm arrangement at that stage he entered into a draft agreement, which still allowed him to keep his options open and bring diplomatic pressure to bear on England. The treaty was signed at Perth in mid July and ratified by Charles at Chinon in November. Charles sought his country's salvation in little Princess Margaret of Scotland; but it was another woman altogether who was destined to save France.

With the negotiations completed Darnley spent his remaining time in Scotland seeking volunteers to come with him to France. When he returned in January 1429 the city of Orleans on the River Loire had become the centre of military operations. This was of vital importance to France: if Orleans fell to the English the whole of the south would be open to attack. However, the siege of Orleans also demonstrated the extreme weakness of the English position by the end of the 1420s: Bedford's forces were thinly spread, and the troops devoted to the reduction of Orleans were barely adequate for the task. The English army was like a spring stretched to the uttermost limit; all it needed was one sharp blow to force it back on itself.

Even before Darnley arrived the Scots were taking an active part in the defence of Orleans. William Douglas of Drumlanrig was killed in the fighting around the town in October 1428 and buried in the cathedral, as was another man by the name of William Douglas. In the garrison there were 169 Scots men-at-arms and 400 archers under a number of captains, including one John Wishart. They were joined by the main Scots force with Darnley and his brother William, who managed to enter the town in February when the English were in winter quarters.

When they arrived they received intelligence that a supply column carrying herrings and other Lenten provisions was on its way to the besiegers from Paris commanded by Sir John Fastolf, an English veteran. Darnley immediately joined with Dunois, the Bastard of Orleans, and other commanders in an attempt to intercept this column. The joint force came across Fastolf at a place called Rouvray St Dennis some twenty-four miles north of Orleans on 12 February 1429. At the same time another French force arrived from the west under Charles de Bourbon, Comte de Clermont, offering a good opportunity for a joint attack. But Clermont held back giving the English commander time to form his wagons into a *laager*, with two openings, one wide and the other narrow. These openings were closed by pointed stakes behind which the archers deployed. Dunois and Darnley began the attack. Unsupported by Clermont their force, mainly Scots, was cut to pieces. A French account describes the last moments of Darnley:

> In the ensuing battle, Sir John Stewart, coming to the relief of
> his brother who was being hard pressed by the English, pulled

him out of danger and, though wounded himself, made a most gallant and persevering resistance. But at length surrounded on all sides by his enemy and covered with wounds, the old warrior sank to the ground. His brother William who had retired from the battle, seeing what was happened flew to confront the enemy once more and was himself slain.

Darnley's body was taken from the field by Dunois and buried in Orleans Cathedral, where it remained until the outbreak of the French Revolution. The so called 'Battle of the Herrings' marks the end of the Scots as a distinct army in the French service. It was also the last English victory in France. Scots continued to serve with the French in much smaller units from this point forward. Even so, the office of Constable of the Scots army still existed, and Darnley was succeeded in this post by Sir Patrick Ogilvy.

After the engagement at Rouvray, Dunois and the remaining Scots fell back on Orleans. Morale was low; the position looked desperate. But already strange rumours were reaching Orleans from the court of Charles at Chinon. Finally, on 30 April 1429, the Scots and French troops on the battlements witnessed the incredible sight of a seventeen year old woman in armour leading a relief force into the town. Her name was Joan of Arc.

Joan, soon to be known as *La Pucelle* or the Maid of Orleans, came with a clear sense of mission. As she herself put it:

> No man in the world — kings, nor dukes, nor the daughter of the Scottish king — can recover the kingdom of France, nor hath our king any succour save from myself...and the deeds I must do, because my Lord so wills it.

It is no part of this book to tell the story of Joan, who properly belongs to the history of France; suffice to say that she taught the French how to fight, and the English how to fear. Orleans was saved and Joan led her countrymen to victory over the enemy at the Battle of Patay; Charles was escorted by her to Reims, the traditional coronation site of the French Kings, and was finally anointed as King Charles VII. During her brief career she was also accompanied by a small body of Scots, who remained loyal to her to the end. In the words of Andrew Lang:

> Alone of all the people with whom she was concerned, the Scots never deserted, sold, betrayed or condemned La Pucelle.

69

The author of the *Chronicle of Pluscarden* stayed with her even after she had been taken by the English, witnessing her martyrdom at Rouen in May 1431. Joan was more than a soldier: she was an inspiration. Her death brought no relief to the English, and simply began the death agony of Lancastrian France. In 1435 Bedford died and soon after the long French civil war ended when Burgundy made peace with Armagnac. Ten years later the French royal army was reorganised and two companies of Scots Guards were formed. These men were present in the final actions of the Hundred Years War in Normandy in 1450 and at the Battle of Castillon near Bordeaux in 1453, when the ancient English Duchy of Aquitaine disappeared forever.

# CHAPTER 5
# Roxburgh

For God's sake, let us sit upon the ground.
And tell sad stories of the death of kings.

*William Shakespeare, Richard II*

When James I crossed the Scottish Border in the spring of 1424 the prospects for a new understanding between England and Scotland seemed to be good. James had been impressed by many features of English law and government, and by the vigour of Henry V. His principle concern, moreover, was to establish himself securely on the Scottish throne. James' return had been opposed by the Albany Stewarts; and while Duke Murdoch was of little account, his son Walter was a much more vigorous individual. Even more seriously, Murdoch's brother, John of Buchan, who represented Scotland's French connection, and who commanded a powerful army in the service of Charles VII, had also been opposed to the ransom treaty. In October 1423 he had concluded an agreement with his nephew Walter, in which the latter agreed to observe the French alliance, prevent a truce with England, and if necessary to open up Dumbarton Castle to a force of French men-at-arms and archers, to be used against unspecified 'enemies or rebels.' James was naturally anxious to be rid of Buchan as quickly as possible, hence his refusal to recall the Scots in France in the treaty negotiations with England or prevent further reinforcements prior to his return.

Once back in his kingdom James had to proceed with caution. A seven year truce was agreed with England to run to 1 May 1431, which was generally well kept, despite some minor infractions. Freed from any concern about the security of the Border, James was left to concentrate on internal matters. The government of the Albany Stewarts, especially Murdoch, had led to a serious fragmentation of authority. It took the King some time to gather together the reigns of power, and he was always mindful of the dangers of baronial opposition, headed by his Stewart cousins. The death of Buchan and his allies at Verneuil greatly improved his political strength in Scotland. By the following year he was ready to move against his enemies.

Murdoch, Walter and their associate the elderly Earl of Lennox were arrested and executed. From this point forward James began to demonstrate a new vigour in both domestic and foreign politics which was to earn him many enemies.

There is absolutely no reason to doubt that James wished to do business with England and his Beaufort relatives; but he was always mindful of his own advantage. Fairly early on his ransom payments began to get seriously into arrears; and with England heavily committed to the French war there was no possibility that she would attempt to enforce collection. Beyond that James had no wish to antagonise the English. While he agreed to the French marriage alliance in 1428, he was initially very reluctant to send his young daughter Margaret abroad. The draft treaty simply offered a way of putting additional diplomatic pressure on England as a way of obtaining further concessions. In other words, James was not fully committed to either party, and was perfectly prepared to play one off against the other. His calculations had an immediate and dramatic effect.

James' agreement with Charles alarmed the English government, especially Cardinal Beaufort, the principal mover behind the treaties of 1423–4, who had gambled his political reputation on James' release tied to an English alliance. All of his calculations now looked as if they were about to come apart. Beaufort had been planning a crusade against the heretical followers of John Huss in Bohemia, a somewhat unrealistic project in view of the military problems in France. Before he could continue with his plans it was vital that he restored the diplomatic balance in the north. With this in mind he came to meet James at Coldingham in early 1429. No records of this meeting have survived. From subsequent discussions it would appear that Beaufort may have suggested the young Henry VI as a bridegroom for Margaret in place of the Dauphin Louis. It is equally possible, though, that this proposal may have come from James himself. Nothing ever came of the suggestion, although it was still being discussed as late as 1434. It seems that the English council simply used this as a way of delaying the French marriage. Doubtless Beaufort also took the opportunity of the Coldingham meeting to remind James of the outstanding ransom; if so his mission was a singular failure, for no further money was forthcoming.

The astonishing recovery of France after the appearance of Joan of Arc had a major effect on the policy of both Scotland and

England. With England now fighting a losing struggle in the Hundred Years War, to be followed on its conclusion by a major dynastic conflict, she ceased to be a serious threat to Scotland for fifty years. The Scots, for whom warfare to date had consisted of plundering raids in the main, took advantage of the new realities by turning their minds towards the recovery of Roxburgh and Berwick, all that remained of the English conquests of the Wars of Independence.

During the discussions of 1430 to renew the truce, due to expire in 1431, the Scots began to demonstrate a new assertiveness, an alarming development for the English negotiators. One of the ambassadors, Henry, Lord Scrope of Masham, reported his perceptions to the royal councillors in King Henry's presence at Calais in July 1430. Scrope was deeply concerned by James' ambiguous conduct. The Scottish King was willing to consider a general truce by sea — thus allowing him to send the promised troops to France — but only a limited truce by land. He also presented James as a potentially dangerous opponent 'a fell, a far seeing man, having great experience.' Not willing to face the prospect of a second front in the north with the situation in France at such a critical stage, the council agreed to accept the Scottish terms, disadvantageous as they were. In December the truce was renewed for a further five years, to run to 1 May 1436.

Peace with England did not deflect James from attending to the defences of the realm. Castles were strengthened and regular wappenshaws — armed musters — were held. The King had also learned much from the experience of the English war machine in France. Parliament passed statues calling on men to master the longbow, a skill that the Scots never acquired despite repeated admonitions. James was also aware of the increasing importance of guns and artillery in the science of war. The money which he gathered for the ransom was used, amongst other things, to purchase fire arms. In 1430 his agents in Flanders, where the best guns were made, were authorised to commission the manufacture of artillery pieces, which included one great assault weapon, or bombard, to be known as the 'Lyon.' Weapons of this kind were used to smash their way through the walls of castle and other fortifications, which would seem to provide a clear indication of James' thinking.

The prospect of a Franco Scottish marriage alliance put James in a very strong bargaining position. Reluctant to antagonise the

Scottish monarch the English made only the most perfunctory requests for the balance of the ransom money. Indeed, as the military situation in France deteriorated still further the English attempted to woo James away from any commitment to Charles by the most comprehensive peace proposal since 1328. In 1433 an embassy headed by Edmund Beaufort, the Earl of Mortain and the Cardinal's nephew, a leading member of the peace party in England, and Master Stephen Wilton came to Scotland with a remarkable offer: in return for a comprehensive peace treaty, involving a break with France, England would return both Roxburgh and Berwick to Scotland, and would abandon all claims of feudal superiority. James was tempted; but on a matter of such importance he would need to take the counsel of the leading men of the realm.

The Mortain proposal was debated for two days by the Council General meeting at Blackfriars in Perth in October. James himself made no direct intervention. His views were no doubt expressed by his confessor, John Foggo, Abbot of Melrose. Foggo argued in favour of the proposal, taking the rather cynical view that, even in the context of the French alliance, the King was still at liberty to make peace with a third party. This kind of Machiavellian politics was not alien to the spirit of the age. However, when it was openly expressed, especially by a churchmen, it had the effect of shocking his audience. Support for the proposal, which had been strong among some of the higher clergy, began to dwindle. Opposition to the Mortain plan was especially fierce amongst the lower clergy, whose views were vigorously aired by Walter Bower, the historian and Abbot of Inchcolm, and John of Inverkeithing, the Abbot of Scone. For these men the peace proposal was totally incompatible with the agreement between James and Charles. England was simply behaving like an artful wolf in its attempts to sow dissension amongst the Scots, and there was no serious intent behind the offer. This argument carried the day. Walter Bower records the outcome of the debate in his *Scotichronicon:*

> ...it was finally agreed that the English were trying in this matter
> to stir up division in our kingdom, since it was very clear that
> they were not really proposing to restore to us what belonged to us.

For his trouble John Foggo found himself accused of heresy. He was forced by the senior Scottish inquisitor, Master Laurence of Lindores, to recant the position he had taken in the matter.

It is difficult to reach a definite conclusion about the sincerity or otherwise of the English proposal. Walter Bower and his colleagues were quite possibly correct in viewing it as a cynical ploy, no more sincere than the proposal to marry Margaret to Henry. But it is also true that in the 1440's the English bought a temporary peace and marriage alliance with the French by surrendering territory in Maine and Anjou. It has to be said that against a background of profound Scottish distrust of English motives, any proposal for a permanent peace, no matter how seriously intended, was almost bound to fail. Few of the nobility or the ordinary people of the realm would have been prepared to drop their French guard in return for English promises, which might easily be withdrawn at a future date. Scots hatred of the English was now well established; and when Aeneas Sylvius Piccolomini — the future Pope Pius II — visited Scotland during the reign of James I he noted that 'Nothing pleases the Scots more than abuse of the English...'

Even while the Mortain mission was underway there were growing reports that the truce was beginning to break down. In July 1433 Scots raiders were operating near Berwick and in Glendale. The English retaliated by attacking Hilton and Paxton. Following the failure of the embassy, conditions became steadily worse. The defences of Berwick and Roxburgh were strengthened. Scots raids continued into the new year, when a greater part of Alnwick, the capital of the Percies of Northumberland was burned. With the cold war getting hotter James took this opportunity to improve security on the Border by dispossessing the Earl of March, an arbitrary action which directly contributed to the downward spiral in international relations.

The traditional view of James is of the lawmaker, the man who came back to Scotland with a mission to restore order and stability. In some accounts he is depicted as the strongest King to occupy the throne since Robert Bruce. But many of his contemporaries had a different view: for them James often behaved in an avaricious, arbitrary and vindictive manner. His destruction of the Albany Stewarts caused alarm. Further arbitrary action followed: the fifth Earl of Douglas, the hero of Bauge, was arrested and imprisoned on two separate occasions; and Malise Graham was deprived of the earldom of Strathearn while he was held as a hostage for a ransom that James had no intention of paying. Finally, in 1434, the turn of the house of Dunbar had come.

Gavin, Earl of March, the son and successor of the man who had defected to Henry IV, was arrested and his castle at Dunbar seized on the King's orders by William Douglas, the second Earl of Angus, William Chrichton and Adam Hepburn of Hailes. Custody of this powerful fortress was given to Hepburn. When parliament met at Perth, Dunbar was formally deprived of his earldom on the grounds that the restoration of his father by Albany in 1409 had not been legal. James attempted to compensate him with the earldom of Buchan; but the Earl's pride was not soothed by this financially unattractive alternative, so he and his family left for England, finally bringing the ancient Dunbar earldom of March to an end. James had no evidence that Dunbar had in any way considered following his father's example. His action greatly weakened the security of the east march at a dangerous time, bringing about the very thing it was supposedly intended to prevent.

Soon both Gavin and his son Patrick were involved in intrigues against James. More militant counsels were now prevailing in England. Henry V's youngest brother, the warlike and hot headed Humphrey, Duke of Gloucester, had achieved a temporary domination of national affairs. His allies the Earls of Northumberland and Nottingham had replaced the more diplomatic Earl of Salisbury in the office of warden of the march. The defection of the Dunbars appeared to offer the same prospect of intervention in Scotland that it had after 1400. Patrick Dunbar was stationed on the Border, and was given armed assistance by Robert Ogle the younger, the keeper of Berwick Castle. The protests of the Scottish government that Ogle was aiding 'Paton of Dunbar, the kingis rebell' were simply ignored. In a possible attempt to raise the Dunbar retainers against the King, Patrick and Robert Ogle crossed the Border with a large raiding force in September 1435, the most serious English incursion for some considerable time. The Scots were fully prepared. On 10 September Dunbar and Ogle were engaged by the Earl of Angus, the warden of the east march, Adam Hepburn of Hailes, Alexander Ramsay of Dalhousie, and Alexander Elphinstone at Piperdean near Old Cambus on the road between Coldingham and Cockburnspath. In the ensuing fight a few knights on either side were killed, before the English were driven off. Dunbar escaped, but Ogle and a number of other Englishmen were taken prisoner.

The Raid of Piperdean did little to improve the tense political atmosphere, although it did not cause a complete breakdown of relations. For a time at least James was willing to keep diplomatic channels open, with a view to a possible extension of the truce, due to expire on 1 May 1436. However, an important change in political circumstances on the Continent persuaded him that the time had come to complete the long delayed French marriage and to allow the peace with England to lapse.

Charles had been concerned by James' negotiations with England, and the rumour of a possible marriage treaty. With the revival of his military fortunes he no longer needed the soldiers requested in the draft treaty of 1428. Neither did he need a better understanding between England and Scotland. In response to French queries James denied that he was seriously considering a marriage agreement between Margaret and Henry. He was still reluctant, however, to lose the advantage he had over both sides by keeping Margaret in Scotland for the foreseeable future. In response to French pressure to send her to the home of her prospective husband, James protested that she was still too young, or that it was too late in the season. But the death of John, Duke of Bedford, which was followed soon after by the reconciliation between Philip the Good of Burgundy and Charles VII helped him change his mind. English fortunes in France now appeared to be in terminal decline. Having little to gain from Henry, and angered by the Piperdean affair, James was now more open to the prestige and advantages offered by the marriage of Margaret and Louis. The twelve year old princess finally sailed from Scotland on 27 March 1436, with an escort of eleven ships and 1000 men. Although the truce still had some weeks to run the English made an unsuccessful attempt to stop her progress, angering James still further. On 25 June she and Louis were married. For Scotland and England this marriage brought war; for Margaret it brought deep personal unhappiness. Neglected and scorned by her profoundly unattractive husband, she died childless at an early age, a political pawn in the history of three kingdoms.

On Charles' suggestion, James made ready to use the troops that he had formerly promised to France to make war in the north. While he had little direct experience of war, James had been present during some of Henry V's siege operations in France. He made ready to use his carefully acquired artillery train in an all-out attack on the fortress of Roxburgh, the occupation of which was a continuing irritant to all Scots. The time was right for such an attack; for Philip of Burgundy, England's former ally, was preparing to invest Calais, the most powerful English base on the continent. With the departure of Humphrey of Gloucester and the main English army for Calais, James seems to have believed that England was denuded of fighting men — a recurring delusion of Scottish kings since the days of David II.

The English were fully aware of Scots preparations for war; although it was not yet clear if the objective was Roxburgh or Berwick. On 27 June orders were issued for the sheriffs of the northern counties to raise the local levies to assist the march wardens. There was particular concern over Berwick, where the walls were in a bad state of repairs and the garrison threatening to mutiny because of arrears in wages. Desertion was commonplace. The Mayor, Thomas Elwick, was so alarmed that he reported the gravity of the situation to a small body of notables appointed to attend to the defence of the north headed by the Archbishop of York and the Earl of Northumberland. Elwick was instructed to return to the town with all possible haste

> ...for to trete the saide souldeours that were last therinne to abide and to acquite thaim so namly in that article of nede as thei myght deserve thanks of us for a tyme till that they myght be better ordened fore. The which Thomas after that he hadde soo doon, conceyyvying the grete scarcite of peple at that tyme left in oure (the King's) said toune and also the simple keepyng of the watches therynne, hired watches for viii days and viii nights and paid thaim of his own money.

Fortunately for English prestige, James decided to begin by attacking Roxburgh.

At the beginning of July, Sir Ralph Grey, the captain of Roxburgh, wrote to Thomas Langley, the Bishop of Durham, saying that he expected to be attacked by King James in person. James finally arrived with his host and siege guns in early August 1436. He had invested his personal reputation in the capture of Roxburgh, also known as the Marchmont, showing his confidence in the outcome of the enterprise by adding the legend 'Marchmont' to the royal signet and creating a Marchmont Herald, an act associated with the acquisition of new royal honours. To make sure the Lyon and the other guns in the royal artillery were properly used he brought with him a number of German experts. Yet, remarkably, despite all these expensive preparations, the siege was abandoned after only fifteen days. All the artillery, acquired at such expense, was left behind. The siege of Roxburgh was a fiasco which seriously damaged James prestige.

What exactly happened at the siege, and why it was abandoned in such haste, is something of a mystery. It is certainly true that Grey carried out an able and tough defence, apparently causing the Scots to exhaust their ammunition at a fairly early stage. Also the English had plenty of advanced warning of James' attack. The whole operation was delayed for far too long, giving the Earl of Northumberland time to assemble an army, which marched to the relief of Roxburgh not long after James began his siege operations. Hardying takes his usual delight at Scottish discomfiture:

> Therle then of Northumberland throughout
> raysed up the lands, and when he came it near,
> The kyng trumped up and went away full clere.

Scots memories of Homildon and Verneuil were certainly fresh enough for them not to wish to take the risk of facing the English in battle. But there also seems to be something more — a suggestion in the Scottish accounts that James may not have been entirely safe in the midst of his army. The details are infuriatingly vague. Mention is made only in the most general terms of 'dissensions' and 'conspiracies'. It is important to bear in mind that James and his successors did not have the financial means to pay for an army, and were dependent for their military force on the nobility of the realm observing their obligation to attend the King with their armed retainers when called upon to do so. This arrangement worked reasonably well when the monarch enjoyed the trust of his magnates. But James was not a popular King. He had been too greedy, too high handed to be at all comfortable amongst such a large number of armed noblemen, who were quite capable of treason or mutiny, as his descendants were to discover in 1482 and 1542. Whatever the exact circumstances of the Roxburgh fiasco, the only thing we know for certain is that conspiracy continued to flourish even after the army had disbanded.

The sudden and ignominious retreat from Roxburgh left southern Scotland open to attack. Fortunately for James, the English had neither the will nor the means to prosecute the war. His first taste of conflict on the Border did nothing to weaken the King's appetite. Over the winter season Adam Hepburn of Hailes was delegated to carry out limited operations on the frontier. When parliament met in Edinburgh in October James was as bellicose as ever, asking for money so that, as a near contemporary account puts it, '...he could levy an army and lead the host against England and take revenge for this injustice by force of arms.'

It was not to be. In February 1437 James was murdered in Perth by a group of noblemen to whom he had caused particular offence, providing flesh to the rumours of treason. He was succeeded by his son the seven year old James II. Conditions on the Border remained unsettled for a considerable time after the assassination of James I. As late as 1438 Thomas Roulle described the general picture 'as youth yt were opyn were (as though it were open war). But with Scotland now preoccupied with the problems of a royal minority, and England beset with her endless agony in France, there was little serious desire for a major Border conflict. The half-hearted conflict was finally brought to an end by a new nine year truce to run from 1 May 1438.

The next few years were a period of relative calm, at least as far as the relations between England and Scotland were concerned, and the truce was extended to May 1454. Henry VI grew to manhood, marrying Margaret of Anjou in 1445, during a period of temporary reconciliation between England and France. By this time most men had the measure of a King who was only a shadow of his great father, and who was not able to stand up in the whirlwind that was soon to beset his realm. Margaret, by contrast, was a woman of single minded determination, but who had the misfortune never to understand her adopted country. In 1449 the young James II — known from a livid birthmark as James of the fiery face — signalled his own entry into manhood by an equally prestigious marriage to Mary of Gueldres, the niece of Duke Philip of Burgundy. James' minority had been a particularly turbulent time. He grew up as a tough and resourceful individual, ready to seize the opportunities that fate was soon to thrust in his way.

The peace between England and Scotland broke down in 1448 for reasons that are not entirely clear; but it was most probably due to one of the many minor Border incidents which always had potential to escalate out of control. Indeed, the intervening years had not been free of incident, including a fairly major breach of the truce in 1446 when Archibald Dunbar, at the head of an English force, took the Hepburn stronghold of Hailes Castle in

East Lothian and, in the words of Robert Lindsay of Pitscottie, 'slew them all that he fand tharin.' He was afterwards ejected by James Douglas.

The Border war of 1448 rapidly acquired a serious character. In May, the town of Dunbar was destroyed by Henry Percy, son of the Earl of Northumberland, and Robert Ogle. This was followed a month later by the destruction of Dumfries by the Earl of Salisbury, the warden of the east march. These attacks did not necessarily represent a declaration of war on the kingdom of Scotland as such; but they most certainly meant war with the house of Douglas, by far the most powerful force on the Scottish march. In retaliation for these raids, William, the eighth Earl of Douglas, together with his kinsmen the Earls of Ormond, Angus and Orkney destroyed Alnwick and Warkworth. Further destructive forays followed into Cumberland as well as Northumberland. The situation was considered serious enough to bring the unwarlike Henry VI north on a royal progress to Durham. Matters, however, were ultimately left in the hands of the Percies and their allies, who were authorised to lead the biggest punitive attack on Scotland for some years.

In October, Northumberland crossed the west march with an army estimated at 6,000 men. He had with him his son Henry, Sir John Pennington, Sir Thomas Harrington, and Magnus Redmane. No sooner had they crossed the River Sark than the army made camp near Gretna, presumably with the intention of fanning out from here across the adjacent countryside. If so, Northumberland showed a deplorable lack of military skill in his choice of base. His army was placed between the Sark and the Kirtle Water, close to where both flow into the Solway, a dangerous, tidal waterway. Near to his camp stood a feature known as the Lochmaben Stone, the lonely survivor of an ancient prehistoric circle. An army caught in this position would effectively be locked into a kind of natural vice.

From the first the Scots were aware of Northumberland's presence. Hugh, Earl of Ormond, a brother of the Earl of Douglas, set about organising the men of Annandale and Nithsdale to resist the invasion. With the help of Sir John Wallace of Craigie, the sheriff of Ayr, the Laird of Johnstone, the Master of Sommerville, Herbert Maxwell of Carlaverock and other Border gentry he gathered about 4,000 men. On 23 October 1448 Ormond's army marched into battle. Northumberland clearly believed that there was no major force in the area capable of resisting his invasion, for he appears to have been taken by surprise. When the Scots appeared he rapidly organised his men into their battle divisions: his left wing, mainly Welsh bowmen, was placed close to the Kirtle Water, under the command of Sir John Pennington; Northumberland himself commanded the centre; and the right stretching towards the Sark was under Magnus Redmane. To the rear of the whole was the mud and marshes of the Solway; what is worse, the tide was beginning to advance. Lochmaben Stone stood in silent witness to the coming battle.

Ormond arranged his own force to match the disposition of the enemy. The left — opposite Magnus Redmane — was under Wallace of Craigie; Ormond faced Northumberland in the centre; and the right was placed under the joint command of Maxwell and the Laird of Johnstone, the ancestor of the Johnstones of Annandale. The English opened the engagement in their usual fashion by a discharge of arrows; and for a brief period it looked as if the battle was going to repeat previous Scottish disasters. But it would appear from the outcome of the struggle that Northumberland had not sufficient time to see that the archers were supported by infantry or cavalry. Perceiving this weakness Wallace of Craigie ordered his spearmen on an immediate charge, which scythed into Redmane's division. Pittscottie provides us with a vivid account of Craigie's charge:

> ...his men wes sa inrageit and ruschit sa furieouslie wpoun the Inglisch wangaird with exis, speris and halbertis and maid sa great slaughter at the first tocoming that they put the Inglisch men cleane abak fre thair standart and compelld thame at last to tak to flight.

Redmane was slain and his division routed. Heartened by Craigie's example the rest of the army followed him into battle. Unable to withstand the onslaught the English found themselves pushed back towards the Solway channel. Pittscottie continues the story:

> ...the filling of the sea, caused many to lose their lyves and perisch in the watteris. Utheris, siean this, doubted quhidder they would fight and die with honour or live with schame, and preferring the on to the other, were cruellie slain upon the water bankis.

According to the *Auchinleck Chronicle* 1,500 Englishmen were slain and a further 500 drowned in flight. Many prisoners were taken, including Sir John Pennington and Sir Thomas Harrington. Henry Percy the younger was also captured after he had success-fully helped his father to escape. All the captives were led off to Lochmaben Castle by Ormond. Estimated Scots losses range from a low of 26 to a high of 600, the most serious of whom was Wallace of Craigie, who was mortally wounded, dying some time after the battle he had done so much to win. The booty which fell to the victors was claimed to have been greater than at any time since Bannockburn.

The Battle of Sark — sometimes known as the Battle of Lochmaben Stone — was an important landmark in the history of Border warfare, although it is now almost completely forgotten, not even meriting the crossed sword symbol on Ordnance Survey maps. For the first time since Otterburn the Scots enjoyed a significant victory over their enemy, helping to wipe out the memory of Homildon. Until the reign of Edward IV they held the military initiative on the marches against an opponent weighed down by foreign and then civil war. But it also had the effect of increasing the prestige of the Douglas clan, a not altogether comfortable outcome for the Scottish government.

Angered by this unexpected setback, the English government ordered an immediate reprisal, paying no heed to the lateness of the season. The levies from Yorkshire, Cumberland and Westmor-land were raised by the Earl of Salisbury, the warden of the west march, and marched towards the Border in November. But after a fruitless three day expedition he retired with his demoralised force, having lost 2,000 horses. Salisbury's inglorious retreat was the signal for a Scottish counter attack, and the neighbourhood of Carlisle was ravaged. In the new year, parliament meeting at Westminster discussed the critical military situation in the north. Reinforcements were sent to the Border, and the King wrote to Sir Ralph Percy, the brother of Northumberland, and Sir Robert Ogle urging them to keep up the struggle against the Scots. James II was later to express the view that the English lost Normandy and Aquitaine because Scots pressure prevented them from sending essential reinforcements to France.

Humiliation in the north and disasters in Normandy considerably weakened the prestige of the Dukes of Somerset and Suffolk, who dominated the government the diffident Henry VI. By the summer of 1450 northern France was lost, a profound blow to national morale. Opposition to Henry's government began to focus on Richard, Duke of York. We can now detect the formation of the opposing parties of Lancaster and York, soon to be involved in a murderous civil war.

In the wake of the French disasters and growing political problems at home there was no stomach for war with Scotland, and negotiations were opened up for a new truce at Durham in September 1449. At first little progress was made because of English insistence on Henry's rights of sovereignty over Scotland, a pointless and empty declaration in the circumstances, designed, no doubt, to salvage some of the country's tattered prestige. The final truce agreement passes this question over in silence. The agreement of this year is of particular interest because it introduces a new term in the relations between the two kingdoms — the Debatable Land.

The ancient western boundary of the kingdom of Scotland was defined by the course of the River Esk; but from the late fourteenth century onwards this was the subject of constant disputes. By the time of the truce agreement of 1449 there was a small area whose ownership was claimed by both lands. The so called Debatable — or Batable — land was situated in the four miles that separated the Esk from the Sark, stretching away some thirteen miles to the north east almost as far as Langholm, embracing the parishes of Cannonbie and Kirkandrews. With the two governments unable to agree on ownership this area effectively was to become a no-mans-land, and in the course of time a kind of 'wild west' of the march where no law ran. By the sixteenth century it was to achieve particular notoriety as a hideout for outlaws and other broken men.

By the early 1450s James II was fully in control of the Scottish government. Freed from any immediate concern about his relations with England his principal worry was the inordinate power of the house of Douglas. In destroying the Dunbar earldom of March the King's father had unwittingly bequeathed to him a major political problem by removing the last effective check on Douglas expansion. While war with England might bring the crown some rewards, it was far more likely to increase the power and prestige of the Douglases, as the victory at Sark had shown. James was confronted by an even more worrying problem when the eighth Earl of Douglas formed an alliance with two powerful northern noblemen — the Earl of Crawford and John, fourth Lord of the

Isles, who had also succeeded to the previously disputed Earldom of Ross in the right of his mother. Douglas refused to break this alliance, and in 1452 he was murdered by James in a fit of passion at Stirling Castle. Thereafter the King was involved in an intermittent struggle with James, the ninth Earl of Douglas, the brother of the dead nobleman, who, amongst other things, was accused of treasonable associations with England.

By 1455 James was moving towards a final showdown with the Earl of Douglas. At the same time England was approaching its own great struggle between the houses of Lancaster and York. Preoccupied as they were with internal affairs, neither country was in a position to take advantage of the weakness of the other; but James gained the upper hand by disposing of his civil war just as the political antagonisms in England were on the point of breaking into open conflict. On 1 May 1455 the Earl of Ormond, the victor of Sark, was defeated and killed fighting against King James' army at the Battle of Arkinholm. Prior to this his brother, the Earl Douglas, fled to England, ready to hand over his last remaining stronghold, the castle of Threave in Galloway, to Henry VI in return for aid against James. Although the English government was later to conclude an agreement with Douglas promising to assist him to recover the lands taken from him by the one 'who calls himself King of Scots', it was able to do nothing in the short term; for on 22 May 1455 the first Battle of St Albans signalled the beginning of the Wars of the Roses with a victory for Richard of York. Amongst the Lancastrian dead was Henry Percy, second Earl of Northumberland.

With the Douglas danger disposed of and his troops still in arms this opportunity was too good for James to miss: no sooner had he heard of St Albans, and the death of Northumberland, than he ordered an immediate attack on Berwick, regardless of the truce. The garrison successfully resisted all attacks. James withdrew on this occasion; but from this point until the end of his life before the walls of Roxburgh five years later he remained poised to gain whatever advantage he could from the political confusion in England.

James showed his new assertiveness the following year when he laid claim to the Isle of Man, which prior to 1333 had been a possession of the Scottish crown. An attack was made on the island which provoked Thomas Stanley, the lord of Man, in alliance with the exiled Earl of Douglas to launch a retaliatory raid on Kirkcudbright, which was plundered and burnt in the summer of 1457. In popular tradition this brief war between James and Stanley over Man coincided with the activities of a Scots pirate from Galloway by the name of Cultar McCulloch, whose depredations had been so bad as to merit a direct appeal for divine intervention:

> God keep the corn, the sheep and the bullock
> From Satan, sin and Cultar McCulloch.

With Richard, Duke of York, in control of the English government after St Albans, James wrote to Charles VII in November under the pretext of supporting King Henry against domestic rebels, suggesting a co-ordinated attack on Berwick and Calais, the last English outpost in France. But Charles, who was anxious to uphold the position of Margaret of Anjou, declined to take part in such an operation. Nothing daunted, James continued his relentless campaign, agreeing to a truce at one moment, only to break it the next. In an aggressive diplomatic exchange in 1456, Richard of York, acting in the name of the feeble Henry VI, revived the claim of overlordship, provoking James still further. In the middle of August he crossed into Northumberland, capturing seventeen towns and small fortresses, and spending six days ravaging the countryside before retiring north.

James' aggressive adventures on the Borders demanded that special measures be taken for the defence of the realm in case of English retaliation. When parliament met at Stirling in October 1455 various defensive measures were agreed: all men between 16 and 60 were to be ready in arms as soon as they received news of the approach of the enemy; by the special request of the King the wealthier noblemen were to provide 'carts of war', a kind of primitive mobile artillery; and a watch was to be kept on the march between Roxburgh and Berwick. But without French support James, who was doubtless running short of money, and having gained no definite advantage, was unable to keep up the pressure. A further unsuccessful attack was made on Berwick in February 1457. Making no progress in his hit and run war James agreed to a truce in June, which was finally extended to July 1468. Even so, the situation in England was simply too volatile to persuade James to settle down to a long term peace, whatever his financial worries were.

In October 1459, after the Yorkist debacle at Ludlow, the Lancastrians were back in control of the English government, with their enemies in exile at Dublin and Calais. Here was a new opportunity for the restless King. Formerly suspicious of York's aggressive ambitions, James entered into negotiations with the rebel Duke, now poised to make his own claim for the crown of England as a descendent of the Earls of March. When the Yorkists invaded England from Calais in the summer of 1460 James was busy with his own preparations. No sooner had he heard of their victory at the Battle of Northampton in July than his own army moved towards Roxburgh, arriving there before the end of the month.

The army that gathered with James at Roxburgh was at least as powerful as that brought by his father in 1436. His artillery train was even stronger. James was an artillery enthusiast, who not many years before had received as a gift from Philip of Burgundy, his wife's uncle, the huge bombard known as Mons Meg, the most powerful gun in the British Isles at that date. There is no record that James brought Meg to Roxburgh. Knowing his enthusiasm for artillery it is not impossible that she was present. Mons Meg and her lesser sisters were now an essential part of siege warfare; but it is difficult to tell who was most at risk from them — those who fired the guns or those who were fired upon. Gunnery was still very primitive. The weapons were prone to cracking. Even more dangerous from the gunners' point of view was the problem of recoil, the backward punch that a big gun gives after it has been discharged. This was dealt with in the fifteenth century by banking heavy guns up with planking and wedges, intended to make them completely immobile, which, not surprisingly, had the effect of building up a tremendous strain. With depressing frequency the weapons burst, killing all in the vicinity.

James positioned his artillery on the north bank of the Tweed to keep up a steady fire on the fortress. We only have the briefest record of what then happened, or indeed who was in attendance. All that can be said for certain is that on 3 August 1460 the King was close to one of his bombards which burst on discharge, killing him instantly. He was thirty years old. James died, in the words of John Major, because he 'was over curious in the matter of engines of war.' Queen Mary is said to have arrived in the camp shortly afterwards with her seven year old son, now King James III, and persuaded the demoralised army to continue with the attack. Roxburgh, which had been continually occupied by the English since 1347, fell a few days later and was razed to the ground. For the second time in Scottish history a dead man had won a fight.

# CHAPTER 6
# Berwick

Indeed, history is nothing more than
a tableau of crimes and misfortunes.

*Voltaire*

News of the Scottish invasion soon reached the victorious Yorkist lords at Canterbury. Now that they controlled the government once again the arrangement that Duke Richard had entered into with James was conveniently forgotten. A few days after the fall of Roxburgh — although the news would not yet have reached the English court — they decided that Richard Neville, the Earl of Salisbury, should raise an army to repel the Scots. Apart from Roxburgh, Berwick was also believed to be under attack, suggesting that there were some Scots troops near the town. But without a decisive guiding hand the war on the Border petered out not long after the fall of Roxburgh. According to Pittscottie part of James' army, mainly Humes and Hepburns, crossed the Tweed and captured Wark Castle. The rest made their way home.

Even if they had remained, it is doubtful if Salisbury would have made it to the Border. King Henry was captured by the Yorkists at Northampton in July; but Queen Margaret and her young son Edward, Prince of Wales, were still at liberty; and there were considerable pockets of remaining Lancastrian support, especially in Wales and the north of England. Moreover, Richard of York had returned from Dublin set to cause a political explosion. Hitherto the Yorkists had been claiming that their struggle was not against the King, but the Beaufort faction of the Dukes of Somerset and their allies. After the victory at Northampton Duke Richard added a new dimension by claiming the crown itself, in right of his superior descent from Edward III through his second son Lionel, Duke of Clarence, the ancestor of the Earls of March. Not having troubled himself to consult his allies beforehand this came as a shock to even the staunchest Yorkist lords, chief amongst whom was Richard Neville, Earl of Warwick, the son of the Earl of Salisbury. Unwilling as yet to depose an anointed King, parliament decided on a compromise: Henry would continue to rule until his death, and would then be succeeded by Richard and his descendants. Edward of Lancaster had thus been disinherited.

Queen Margaret received news of this arrangement at Denbigh Castle in Wales, where she had taken refuge with Jasper Tudor, her husband's half brother. For Margaret, one of the most single minded and courageous women in English history, there was only one course: the house of Lancaster had to be saved, whatever the cost. With her supporters still too scattered to offer an effective resistance the only option open to her was to sail to Scotland to appeal for aid from the government, now headed by Mary of Gueldres.

Margaret with Prince Edward landed in Dumfriesshire in December 1460, and their presence made known to the Queen Regent. This created a dilemma for Mary. The English civil war had caused a new split between France and Burgundy, with King Charles supporting Lancaster, and Duke Philip taking the side of York. Mary was naturally bound to take the lead set by her uncle, Philip of Burgundy; but she also had to act in the best interests of her son. A strong and competent woman, she tended to follow the line set by her husband in foreign policy, seeking to obtain the greatest advantage from whichever side appeared to offer it. Although family loyalty should have inclined her towards the Yorkists, she was prepared to subordinate her personal attachments to obtain the greatest advantage for her adopted nation. She therefore came to meet Margaret at Lincluden Abbey, and here these two remarkable women spent some ten or twelve days discussing the possibility of Scots aid for the Lancastrian cause. The exact details of their meetings are unknown, though Margaret held out the prospect of Edward marrying Princess Mary, King James' sister. She appears also to have made some territorial concessions, chief amongst which was to promise the return of Berwick to Scotland. It seems likely that Mary was reluctant to commit herself at first to what appeared to be a lost cause. This changed at the beginning of the new year when she and Margaret received an astonishing piece of news — Duke Richard had been killed on 30 December 1460 by the northern Lancastrian lords at the Battle of Wakefield. On 6 January 1461 the Treaty of Lincluden was hurriedly concluded and Margaret rushed south with her Scots auxiliaries to meet her victorious allies.

The Lancastrian army assembled at York, where Margaret persuaded the nobles to endorse the terms of the Lincluden meeting. Her Scots troops, now far deeper into England than any of their countrymen had been for many years, were naturally anxious to begin plundering; but they were held in check with the rest of the northern army until they all passed south of the Trent, after which all were allowed to pillage and destroy at will. London was badly frightened by the approach of Margaret's wild northern host; a fear which was intensified by her victory over the Earl of Warwick at the second Battle of St Albans in February. Here Margaret was reunited with King Henry, who had been brought to the battlefield by the Yorkists. The Scots thirst for booty and mayhem reduced their military effectiveness, and they appear to have made only a limited contribution to the Lancastrian victory. With such an unpredictable and badly disciplined army Margaret was unwilling to press on to London and risk the irretrievable damage a wholesale sack of the capital would have done to her husband's cause. Instead the army returned north, leaving the capital to a second Yorkist army approaching from the west under Edward, Earl of March, the eldest son of Duke Richard. With Henry now in the hands of their enemies the Yorkists dropped the last pretence of loyalty to the house of Lancaster. At Westminster on 4 March 1461 the Earl of March was crowned as King Edward IV.

After St Albans the Scots returned home, leaving Margaret and the Lancastrians to suffer a devastating defeat at the hands of Edward at the Battle of Towton on 29 March. With his wife and son and the other refugees from the battle, the wretched Henry fled towards the Scottish Border. From Alnwick Margaret sent a plea to the Scottish government to be allowed to cross into Scotland. This put Mary in a difficult position: it was clear that the Lancastrians had been thoroughly beaten; open support for a lost cause was likely to bring major English reprisals; and her uncle was beginning to put pressure on her to abandon her support for Margaret and Henry. But the promise of Berwick, still firmly in Lancastrian hands, was too great a temptation, so the royal family and 1000 of their supporters were given refuge in Scotland.

From early in the year Edward had been aware of the importance of Scotland in keeping Henry's cause alive. He therefore wrote to Duke Philip of Burgundy asking him to persuade Mary to adopt a different course. In response Philip sent Louis de Bruges, Seigneur de la Gruthuyse, a senior diplomat, to the court of Queen Mary to undermine the Scots Lancastrian alliance. But there were other pressures on Mary at this time. James Kennedy, the Bishop of St Andrews, who had been abroad at the time of James II's death on a diplomatic mission, returned to Scotland charged by Charles VII with ensuring that the Queen Regent adhered to Henry and Margaret. Mary was well able to make up her own mind. The factor that persuaded her to adhere to the course set earlier in the year at Lincluden was Margaret's territorial promises: in addition to Berwick the exiled Queen now promised to hand Carlisle over to Scotland. In fulfilment of the first part of this promise the Lancastrian garrison allowed the Scots to occupy Berwick on 25 April 1461, the first time that they had held both the town and castle since these had been lost to England in 1333. As a mark of the triumph young King James came to a place that his father had referred to as 'our town, long wrongfully detained by the English.'

The recovery of Berwick was of considerable strategic importance to Scotland. It greatly increased the security of the east march, while weakening that of north eastern England by removing an important buffer zone. Edward IV was not yet secure enough on his throne to attempt to recover it by force. In any case it would have been dangerous to march with an army through Northumberland, an area strong in Lancastrian sympathies, and a source of much trouble for the Yorkist monarch for the next few years. However, Margaret's attempts to buy Scottish support in this way did at least give him an important propaganda advantage. For the Lancastrian Queen the recovery of the crown was an overriding objective which blinded her to the passions and prejudices of most of her countrymen. She underestimated the extent of English hatred and suspicion of the Scots, and the extent to which any cause which depended on their support would be fatally weakened. Edward, who was still far from being accepted as the lawful King by a large number of Englishmen, was now able to drape himself in a cloak of patriotism, happily exaggerating the extent of his enemies concessions:

> ...Margaret, in the name of Henry, lately called king, our great traitor and rebel, hath granted unto...the King of Scots, to his heirs and successors, seven sheriffdoms in our realm of England, and her son Edward in marriage to the sister of the said king.

Edward proceeded in the same letter to increase the blood pressure of his subjects by saying that the archbishopric of Canterbury had been promised to the Bishop of St Andrews, and that in the event of Henry's restoration England would be tied to the Franco-Scottish alliance.

Although Margaret had effectively given Edward a decided political edge by her reliance on an old enemy, Scots support for Lancaster left the north in a dangerous and volatile state, keeping a cause, fatally wounded at Towton, alive and active for a number of years. At the end of May Margaret with Prince Edward, John Holland, Duke of Exeter, and others advanced with a powerful Scots force to take Carlisle. On the east march the situation was equally critical, where one of the Paston correspondents reported that 'Berwyk is full of Scottys, and we loke be lyklyhood for another batayll now be twyx Skotts and us.' Edward was alarmed enough to postpone both his coronation and a planned parliament, declaring that he would come north himself to take charge of the army; but before he arrived the emergency passed. At Carlisle, Margaret and the Scots were defeated with heavy losses by John Neville, Lord Montagu. In the following month a raiding party, with Henry VI in tow, penetrated as far as Branspeth in County Durham, but enjoyed no more success.

Edward decided that the best way of responding to these provocations was to nurture long standing political divisions in Scotland. The Earl of Douglas was a useful tool in this regard; as, of course, was England's old ally, the Lord of the Isles and Earl of Ross, ready to take advantage of a new royal minority to assert his independent power. On 22 June 1461 the King issued a commission to Douglas and his brother John, Lord Balveny, with Sir William Wells and two others to open negotiations with Ross and his cousin Donald Balloch. John of the Isles was flattered by Edward's overtures, and, in the style of an independent prince, granted from his castle of Ardtornish a commission on 19 October to Ranald of the Isles and Duncan, Archdeacon of the Isles, to treat with the King of England. They accompanied Douglas to London, and on 13 February 1462 concluded a treaty with Edward at Westminster, which envisaged the conquest and division of Scotland. Ross agreed to become the vassal of the English crown in return for which Edward promised to assist him in conquering all Scotland north of the Forth — 'beynde Scottishe see.' Edward further promised to restore Douglas in his lands in southern Scotland, with presumably the whole area forming part of the kingdom of England.

The Treaty of Westminster is not an especially convincing document. Edward certainly intended to cause trouble for Scotland, though he made little practical effort to enforce its terms. Indeed,

England had neither the means nor the will to implement this grandiose, overblown scheme for conquest and partition. It simply offered a way of destabilising the country at minimum expense. Ultimately Edward used Douglas and Ross as a way of concentrating minds in Scotland: at the same time as he was negotiating the partition treaty he was also opening up negotiations with Mary.

The Lord of the Isles certainly took the Westminster agreement seriously. In a fit of hubris he set off on the conquest of northern Scotland, not troubling himself to wait for Douglas and his English allies. He mustered the vassals of the lordship and the earldom of Ross, who were placed under the command of Angus Og, his illegitimate son, and Donald Balloch, a tough and experienced soldier. Inverness Castle was captured, and proclamations issued in John's name to the inhabitants of the sheriffdoms of the north to acknowledge Angus Og as his lieutenant under pain of death. It was further declared that his officers would collect all taxes formerly paid to the crown, and that all those within his jurisdiction were to refuse to acknowledge the authority of King James. Yet without substantial English aid the rebellion of the Lord of the Isles, potentially of extreme danger, had little more than local significance, coming to an end with the Anglo-Scots truce of 1464. The Treaty of Westminster failed for the simple reason that Edward's principle enemy, Margaret of Anjou, left Scotland not long after it was signed.

As well as his attempts to make use of Douglas and Ross, Edward also exploited the divisions within the Scottish government. Mary had been happy to accept the gift of Berwick; but the failure of the Carlisle and Durham operations opened her to the dangers that Scotland faced in holding to a cause that was so obviously lost. A second Burgundian embassy appeared in Scotland warning of the risks of the government's present position. There was really no need for this; for Mary had already decided to adopt a more pragmatic attitude. She was followed in this by a group called the 'young lords', who favoured Burgundy and York. They were opposed by the 'old lords' round Bishop Kennedy, who adhered to France and Lancaster. It was clear by the end of 1461that Kennedy and his allies were in an indefensible position: for one thing, most of the Scots lords accused him of putting the country in jeopardy in the interests of France; and for another, Charles VII had died, leaving a successor, Louis XI, whose only measure of any cause was how useful it was to himself.

Margaret's continuing presence in Scotland was the main obstacle to peace. Realising that she was likely to get little more in the way of assistance from Mary she decided to go to France to make a direct appeal to King Louis. Delighted to see the back of her politically damaging guest Mary provided her with the necessary funds, allowing her to sail for Kirkcudbright in April 1462. No sooner had she gone than negotiations were opened up at Dumfries with the Earl of Warwick, as King Edward's representative. But Mary's position was weakened by the continuing activity of Kennedy, who offered Margaret a bridgehead back into Scotland, and who made every effort to abort the discussions with Warwick. He was successful in having them broken off for a time, causing Warwick to lead his army across the Border in early summer, when he captured an unnamed castle. Unable to deal with both Warwick and Ross the Scots soon resumed the talks. The Queen Regent's approach was welcomed by Edward, who left Ross to his own devices in the north, and ordered Douglas to stop his ravages on the Border. The exiled Earl was sent south, and, in the words of one contemporary account:

> Earl Douglas is commanded to come hence, and as a sorrowful and sore rebuked man lieth in the abbey of St Albans; and by the said appointment shall not be reputed nor taken but as an Englishman, and if he come in the danger of the Scots, they do slay him.

A short truce was also agreed and it was rumoured in England that the Scots were ready to hand over Henry, an unlikely move in the face of Kennedy's fierce opposition. All discussions came to a premature end when Margaret arrived back in the north towards the end of the year with a small French expeditionary force under the command of Pierre de Brézé — all that Louis was prepared to allow her in return for a promise to cede Calais to France.

Margaret landed in the north coast of Northumberland with her little French army, hoping to incite a Lancastrian uprising. To her disappointment all she managed to do was to establish an uncertain bridgehead at the castles of Alnwick, Bamburgh and Dunstanburgh. With Warwick approaching she realised how dangerously exposed she was. She then sailed on to Scotland, to collect King Henry and appeal for further aid. Although she could do nothing to prevent Margaret's re-entry into the kingdom, Mary offered no assistance, forcing her to appeal to the nobles to enter into private treaties. While she was away, Bamburgh and

Dunstanburgh were retaken by Warwick, who then moved to besiege Alnwick. The best Margaret could achieve in Scotland was an agreement with the Earl of Angus, one of the old lords, who was promised an English dukedom as the price of his assistance. In London, Edward received reports that Angus was massing troops on the Border, ready to enter Northumberland in January 1463. He wrote to Archbishop William Booth of York informing him that Angus planned to rescue 'our enemies of France closed within our castle of Alnwick.' Yet despite this advanced warning nothing effective was done to stop the Scots. Angus and de Brézé managed to rescue most of the garrison and bring them to Scotland. Nothing more was attempted for the time being.

Edward's first response to the new Scots aggression was to allow Douglas to return to the Borders, armed with letters of assurance and plenty of money for any Scots who were prepared to join him. Soon he had managed to buy over, in the words of Kennedy, 'a great number of wicked people who did much damage.' Basing himself in the hills of Galloway from March 1463, he soon enjoyed some notable successes, continually attacking his enemies, capturing the Earl of Crawford, Lord Maxwell and other notable prisoners in an encounter where many were slain. His depredations continued throughout the summer. By July it was rumoured that Lord Hailes and some other magnates were on the point of joining him.

Although the Lancastrian cause in Scotland received a blow when Angus died in March, Margaret was able to organise sufficient force to launch yet another attack across the eastern Border. Sir Ralph Percy allowed a Franco Scots force to occupy once again the castles of Bamburgh and Dunstanburgh, an example that was followed by Sir Ralph Grey at Alnwick, thus completely unravelling Warwick's hard won winter successes. These minor victories in the field were backed up by a political triumph in Scotland, where Kennedy and his party appear to have gained the upper hand in their contest with the by now ailing Queen Mary. To demonstrate practical support for King Henry an army was assembled, and in the company of the young King James, Queen Mary, King Henry and Queen Margaret crossed the Tweed in the summer to begin the siege of Norham Castle, the last important stronghold in the north east still in Yorkist hands.

For Edward the situation was critical. With Berwick gone and Bamburgh, Alnwick and Dunstanburgh occupied by the Scots and Lancastrians, and Wark still in ruins after the raid of 1460, the fall of Norham would punch a huge hole in the defences of northern England. This was simply too serious for the King to leave to Warwick and the northern levies, so he proposed to come north in person. He only made it as far as Northampton, where he received news that Warwick and his brother Lord Montague had broken the siege and driven the enemy back into Scotland.

Warwick reacted to the emergency with speed and skill. Relying on Douglas to keep up his diversionary pressure on the west march, the Earl assembled all available forces, including the clergy of the archbishopric of York. He advanced rapidly to the vicinity of Norham, forcing the Scots to withdraw in some haste rather than risk a battle. Warwick followed this up with a major raid into south east Scotland, ravaging the countryside as far north as Dunbar.

Shortly after the retreat from Norham Queen Mary retired from politics. She died before the end of the year, leaving Bishop Kennedy in sole control of the Scottish government. Undeniably a man of strong principle and unbending loyalty, he lacked the foresight to see the extreme danger into which Scotland was being drawn by his support for a dying cause. The attack on Norham was a tactical disaster; what is worse, it threatened to bring about the most serious English invasion of Scotland for over sixty years.

By the late summer Edward was so exasperated by the continuing Scots support for Henry VI that he began to contemplate a major campaign against the kingdom. In July he wrote to the mayor of Salisbury from Fotheringay Castle, saying that he intended to be at Newcastle by 13 September 'toward our voyage against our enemies of Scotland.' The Earl of Worcester was authorised to begin naval operations, and soon the alarm spread as far north as Aberdeen, where a constant watch was kept for English ships. By September the King was in York. In the meantime Douglas and his guerrilla army continued to harry their fellow countrymen. The situation was so grave that Kennedy proposed to head the army in person in the company of his young sovereign. But as the season progressed the crisis passed. On the west march the Earl of Douglas was defeated in battle by a group of Border gentry, headed by the Scotts and Turnbulls. His bother John, Lord Balveny, was brought to Edinburgh and executed along with other Douglas supporters. King Edward himself came no closer to the Border than York.

The reasons why Edward failed to appear in Scotland are not entirely clear. Douglas' defeat is likely to have been a contributory factor; but the King, while he was a first class general, had acquired by this time a preference for the comforts of court over the hardships of the field. More to the point, his mortal enemy, Margaret of Anjou, had left the north in August with her son Edward heading once more for the court of Louis XI. While Henry still remained, first in the keeping of the Bishop of St Andrews, and then with the rump of the Lancastrian faction in England, he himself represented no direct danger, and could be dealt with by Edward's northern lieutenants. Besides, Edward had nothing to fear from any approach that Margaret intended to make to Louis; for in October both Kings had concluded a year long truce. Louis, true to his nature, did not trouble himself to consult Kennedy, or to include Scotland in an way in his deal with Edward, thus establishing a pattern that he was to repeat throughout his reign, during which the Auld Alliance reached the lowest point in its history.

Louis' treachery opened Kennedy at last to the new realities of international politics. With Margaret gone there was simply no further point in keeping up a hopeless struggle. Towards the end of the year envoys were sent to meet Edward at York. Edward realised that England needed to rest after a long period of war and civil strife, and was pleased to receive Scottish truce proposals. Douglas, an obvious obstacle to peace, was packed off to Ireland as the warden of Carrickfergus Castle. On 9 December 1463 a short ten month truce was agreed as a preliminary to further discussions to be held at Newcastle in April 1464. As a condition of this truce it was agreed that:

> The King of Scotland should give no further assistance to Henry, calling himself King of England, to Margaret his wife, Edward her son, or any of his friends or supporters.

Kennedy, in the fashion of many sudden conversions, was now an active advocate of a policy he had formerly despised. He wrote to Louis in March saying that while he intended to uphold the Auld Alliance he now saw the necessity of peace:

> ...for in God's truth the Kingdom ( of Scotland) has often been placed in great peril of perdition by occasion of the wars which have lasted so long between the two realms in times past.

In an attempt to prevent these negotiations the Lancastrian forces in the north east rallied under Sir Ralph Percy; but they were defeated by Lord Montague at the Battle of Hedgley Moor. Thereafter the existing truce was extended for a further fifteen years to 31 October 1479.

No sooner had the peace been concluded than it came close to collapse. King James' younger brother Alexander, Duke of Albany, was returning in the company of Thomas Spens, the Bishop of Aberdeen, from a visit to his maternal relations in Guederland when his ship was intercepted by an English privateer, *La Katerine Duras*, commanded by one Robert Spofford. The new truce had recently been agreed, and Albany had an English safe conduct, unlike Prince James in 1406. Nevertheless, Edward considered taking advantage of this act of piracy and breach of good faith by keeping Albany captive, to be held against a possible exchange for Henry VI, whose whereabouts were unknown at this time. Kennedy protested vigorously. Rather than risk a breakdown in relations Edward agreed to release Albany, although Bishop Spens was retained to ensure that no further help was given to Henry. However, relations between the two countries were eased still further when the fugitive King was finally tracked down in Lancashire in July 1465. This tragic and pathetic man, the tool of others for most of his life, was taken to the Tower of London, where he was lodged for the next five years. He was never to see his wife and son again. With Henry conveniently out of the way fresh Anglo-Scots negotiations in December extended the truce until 31 October 1519, an unprecedentedly long period, suggesting that it was intended as the first stage of a more permanent settlement.

There was good reason for the Scots to keep the peace at this time. In the person of Louis XI the French throne was occupied by the most devious and faithless of all the Valois kings. The Bishop of Glasgow had received information that during his negotiations with the English in 1463 Louis had openly said that he had no great regard for the Scots, and that once he had reached agreement with Edward he would help him to enforce his claim to homage over their land, by force if necessary. So it was perfectly clear that Scotland could no longer rely on France. Moreover, the political upheaval following the death of Bishop Kennedy in May, when Lord Boyd of Kilmarnock seized James III to secure his own hold on the levers of power, demanded that the country enjoyed good relations with its southern neighbour.

For the first time in its history Scotland was beginning to move away from France towards an alliance with England. This was a process that was at first slow and hesitant. It finally found full expression when James III began to rule in his own right.

For the next few years relations between the two kingdoms were good. The Scottish government made no attempt to take advantage of the renewal of the Wars of the Roses in the period between 1469 and 1471, despite Louis' best efforts to get it to intervene in support of Henry VI. For a brief period King Henry was restored to the throne and Edward fled abroad. With the help of the Duke of Burgundy he returned to England and defeated his enemies in 1471 at the battles of Barnet and Tewkesbury, where Edward, the Lancastrian Prince of Wales, was killed. He returned to London in May. Soon after King Henry was murdered, and the Lancastrian dynasty was extinguished from history. The only alternative to Edward IV was an exile by the name of Henry Tudor, Earl of Richmond, who had a flimsy claim to the crown in the right of his mother, Margaret Beaufort, a descendent of John of Gaunt. Few Englishmen took Richmond seriously. But for the ambition of one man, Richard, Duke of Gloucester, King Edward's youngest brother, the Sun of York might have shone forever.

With Edward firmly back on the throne of England he turned his gaze in anger across the Channel to Louis, who had been the principal mover behind the brief Lancastrian restoration. With England and France moving towards war, James III, now fully in control of the nations affairs, was placed in a uniquely advantageous position. Having no emotional or practical commitment to the France of Louis XI, James was ready to exploit the situation to his best advantage, and in the process was to bring about a revolution in Scotland's foreign policy.

His opening move was conventional enough. For a time relations between England and Scotland were frosty because the Scots had given refuge to the Lancastrian nobleman John de Vere, Earl of Oxford, after the Battle of Barnet; and the English likewise had opened their door to Lord Boyd of Kilmarnock, whom James considered a traitor. Aware of Edward's preparations against France he sent an embassy to the court of King Louis in May 1473. The representative of the Duke of Milan at the French court reports their mission:

> The ambassadors of the King of Scotland have been here some
> time, with offers to wage active war on the King of England if he

99

chooses to land in this kingdom, and they promised his Majesty that they will adhere to their ancient league and confederation, but that they must have what his predecessors ( King James') had received from the crown of France in the past, to wit a pension of some 60,000 crowns a year...

But Louis, believing that war between Scotland and England was inevitable, thought he could create a diversion on the cheap. All he was prepared to offer was 10,000 crowns in total, and then only once it was clearly established that James had been successful in keeping Edward at home. In other words, Scotland was to bring down upon itself the full might of the English war machine, without active French support, in return for the promise of a one off payment. Naturally enough, James declined this offer and prepared to do business with Edward.

For Edward to proceed safely against Louis he had to be sure that the peace in the north would hold. The best way of achieving this, he believed, was by means of a marriage alliance, the common currency of international relations at this time. This proposal was first raised not long after the birth of Prince James — the future James IV — in March 1473. It was raised again the following year and in July a commission was appointed to treat for a marriage between Prince James and Princess Cecily, a younger daughter of Edward IV. The negotiations went well: on 26 October 1474 the betrothal of James to the four year old Cecily was celebrated at Greyfriars Church in Edinburgh. Cecily came with a promised dowry of 20,000 English marks, to be paid in annual instalments, beginning in February 1475. This was the closest the two countries had come to a full peace since 1328.

As a sign of his good faith Edward revealed the terms of the secret Treaty of Westminster with the Lord of the Isles. John was thereupon summoned to appear before parliament on a charge of treason. When he failed to come he was formally forfeited. The sentence was reversed when he submitted to the King in 1476, but he was not allowed to retain the earldom of Ross, which reverted to the crown. He also lost Kintyre and Knapdale. Moreover, from this point forward the title of Lord of the Isles was to be granted by the crown rather than assumed by an independent prince.

For Louis the marriage treaty was a diplomatic disaster. As late as the summer of 1474 he had held to the belief that war between Scotland and England was inevitable. Now, in desperation, he tried to prevent the proposed marriage by searching around for an alternative bride for James, attempting with no success to persuade the Duke of Milan to offer one of his own daughters. Having alienated France's oldest ally he was left to face the English invasion of 1475 with no foreign support, and was forced to buy Edward off for considerably more than James had asked for two years before.

The Anglo-Scottish marriage treaty tied to a lengthy peace seemed to offer a new beginning in the relations between the two kingdoms. Edward, as time was to show, held to it because it suited him. For James, in contrast, it became the defining moment of his kingship. Setting aside the question of the Debatable Land, Scotland for the first time in many years had no outstanding territorial claims against England. Peace was an obvious policy, preventing any English attempt to recover Berwick. But James was not a popular King, and peace with England was not a popular policy, especially with the powerful lords on the Border, for whom war and plunder had become an essential part of their lives. The general mood of the times, moreover, was not in favour of good relations with England. As if to remind Scots of past English enormities the poet Blind Harry composed his great work *The Wallace* in the mid to late 1470's, an epic that, perhaps, reveals more about his time than it does about the life of the victor of Stirling Bridge:

> Our antecessowris, that we suld of reide,
> And hald in mynde thair nobille worthi deide,
> We lat ourslide, throw werray sleuthfulnes;
> And castis ws euir till uthir besynes.
> Till honour ennymis is our haile entent,
> It has beyne seyne in the tymys bywent;
> Our ald ennemys cummyn of Saxonys blud,
> That neuyr yeit to Scotland wald do gud,
> Bot euir on fors, and contrar haile thar will,
> Quhow gret kyndness thar has beyne kyth thaim till.
> It is weyle knawyne on mony divers side,
> How thai haff wrocht in to thair mychty pryde,
> To hald Scotlande at wndyr euirmair.
> Bot God abuff has maid thar mycht to par:
> Yhit we suld thynk one our bears befor
> Of thair parablys as now I say no mor.

After the conclusion of his 'phoney war' with Louis, Edward had no real need for the Scottish alliance; but for the time being he kept to his side of the bargain, and the instalments of Cecily's dowry continued to be paid up to 1479. By the beginning of the 1480's, however, the peace was showing signs of breaking down. The exact reasons for the collapse of the truce are uncertain. It seems to have involved a combination of renewed aggression by the Scottish Border lords, French intrigue, and a loss of commitment on the part of the English.

Opposition on the Border to James' peace policy was headed by his brother, Alexander, Duke of Albany, the warden of the march, who was arrested and charged in 1479 with breaking the truce 'be slaucteris, reiffs and hereschipps tresonable committit contrar to the king and the commne gud of this Realme.' Albany managed to escape from his prison in Edinburgh Castle and made his way to France. This offered Louis an ideal opening into Scotland. He was now involved in a major dispute with Maximilian of Habsburg, a future Holy Roman Emperor, over the inheritance of Charles the Bold, the last Duke of Burgundy, who had been killed in battle in 1477. Keen to prevent an alliance between Maximilian and Edward it suited Louis' interests to stir up trouble between England and Scotland. He sent John Ireland, a Scots professor at the Sorbonne, to Scotland charged with bringing about a reconciliation between the royal brothers, and to request that James, his 'dearest ally,' help prevent England making war on France. In response James sent his own mission to Paris under James Stewart, Earl of Buchan, which only served to increase Edward's anger, driven close to breaking point by the free lance aggression of the Scottish Borderers.

Albany's departure had done little to ease the tension on the Borders; for he had left others of a similar frame of mind, all too ready to make trouble. Chief amongst these was Archibald Douglas, Earl of Angus, Sir William Wallace of Craigie and Sir John Liddale of Halkerstone. It seems certain that while James was desperately trying to shore up the crumbling peace Louis was intriguing with the Scottish nobility to bring about war with England. Edward's patience was at an end, and the renewed Border disturbances provided him with an excuse to break his treaty arrangements with James.

In early 1480 Alexander Legh, Edward's envoy, came to Scotland with an alarming message:

> ...the King, upon grete grounds and urgent causes, is determined
> by the deliberacion of his counseill and the hool assent of his
> land, to make ayeinst the said Scottes rigarous and cruel werre,

for soo it is that the King of Scottes, contrearie to his promised trewes and also thassured mariage of his sone, for whiche mariage he hath receyved of the King grete and notable soumes of money, hath doen the Kinges subgietes by his subgietes to be invaded, murdered and slayne without cause or sommanicion ayeinst all honour, lawe of armes, and good conscience.

Legh proceeded to put forward Edward's ultimatum: Prince James had to be handed over as a surety for the marriage; James had to surrender Berwick, Roxburgh and other lands in Scotland which rightfully belonged to England; the Earl of Douglas was to be restored; and Edward was to be recognised as the lawful overlord of Scotland. The least Edward was prepared to settle for was Prince James and Berwick. There was simply no basis for compromise here: England wanted war. And, of course, so did Louis of France.

Almost immediately preparations for conflict were underway. On 12 May 1480 Richard, Duke of Gloucester, was appointed as the King's lieutenant on the marches, with power to call out the northern levies. The fleet was made ready, and artillery brought from Nottingham to Norham. Before Gloucester could organise his forces the Earl of Angus launched a raid across the Border, advancing as far south as Bamburgh, which was left in flames. In retaliation, Gloucester and the Earl of Northumberland attacked Berwick, but were soon driven off. Despite these acts of aggression James continued to fight a rearguard action for peace. He sent messengers to London suggesting that mutual grievances might be settled by discussion. His proposals were brusquely rejected. In November Edward announced that he planned to lead his army into Scotland in person the following year. Douglas was brought back to the Border to stir up trouble. An approach was even made to Edward's former ally, the Lord of the Isles. Considering the political embarrassment that Edward had caused him in 1474 it's of no surprise that he refused to be drawn on this occasion, preferring to remain loyal to King James.

In military terms the year 1481 came in with a bang and out with a whimper. Not willing to leave matters to Gloucester and Northumberland, King Edward made many lengthy and expensive preparations for an invasion which in the end never came. The two commanders waited patiently for the arrival of the King, who set out from London on his painfully slow northern progress in September. By the end of October he had only come as far as Nottingham, the closest he got to the frontier. It was now far too late in the season for a major campaign. The precise reasons for Edward's failure to take more decisive action are unclear: it seems that he was reluctant to take his eyes off events on the Continent. Above all, he did not want to turn his back on the slippery Louis XI any longer than was necessary.

While the King was at Nottingham he renewed the Anglo-French truce of 1477. Louis was alarmed that the English army might be sent to Europe to aid Maximilian. He was delighted to be told that Edward would continue with his offensive against Scotland in return for Louis' agreement to keep up the pension instalments promised in 1475. In addition negotiations were to be opened up for the marriage of the Dauphin Charles to Princess Elizabeth of York, Edward's eldest daughter. Louis had effectively achieved all he wanted: to keep the English at home he had involved Scotland in a potentially disastrous war, and then nimbly stepped aside, ignoring all pleas for aid. James' letters to his French ally were simply left unanswered.

While there was no major offensive in Scotland during 1481, the year was not without incident. Lord John Howard, the future first Duke of Norfolk, was given charge of an naval squadron and instructed to 'brenne the Leith and other villages along the Scottish Sea'. Howard sailed up the east coast in the company of the Earl of Douglas, entered the Firth of Forth and destroyed shipping at Leith, Pittenween and Kinghorn. He then proceeded to Blackness, where he landed, setting fire to the town and 'ane greit barge ship lyand besyd.' A second expedition later in the season was less successful after it was driven off by the Scottish sailor, Sir Andrew Wood.

To compensate for his brother's absence Gloucester kept up some limited actions on the marches, although he seems to have achieved very little and was unable to prevent Scottish reprisal attacks on northern England. The biggest operation of the period was his attempt to lay siege to Berwick over the winter. Lesley describes this in his *History of Scotland:*

> The King of England causit siege Berwick asueill be see as be land all the winter, and kest doune ane new biggit wall about the same; bot the sane wes sa stoutlie and courageouslie defendit be the Scottishmen, being thairinto that they kept it still in thair handis.

Berwick was especially prized by King James, the first Scottish monarch to set foot in the town since Robert Bruce. When parliament met in April 1481 to plan the defence of the realm, Berwick occupied a place of special importance. The King had taken special measures to strengthen both the town and castle walls. In addition, he had supplied the castle with artillery and was maintaining a garrison of 500 men, all at his own expense. Approving of this action the Estates agreed to levy a tax of 7,000 marks for the victualing and defence of the town. They further agreed to back up the royal measures by instructing the Border barons, and those whose lands lay near the coast, to see to the defence of their own strongholds, special mention being made of Tantallon, Hailes, Dunglass, St Andrews, Aberdeen, Hume, Edrington and Hermitage. The kingdom in general was warned to make ready for invasion, and all able bodied men were to be ready to assemble for the defence of the kingdom on eight days notice.

Of all the wars between England and Scotland, Edward IV's is perhaps the most puzzling. The war aims had been clearly set out by the Legh embassy in 1480. All Scottish attempts at compromise were brushed off; yet by the spring of 1482 nothing had been achieved. The reasons for this are not too hard to find. From the outset Edward had been torn between Scotland and Europe, not sure which direction to take, and failing to set clear objectives for his generals in the north. He was short of cash. Parliament was not willing to fund a long and expensive campaign, forcing the King to resort to borrowing. Supply problems had been intensified by the poor weather and bad harvest of 1481; and the large troop concentrations on the frontier were creating severe food shortages. Something more decisive was clearly required; yet the English had neither the time nor the resources for a prolonged military operation. The obvious way out of the deadlock was to make use of a native fifth column, a tactic tried with some success in the past. This time someone more significant and less compromised than the Earl of Douglas was required. In the spring Duke Alexander of Albany, James III's estranged brother, came to England from his French exile. Louis made no attempt to stop him.

For Edward, Albany represented something greater than Douglas or the Lord of the Isles: more than a rebel he was an alternative to the King himself. James was known to be unpopular with many of his nobles. With Albany set up as an alternative king the ensuing political upheaval in Scotland would help England achieve its war aims at far less cost than might otherwise be incurred. At Fotheringay on 11 June 1482 a treaty was concluded in which Albany was recognised as 'Alexander King of Scotland be the gyfte of the King of England.' In return for English support 'Alexander IV' was prepared to surrender Berwick, Lochmaben, Liddesdale, Eskdale and Annandale. Furthermore, he promised to break with France, recognise Edward as his liege lord and contract a marriage with Princess Cecily, still formally betrothed to his nephew, Prince James.

It is open to debate if Edward ever took 'King Alexander' seriously. The two treaties he negotiated with him — Fotheringay in 1482 and Westminster in 1483 — were not signed and sealed by the King. But Albany had useful allies amongst the Scottish nobility — the most important of whom was the Earl of Angus — and provided a way of unsettling James. With this purpose in mind he was packed off to the north in the company of the Duke of Gloucester. Edward once again reneged on his promise to lead the projected invasion, indicating that his health was starting to break down.

When the Scottish parliament met again in March 1482 James once more proclaimed his desire for peace; but the feelings of his fellow countrymen were made plain when they openly denounced the 'Reavare Edward calland him King of England.' Having attended to the defence of the Border the King made ready to assemble the national host to meet the invasion expected in the summer.

Gloucester had already signalled his intentions by leading a reconnaissance in strength across the west march, setting fire to Dumfries. After meeting Edward and Albany at Fotheringay he returned to the march to make his final preparations, authorised, on the King's mandate, to act as commander-in-chief. By the middle of July he had assembled a large army at Alnwick. Some sources claim he had 20,000 men, probably an inflated estimate. It is possible, though, that his force was at least as strong as the royal armies of 1385 and 1400; it is certainly true that this was the most serious threat that Scotland had faced in eighty years.

Paying for so many men over a long period was ruinously expensive. The troops were contracted to serve for only forty days, so speed and quick results were essential for the success of Gloucester's invasion. With Albany, the Earl of Northumberland, the Marquis of Dorset, Lord Stanley and Sir Edward Woodville, Gloucester crossed the east march towards the end of July 1482 making for Berwick. Intimidated by the size of the English army the town quickly surrendered, apparently with no attempt at resistance. It is possible that one of the wardens, Andrew Lord

Grey — a partisan of Albany and Angus — opened the gates by prior agreement, although this cannot be proved one way or the other. In contrast, the castle, commanded by Patrick Hepburn of Hailes, held out and offered a determined defence.

On receiving news of the English advance James assembled his own army and advanced to the relief of Berwick. He only got as far as Lauder, where on 22 July he was arrested by some of the leading magnates, headed by his three half uncles John, Earl of Atholl, James, Earl of Buchan, and Andrew, bishop elect of Moray. Buchan, in particular, as warden of the middle march and, as such, responsible for all the troops in the area, was ideally placed to carry out this *coup* against the King.

The reasons for the treason at Lauder are far more complex than the rather silly traditional tale of noble hostility to base born favourites suggests. James, like his grandfather, was not a popular monarch. With the magnates gathered in arms once again the rumours of conspiracy that had beset James I at Roxburgh in 1436 took on a more definite shape at Lauder. The principal charge against him was that he had debased the currency, a measure forced upon him to pay for a war that he had never wanted. Moreover, few of the nobles shared the King's enthusiasm for Berwick, and were unwilling to take the risk of facing the English in open battle in its defence. The English chronicler Richard Grafton puts this point well:

> ...if they should come to rayse the siege, that the Duke of Glocester woulde with them shortly encounter, and that if they lost the field, bote the strength of the realme was brought to an imbecilitie, the nobles sore minished, and the Castell lost and taken. And on the other side, if they obtenyed victorye, nothing was gotten but the pore town of Barwicke, and they were likely sone to be invaded wyth a greater powre shortly agayne..

It is also possible that Angus and the Albany faction may have played some part in inciting treachery against James, to what degree remains uncertain. What is beyond doubt is that the action at Lauder punched a huge hole in the nation's defences, leaving the country wide open to Gloucester. James was taken as a prisoner to Edinburgh Castle under the custody of his uncles, where he was to remain for some time in fear of his life.

Gloucester and Albany were still at Berwick when they learned of James' arrest. This was an astonishing turn of events, and is likely to have led them to conclude that some form of revolution on behalf of 'King Alexander' was underway. Leaving a covering force at Berwick Castle the rest of the army advanced to Edinburgh through the undefended countryside. Yet it soon became apparent that, whatever hostility there was against James, there was no real enthusiasm for Albany. While the seizure of the King and the dispersal of the Scots allowed Gloucester to enter Edinburgh without opposition, it had also created a major problem for the overall success of his enterprise. For James was now safely tucked away in Edinburgh Castle and Duke Richard had neither the time nor the equipment to reduce the stronghold. Moreover, as there was no sign of the Scots acclaiming King Alexander IV he was anxious to negotiate a quick agreement from his position of temporary strength.

Eager to complete his task at Berwick, Richard entered into negotiations with some of James' former ministers at Edinburgh on 2 August. Albany was promised not a kingdom, but his lost lands and an offer of reconciliation with his brother, a proposal which he readily accepted. Gloucester agreed to this breach of the Treaty of Fotheringay, although it is possible that Albany may also have made a secret promise to carry out the terms of the pact as soon as circumstances allowed. Two days later the provost and town council of Edinburgh, anxious to be rid of the English, promised to repay Cecily's dowry payments.

Having obtained the best agreement that circumstances allowed Gloucester returned to Berwick by way of the Lammermuir Hills. On 11 August he dismissed the bulk of his army, confident that he faced no further threat from the Scots. Hepburn was in an impossible position: his King was a prisoner and his country without an army. With no possibility of relief the only choice he had was to negotiate an honourable surrender. On 24 August 1482 Berwick was once more in English hands after a gap of twenty one years. This time it was lost to Scotland forever.

# CHAPTER 7
# None Dare Call it Treason

...the Scots are to be kept in readiness
to be let loose on the English on every
occasion.

*Sir Thomas Moore*

For England the war of 1482 had ended well. Berwick was once more in her hands, considerably improving the security of the north east. The military ascendancy established by the Scots in the years after the Battle of Sark was over. Although the Fotheringay agreement had come to nothing, the restoration of Albany would mean an increase in English influence north of the Border. The victory was celebrated throughout the realm; and as far away as the outpost of Calais the governor ordered the guns to be fired in salute.

Yet there is good reason for believing that Edward was not completely satisfied. The war was less destructive and the victory less complete than he would have wished. There is a hint of this in a letter he wrote to Pope Sixtus IV after Gloucester's return:

...the army which our brother lately led into Scotland, traversing
the heart of that kingdom without hindrance, arrived at the royal
city of Edinburgh, and found the King with the other chief lords
of that kingdom shut up in a most strongly fortified castle,
nowise thinking of arms, of war, of resistance, but giving up that
right fair and opulent city into the power of the English, who,
had not their compassion exceeded all human cupidity, would
have instantly doomed the same to plunder and the flames.

Berwick was a welcome prize; but Edward still looked for the additional territories promised by the Treaty of Fotheringay. While he held to the short truce Gloucester made before he left the north, no attempt was made to extend it when it expired in November, and the Border war was soon underway once more. English designs on Scotland were aided by fresh treasonable conspiracies against King James.

James was released from captivity in September and outwardly reconciled with his wayward brother. Beyond this there was little more. Albany clearly looked for political power, and parliament went so far as to recommend that he be appointed as the King's lieutenant general, with responsibility for defending the marches. Although the King still had to move with care, he effectively ignored this suggestion as he became more confident in his resumption of power.

Albany retired early in the new year to his castle of Dunbar, where he plotted a fresh coup against James. Aware that the support he enjoyed in Scotland was too narrow to guarantee success, he put out feelers to King Edward, suggesting a fresh agreement. In February 1483 three of his agents — the Earl of Angus, Andrew Lord Grey and Sir John Liddale of Halkerston — came to Edward to renew the terms of the Fotheringay pact.

Edward was delighted to receive them. Already he was planning a renewal of the war. When parliament met in January it had expressed its gratitude to Richard of Gloucester for his successes the previous summer by granting him a new hereditary principality in the north to embrace Liddesdale, Eskdale, Ewesdale, Annandale, Wauchopdale, Clydesdale and any other lands he might gain control of in Scotland. Albany's willingness to make substantial concessions in return for English assistance would help to make these dreams into reality. At Westminster on 11 February Albany renounced his allegiance to the Scottish crown, and promised to assist England in the conquest of Scotland, break the Auld Alliance, recognise English territorial rights on the marches and restore the Earl of Douglas, still languishing in interminable exile. In return Edward agreed to make Albany King of Scotland. This new treaty would provide the English with a pretext for renewing the war.

Amazingly, Albany and his brother were reconciled once more, even after this fresh evidence of treason. But, driven on by the devil of ambition, he continued his intrigues; and, after having exhausted the patience of his countrymen, he was finally attainted by parliament. Before this he had fled to England, after handing Dunbar Castle over to a party of English troops. But his endless plotting came to nothing when Edward suddenly died in April 1483. He was succeeded by his twelve year old son, Edward V. Beset by the problems of a royal minority, England had no further interest in Scottish affairs for the time being.

Richard of Gloucester, named as the young King's guardian by Edward IV, hurried south to engage in a power struggle with his chief rival Richard Woodville, Earl Rivers. By the early summer Gloucester was supreme. The marriage of Edward IV to Elizabeth Woodville was declared to be invalid, and their two sons, Edward V and Richard, Duke of York, were pronounced illegitimate. With the little princes securely held in the Tower their uncle was crowned King Richard III. As long as they were alive Richard's nephews represented a danger to his hold on power. They were seen with decreasing frequency; and after July 1483 they were seen no more. Soon after the story spread that they had been murdered. Many began to look across the Channel to the exiled Henry Tudor. This was the beginning of the end not only for the house of York but also for the ancient Plantagenet dynasty.

James initially tried to exploit the political uncertainty in England by renewing the peace offensive. Richard, not yet secure on his throne, was responsive, and the truce was renewed for a short period. Essentially James was seeking to return to the relations the two countries had enjoyed between 1474 and 1479. Dunbar and Berwick, he hoped, could be recovered by negotiation, and a new understanding cemented by yet another marriage alliance. But once Richard had successfully disposed of a rebellion led by his former friend the Duke of Buckingham, he began to adopt a more aggressive posture. For one thing, he depended on the support of the northern nobility, as ever eager for conflict with Scotland; and for another, a foreign war offered a release from domestic political tensions. By February 1484 Richard was announcing that he intended to march north with the army during the coming summer to destroy 'our enemies and rebels of Scotland'. Douglas and Albany were once more welcomed at the English court.

Disappointed by Richard's attitude James turned to France. Louis had died the previous summer, to be succeeded by his young son Charles VIII. The new French government was much more responsive to Scotland than Louis, and the Auld Alliance — which appears to have been in hibernation since the time of Charles VII — was formally renewed on 13 March 1484. This was especially dangerous for Richard as the French were also giving support to his main rival, Henry Tudor, Earl of Richmond. James seized the initiative by beginning an assault on the English garrison at Dunbar. Richard was now too preoccupied by a possible invasion of England by Richmond to come to Scotland as he had promised. All he was prepared to do was to give

Douglas and Albany permission to raise their own force, with a view to crossing the Border and inciting rebellion against James.

With some 500 horsemen the two exiles crossed the west march on 22 July 1484, advancing towards Lochmaben, where the annual fair was underway. This was once Douglas territory, and the Earl clearly hoped that he would be able to count on the old loyalties towards his family; but he had been away for too long, and his influence in the area had long since died away. When he and Albany entered the town people took to arms, believing this to be just another English raid. Soon a bloody battle was raging through the streets and the adjacent country-side, which continued from the middle of the day to dusk. News of the fight quickly spread, and the townspeople were reinforced by the local gentry headed by Robert Chrichton of Sanquhar, Cuthbert Murray of Cockpool and John Johnstone. Unable to withstand the mounting pressure the English force broke and fled. Albany owed his own escape to the swiftness of his horse. With no further help coming from the beleaguered Richard he returned to France, where he was accidentally killed the following year, leaving a young son who was destined to make his own impact on Scottish history. Douglas was taken prisoner by Alexander Kirkpatrick, who was suitable rewarded by the grateful King. Towards Douglas, now an elderly man, James behaved with remarkable compassion, overlooking his many treasons. He was sent to the abbey of Lindores in Fife, where he lived his life out in peace, dying in April 1488, the last Earl of Douglas.

After the Battle of Lochmaben Fair Richard allowed no further adventures in the north. With Henry Tudor attracting more and more support, even from former Yorkists, he agreed to new peace negotiations with James. These discussions were held at Nottingham in September. James desire for peace was ably expressed by his secretary, Archibald Whitelaw:

> It is an unnatural thing that war should be fought between us —
> we who are bound together within a small island in the western
> sea, and who are linked by living in the same climate and in
> neighbouring lands, sharing similarity of physique, language,
> appearance, colouring and complexion.

Although progress was initially delayed by the problem of Dunbar, a new three year truce was eventually agreed to include all forts and outposts, excepting Dunbar, which was to be left for six months, after which James was to give notice of his intention of recapturing the castle. A marriage treaty was also agreed, by which Prince James was betrothed to Richard's niece Anne de la Pole, the daughter of the Duke of Suffolk. Most important for Richard, the two Kings also pledged themselves to give no aid to rebels of either side.

True to his word James took no part in the final crisis of Richard's reign. There were, however, still Scots in the French service, and a party of these men, led by Sir Alexander Brunton of Earlshall landed with Henry Tudor at Milford Haven in August 1485. From here Richmond and his army marched into central England. On 22 August King Richard died defending his crown at the Battle of Bosworth Field, the last of the Plantagenets. The house of Tudor was now victoriously established in his place in the person of Henry VII. Soon after he married Edward IV's daughter, Elizabeth of York, hoping to end the dynastic wars forever.

Naturally enough the defeat and death of Richard caused much confusion in the north. James took the opportunity to lay siege to Dunbar, now a forgotten outpost of English power, which fell in the early months of 1486. Henry's hold on the throne in the months after Bosworth was highly uncertain. There were still many in the north of the country, where Richard had retained some popularity, who looked upon the new King as a usurper. Henry was particularly fearful of a possible invasion from Scotland, and in September he ordered the Yorkshire levies to assemble for the defence of the Border against 'the King's old enemies of Scotland'. The position was no better in October, when Henry announced:

> ...divers the subgettes of our cosyne James, kyng of Scottes, in great nomber and multitude, ben in ful purpose to invade and enter this our realme, entendyng to leaye seege to our town and casle of Berwick, and the townships and mansions of our liege peaple in our marches there to brenne, wast, and distroye, and the same our liege peaple there dwellyng to take, slee, and emprisone and devoure...

Yet Henry and James, both in different ways uncertain of their hold on their thrones, soon drew closer to one another. In July 1486 a three year truce was concluded which was intended to be the first stage in more comprehensive peace treaty. For James peace was a policy he had pursued consistently all of his adult life. As in the past he considered a marriage treaty as the best means of bringing this about. Recently widowed, he put himself forward as a prospective bridegroom for Elizabeth Woodville, the widow of Edward IV. But while he wanted peace he also wanted Berwick. When parliament met in Edinburgh in January 1488 the marriage settlement was firmly linked to the future of Berwick. Scotland's ambassadors were instructed to:

> ...have ye castel and toun of Berwik either deliverit to our soverane lord or else destroyit and cast doun...falyeing thereof that they sal not conclude upon the seid mariage in na wise in Ingland.

Aware of this declaration Henry ordered the Earl of Northumberland to be prepared to defend the town against a possible siege. But, important as it was, the question of Berwick was not an insuperable barrier to better relations between the two kingdoms. James and Henry planned to meet in July to discuss all outstanding problems, which would have been the first summit meeting between Scottish and English heads of state for a great many years. Unfortunately, while James was well disposed towards Henry and the English, the general line of his foreign policy was no more popular with his countrymen than it had been in the 1470s. In his *Anglica Historia* Polydore Vergil makes the following claim in regard to James:

> He neither refused nor granted the treaty of peace which his ambassadors sought, but replied by confessing frankly that his counsellors and his people were not fond of the English and neither desired nor deemed it practicable that peace with them should last for long.

James was a man in many respects ahead of his time. The tragedy was that he had neither the popularity nor the authority to carry off a major departure in the country's traditional policy. He was the first King in Scottish history to realise that the Auld Alliance did not always work for the nation's benefit; but it was only after the disaster at Flodden that others began to open up to this uncomfortable conclusion. On the Borders there were many who had built up little semi-independent domains that thrived on war and the pickings of war. For them peace with England would only bring an end of a lucrative way of life and an increase in outside interference.

Unable to master the forces ranged against him the unhappy and paranoid King was faced with a major rebellion by the spring of 1488. The Earl of Angus, a man who seems to have made treason a life long profession, and the Border families of Hepburn and Hume were heavily involved in the rising. Sadly for the King, so was his fifteen year old son James, Duke of Rothesay. In June the royal army was defeated at the Battle of Sauchieburn, and James was murdered in mysterious circumstances shortly after. His son then mounted the throne as James IV.

King Henry was immediately suspicious of the new anti-English government in Scotland, which held that James III's principal crime had been the 'inbringing of Englischmen'. As a sign of his distrust he gave willing refuge to 'the divers Scotts that come to the king for relief', who included John Ramsay, Lord Bothwell, soon to be an important English agent in Scotland. In response the Scots gave refuge to a number of Yorkist refugees who had fought against Henry at the Battle of Stoke in 1487 on behalf of the pretender Lambert Simmnel. But James IV was not yet stable enough on his throne to desire any real confrontation with Henry, so the truce was quickly renewed.

Despite the new truce the political situation remained tense. Another of James III's friends, Alexander Gordon, Master of Huntly, wrote to Henry asking for assistance against the government of his son in the rising of 1489. Although bound by the truce Henry may have considered the possibility of direct involvement in Scotland when he entered into an agreement with the Earl of Northumberland for 'the keepyng owt of the Schottys and warryng on them.' Any further moves in this direction were effectively ended when Northumberland was killed in April during a brief insurrection in Yorkshire. Besides, Henry was now involved in a dispute with Charles VIII over the duchy of Brittany which prevented any serious intervention in the north.

English aggressive actions at this time were limited to a semi-official naval war. A small squadron of five English ships had been attacking coastal towns in the Firth of Forth. In response the Scottish seaman, Sir Andrew Wood, with his two ships, the *Flower* and the *Yellow Carvel*, intercepted it off Dunbar, capturing all five of the enemy vessels, which were then carried back to Leith. Angered by this humiliation Henry commissioned one Stephen Bull to capture Wood and bring him to London. With three warships Bull waited off the Isle of May on 10 August 1490, ready to intercept the Scottish commander on his return from a voyage to Flanders. Catching sight of his enemy Wood prepared for battle. The fight continued for the whole day, only to be broken off at nightfall. It began again the following day, round the coast of Fife and into the mouth of the Tay, where all three of the English ships were grounded on sandbanks and captured. Wood was well rewarded for this service and it is said that his name 'became a byword and a terror to all the skippers and mariners of England.'

With the truce due to expire in October 1491 Henry sought to make use of those who continued to be loyal to the memory of the murdered James III. In April John Ramsay and Sir Thomas Todd promised to kidnap James and his younger brother, the Duke of Ross, with the intention of carrying them to England. When nothing came of this Henry turned to the veteran conspirator, Archibald Douglas, Earl of Angus. Angus entered into an agreement with the English, promising to try to prevent James from going to war. If he failed in this he further agreed to hand over his castle of Hermitage in Liddesdale in return for English lands of equal value. James, who was well used to Angus and his methods, took control of Hermitage and removed the untrustworthy noblemen further away from the sensitive Border area. Angus subsequently retired to his fortress of Tantallon on the East Lothian coast. Here he was besieged for a time by the King, who may have suspected that he was on the point of turning it into an English bridgehead.

Relations between England and Scotland continued to be poor at this time, although formal diplomatic relations had been resumed. In October 1491 the English parliament expressed strong anti-Scottish sentiments, saying that James' promises were effectively worth nothing, and that an open state of war was preferable to an artificial peace.

To counter possible English aggression the new government turned to France. One of James' principal lieutenants, Patrick Hepburn of Hailes, the former defender of Berwick Castle and now the Earl of Bothwell, arrived in Paris in 1491 charged with renewing the Auld Alliance. The new treaty had the effect of almost immediately involving Scotland in a possible conflict in which it had absolutely no direct interest. England and France were close to war over Brittany, and before the close of 1491 Henry was writing to the Pope complaining that Charles was encouraging the Scots to attack England. No sooner had James ratified the new defensive alliance than Charles made peace with Henry in the Treaty of Etaples without troubling himself to consult his ally. Thereafter relations on the Border settled down for a time.

Henry VII was in many ways a unique figure amongst the late medieval kings. A shrewd and careful man he considered war for its own sake to be economically wasteful and a failure of policy. For him security was of the first importance, especially security within the British Isles. James III was clearly the kind of man with whom he could do business; but the early policy of James IV upset his calculations. He was aware how close French intrigues had brought him to a major conflict at home, so it was important for him to close his northern backdoor at the earliest opportunity. As always, a marriage treaty offered the usual way of bringing about a better understanding.

In May 1494 Henry sent proposals for a 'perpetual peace', the first time this term had been used, which would be guaranteed by a marriage between James and Catherine Butler, the daughter of the Countess of Wiltshire. The Scots refused to commit themselves either to the peace or to the marriage; but they agreed to a new truce to last until April 1501. In 1496 Henry upped the marriage stakes considerably by offering, for the first time, his eldest daughter Margaret. This was an astonishing offer because it would bring James and his descendants into the English succession. Even so, it was rejected because James was about to embark on the first big adventure of his career.

Henry showed his good faith in another important way by refusing to get involved in a new rising by the Lord of the Isles. The MacDonalds had never reconciled themselves to the loss of the earldom of Ross. In 1491 the elderly John agreed to pass his title to his nephew Alexander of Lochalsh, who then determined to regain Ross by force of arms. In alliance with Clan Chattan he launched an attack on the royal castle of Inverness. The rising soon collapsed when he and his allies were defeated in battle shortly afterwards by the Mackenzies and Alexander was taken prisoner. Exasperated by this latest episode parliament declared the title and possessions of the Lord of the Isles to be forfeit to the crown in May 1493. John appealed to Henry in vain. The following year he accepted the inevitable and voluntarily surrendered his titles to the King in return for a pension. He died in Paisley Abbey in 1503 and his remains were buried on Iona. But the lordship of the Isles had not quite made its final exit from the stage of history.

In his dealings with rebels James proved himself far less scrupulous than his English counterpart. Although Henry had successfully fought off a challenge from one Yorkist pretender in 1487, by the beginning of the 1490's he was faced with a more serious threat from a man by the name of Perkin Warbeck, who was of Flemish origin. One of history's great clowns, Warbeck set himself up as the Yorkist alternative to the new Tudor dynasty, claiming, first of all, to be a bastard son of Richard III, then Edward, Earl of Warwick, the nephew of Edward IV- who was, incidentally, still held in the Tower of London by Henry — before he achieved his final metamorphosis as Richard, Duke of York, the younger brother of Edward V. It is difficult to accept that anyone could have taken this rather ridiculous figure seriously. He was, however, a useful tool for Henry's enemies, the most implacable of whom was Margaret, the dowager Duchess of Burgundy and the sister of Edward IV. With Margaret's help Warbeck moved from place to place, to be supported, when the occasion suited them, by Charles VIII and Maximilian of Austria. With James now mature enough to play the role of sovereign in the fullest sense, Warbeck appeared to offer a way for him to cut a figure on the European stage.

In November 1494 Margaret wrote to James telling him that the 'Prince of England' wished to visit. James readily agreed, regardless of the truce with England or the effect this unfriendly act was likely to have on Henry. Warbeck was duly received by James at Stirling on 20 November 1495. In the following January he was married to the King's kinswoman, Lady Katherine Gordon — a prestigious match for a Flemish adventurer, but much less so for a prospective king of England.

Warbeck was delighted. For him the reception by the Scottish King marked the peak of his career. But what did James expect to gain? In military terms he had put himself in a dangerous position because with Charles VIII now involved in his Italian war, and therefore anxious for good relations with Henry, he was likely to face an English backlash without any foreign support. It is doubtful if he ever really accepted the Warbeck pretence any more than Charles of France had; but for a time his support for 'Richard IV' brought him to the front of European diplomacy, offering the prospect of a rich Imperial or Spanish marriage. Yet while James was prepared to play the diplomatic game up to a point, he was also looking for something more — military glory.

118

It seems he genuinely believed that there might conceivably be a rising in northern England in support of the pretender. As the price of his assistance, Berwick would be returned to Scotland. As far away as Venice it was reported that the Scots were seeking an alliance with Maximilian against England:

> ...hoping thus to recover Berwick and certain other places belonging to their King, which have been held for the English for many years.

Henry was seriously alarmed by Warbeck's arrival in Scotland. Troops were sent to help defend the Border. During the parliamentary session from October to December 1495 the defence of Carlisle and Berwick was discussed. In the following April commissions were issued for the raising of troops in nine northern counties. Henry also approached Charles, who had offered him support, asking for the nine year old John Stewart, Duke of Albany, the orphaned son of Alexander, as a counter to Warbeck and James IV.

Despite all this, he still wanted peace. In May 1496 he offered James his six year old daughter Margaret as a prospective bride. For the twenty-three year old Scottish King this was hardly an attractive prospect. Besides, he had no reason to accept the sincerity of Henry's proposal, especially in view of the Scottish experience of English marriage treaties during his father's reign. In any case, James looked for a Spanish rather than an English marriage.

Ferdinand and Isabella, the King and Queen of Spain, were hoping that Henry would join in a new league designed to arrest French aggression in Italy. With Henry worried about the security of his northern frontier there was no prospect of this. Holding Warbeck as a kind of Sword of Damocles over the head of Henry VII, James began negotiations for the hand of a Spanish princess. Although he was spun along for some time, it eventually became clear that no such princess was available. James therefore decided on war. All the political and diplomatic advantages he held in his dealings with Henry and the other European powers were finally and completely lost when he crossed the English Border in September 1496, set to renew the Wars of the Roses. It was a fiasco.

Since July James had been making active preparations for an invasion of England. Greatest priority had been given to the construction of an artillery train. Guns and shot had been made in Edinburgh Castle and in the Kings Wark at Leith, while some existing artillery pieces had been recovered from Sir Andrew Wood's ship, the *Flower.* By 12 September most of these preparations were complete, and the big guns were concentrated at Restalrig under the command of John Sandilands, who had the support of professional artillerymen from Flanders.

Henry was kept informed of developments by his spy John Ramsay, the former Lord Bothwell, who, although he had been allowed to return to Scotland, had not recovered his former title or estates. With James on his way to the Border Ramsay sent the following report to the English King:

> ...I ondirstand without dout yis instant 15 day of September the King, with all ye haill peple of his realm he can mak, wilbe at Ellam kyrk within 10 myll of ye marches of England, and Perkin and his company with hym...and without question has now concludit to enter within yis zour Realm ye 17 day of ye same month in ye quarrell of yis said fenit boy, notwithstanding it is ayens ye mynds of ye hall noum of his barrons and peple ba (both) for ye danger that therof myght follow, and for ye inconvenience of ye ceaison...

The last part of this letter is undoubtedly wishful thinking on Ramsay's part; for there were many, especially in the Borders, who were only too happy for the opportunity of gathering plunder in England. Before the Border was crossed James told Warbeck of his own price — the immediate return of Berwick and 100,000 marks, payable within five years. Warbeck and his tiny court accepted the loss of Berwick. The sum asked for was reduced to 50,000 marks: it might just as well have been raised to a million for all the chance the pretender had of making payment.

With the heavy artillery in tow progress towards the Border was painfully slow. Not until about 20 September did James' army finally cross the Tweed. Almost at once it was plain that the whole enterprise had been a mistake. Like Margaret of Anjou in the 1460's, Warbeck discovered that any cause that relied on the support of a Scottish army was fatally flawed in English eyes. Besides, the north of England was too far away from the main centre of power for an invasion here to have any chance of success. Henry Tudor had avoided this error in 1485 when he had struck at the heart of England through Wales. James' own military objectives are not clear: it would appear that, in view of the direction he took and the lateness of the season, he intended his invasion to be no more than a launch pad for Warbeck, who would then have to pursue the matter on his own. Above all, he needed a quick return on the expense he had gone to in maintaining Warbeck and mounting an invasion on his behalf.

Whatever fears Henry may have had about the entry of 'Richard IV' into England must soon have been eased; for the pretender attracted absolutely no support whatsoever in Northumberland. James was quickly disillusioned and the campaign degenerated into a large scale plundering raid. Warbeck was shocked by the lack of restraint among the Scottish troops and worried by the effect this might have on his flagging cause. But when he asked James to bring his men back to order he was put firmly in his place by the cynical King. Polydore Vergil reports what happened:

> The King is said to have replied that by all appearances Peter was meddling in other people's business and not in his own: for Peter called England his country and the English his countrymen, but none rushed forward to lend him their aid. Thus the King exposed the man's foolish impudence. Thereafter, as time went on, he paid less and less attention to him...

The chastened Warbeck retired back to Scotland, having spent all of one day in England. James, on the other hand, no doubt anxious to show off the power of his guns, continued to campaign in the Tweed and Till valleys. The towers of Tilmouth, Howtell, Branxton, Shoreswood, Twizel, Duddo and Lanton were reduced to rubble. Beyond this nothing was achieved, and the army withdrew back across the Border on 25 September on hearing of the approach of an English force under Lord Latimer from Newcastle.

By this raid James had thrown away all of the diplomatic advantages he had held earlier in the summer. More seriously, he had also created considerable anger in England. His dangerous and foolhardy adventure had brought no military, political or territorial advantage; what is worse, it had brought in its wake the threat of major retribution. Henry, for once, abandoned all caution and prepared for a full scale campaign against Scotland. A council of war was held at Sheen in October, where it was decided:

> ...to make by see and by lond two armees Roiall for a substantiall warre to be contynued vppon the Scottes unto such tyme as We invade the Realme of Scotland in our owne person and shall haue with goddes grace revenged ther grete outrages don vnto us our realme and subgettes forsaid so and in such wise as we trust

the same our subgiettes shall leve in rest and peace for many years to come.

At the same meeting Sir Robert Litton, the treasurer of war was instructed to:

...make serche of the presidents of the warres (into) Scotland aswele for the defense of owre owne marches there: as of the great armees that have been made into the same land in the tymes of owre noble progenitor king Edward the third and frothens unto the days of our fadre (in-law) king Edward the IIII...

After the war conference at Sheen a Great Council was held at Westminster which granted Henry the huge subsidy of £120,000, later ratified by parliament, to be used in raising an army and fleet. Almost at once the government began to gather weapons: an ordinance corps was built up at Mile End in April and May 1497, and ammunition stockpiled. James had begun a war of guns which Henry intended to finish. The King also ordered the preparation of 'Greek Fire', a kind of medieval napalm. Orders were also given for the employment of continental mercenaries. The fleet was put under the command of Lord Willoughby de Broke, who sailed from Portsmouth on 16 May, arriving at Berwick on 21 June. Soon after operations began in the Firth of Forth. The garrisons at Berwick and Norham were both strengthened.

James was not blind to the danger he faced. In November he held his own council of war at the Hume castle of Hirsel, where he spent ten days making defensive preparations. In February 1497 he took part in a cross Border with the Humes. No details of this 'Raid of Hume' have survived; it probably increased Henry's anger still further. There was no longer any pretence of supporting Warbeck: this was war for the sake of war.

In the end, Henry's invasion plans collapsed under their own weight. His scheme was simply too ambitious. For many Englishmen the burden of taxation required was too great to bear, especially for those in Devon and Cornwall, who saw no reason why they had to pay for a war which was so remote from their own daily concerns. In the spring the west country rose in revolt and thousands of armed peasants advanced on London. Henry was now faced with a far greater challenge to his authority than Warbeck had ever been able to mount. He was immediately forced to recall part of the army he had been planning to send north with Lord Daubeney. While the immediate danger passed when the rebels were defeated at the Battle of Blackheath on 17 June, the country still remained unsettled for the remainder of the year.

For Henry the west country rising was a worrying reminder that the Tudors were still uncertain occupants of the throne. Full scale war was clearly too much of a risk, and he quickly withdrew back into the shell of security. Rather than invasion and ruin James was offered peace. Not long after Blackheath Richard Fox, Bishop of Durham, was appointed to head an embassy charged with coming to terms with the Scottish King. Fox was to ask for the surrender of Warbeck, although this was not made an essential condition of the peace talks.

The men of Cornwall and Devon had saved James from the consequences of his pointless war. But rather than take advantage of the new peace offensive the King attempted to use Henry's domestic problems as a way of furthering his own aggressive aims. Warbeck was packed off from Ayr on 6 July in a ship named the *Cuckoo*, heading eventually for Cornwall in an attempt to rekindle the rebellion against Henry. Meanwhile, James made ready for another assault on northern England. Even before the Battle of Blackheath he had mounted a foray across the Border from Melrose. Another attack followed before the end of June. James' aggression was encouraged when a party of English raiders was defeated in a skirmish with the Humes at Duns in the Merse. He was convinced that northern England was vulnerable to attack. The time for something more ambitious had come.

In July James issued orders for his army to assemble at Melrose. In addition, all of the big guns were to be brought to the Border, including the majestic Mons Meg, which was trundled down Edinburgh's Royal Mile accompanied by musicians and much ceremony. The sheer effort required to carry Meg and her sisters over bad or non existent roads was impressive: huge teams of oxen and horses were accompanied by 110 drivers, 221 workmen, 61 quarrymen, as well as masons, carpenters and gunners. Meg on her own required 100 workmen and 5 carpenters. Not surprisingly, she did not reach the Border until early August. The guns were then all arranged on the north side of the Tweed to begin a systematic assault on Norham Castle, while the army crossed over to begin a campaign of widespread destruction.

After the main part of Henry's army was detached to deal with the west country rising, the defence of the Border was left to

Thomas Howard, Earl of Surrey. Surrey was an experienced soldier who had fought for the Yorkist cause at Barnet and Bosworth, where his father, the Duke of Norfolk, had been killed. Initially imprisoned by the new Tudor King for his political associations, Surrey was soon restored to favour and appointed as Henry's lieutenant in the north and deputy warden of the marches in 1489, after the death of the Earl of Northumberland. It was to Surrey that the task of dealing with the Scots attack on Norham fell.

Norham, an outpost of the bishopric of Durham, was a tough old nut, defying the best efforts of the thundering Scottish guns. Bishop Fox had not neglected his charge, and the castle's defences had recently been substantially improved. To encourage the garrison he remained with them throughout the siege, while the defence was ably conducted by the captain, Thomas Garth. All assaults were successfully beaten off. Having achieved no more success than Bishop Kennedy had in 1463, James withdrew after ten days on hearing of Surrey's approach with a relief army. Although the King had fought on the campaign as a brave soldier, he had also proved himself to be an indifferent commander. The Spanish ambassador, Don Pedro de Ayala, who accompanied James on the Norham expedition, composed a good summary of his conduct and character:

> He is courageous even more so than a King should be...I have seen him often undertake the most dangerous things in the last wars. I sometimes clung to his skirts and succeeded in keeping him back. On such occasions he does not take the least care of himself. He is not a good captain, because he begins to fight before he has given his orders...

After driving James off from Norham, Surrey followed this up on 16 August by invading south east Scotland. Coldstream Castle and the peel towers of Sawmills, Edrington and Fuldean were all destroyed. The following day the English army pressed on towards the north, advancing in deteriorating weather conditions towards Ayton Castle, some eight miles into Scotland. Ayton held out for a while, but had to surrender after a heavy bombardment. Although James was less than a mile away his army was too weak to face Surrey in battle. Rain fell without interruption, affecting the morale of both the Scots and English soldiers alike. There was some posturing between the Earl and the King over single combat or battle to decide the fate of Berwick; but Surrey would not be drawn into a face to face fight, and James could not risk battle. Unable to force the issue, and with his supplies running short, the Earl returned to Berwick on 21 August, where his army was disbanded. James, now realising how little real glory there was in war, agreed to Henry's proposals for a cease fire. On 30 September 1497 a seven year truce was concluded at Ayton, which was extended the following year to last for the lifetime of both Kings. As for Warbeck, his attempts to kindle a fresh rising in Cornwall were a miserable failure. He was taken prisoner in October and finally hanged at Tyburn in 1499.

The Peace of Ayton was the beginning of an important new stage in Anglo-Scottish relations. Although the two sides were initially distrustful of one another, a better understanding began to take shape, helped by James' adoption of a more pragmatic approach to diplomatic relations. Even an incident at Norham Castle in July 1498, when a group of Scots were killed by the garrison, did not seriously disturb the new equilibrium. The English were conciliatory, and Bishop Fox, who came to see James, proved himself to be an especially skilled diplomat. Besides, it is likely that James was opening up to the folly of his previous adventures. The Spanish diplomatic records of this time note that:

> The peace with Scotland is not yet broken; it even seems to improve. The King of Scots has seen the ears of the wolf, and is now endeavouring to make a bed of roses for the King of England. Two or three months ago the English killed a great number of Scots, but King James would not permit the Scots to kill an equal number of English.

Towards the end of 1499 Bishop Fox was appointed to reopen negotiations for a marriage treaty. Although James was initially reluctant, he finally agreed in October 1501. The proposed marriage between James and Margaret Tudor was also to bring about the first full peace treaty between England and Scotland for over one hundred and seventy years. For the long dead James III it represented something of a posthumous triumph. But unfortunately for all, the Perpetual Peace fell under a long shadow cast by the mountains of Italy.

# CHAPTER 8
## The Flowers of the Forest

The stubborn spearmen still made good
Their dark impenetrable wood.

*Sir Walter Scott*

In August 1503 James IV and Margaret Tudor were married at
Holyrood Abbey, and the spirit of a new age was celebrated by
the poet William Dunbar in *The Thistle and the Rose*. The union
was the outcome of the Treaty of Perpetual Peace, concluded the
previous year. In many ways the most important political marriage
in Scottish history, it was to bring a Stewart King, the great
grandson of James IV, to the throne of England one hundred
years later. Indeed, there were many in England who were worried
by the implications of the marriage, including some in the Royal
Council. Henry is said to have replied to their fears that:

> ...our realme wald receive na damage thair thorow, for in that
> caise Ingland wald not accress unto Scotland, bot Scotland wald
> acress unto Ingland, as to the most noble heid of the hole yle...evin
> as quhan Normandy came in the power of Inglis men our forbearis.

The peace itself involved arrangements for regular diplomatic
contacts on the marches to ensure that no Border incident could
escalate into a cause for war. All future monarchs were to renew
the treaty within six months of their accession. It was also
backed up by a papal guarantee, declaring that the first to breach
the peace would be subject to immediate excommunication.

James was a popular and authoritative King, who had proved
himself as a warrior. It was because of this that he was able to bring
about a major revolution in Scotland's traditional policies, whereas
his father had been ruined in a similar attempt. But he was not
prepared to cast off all the chains of the past. In the negotiations
leading up to the treaty of 1502 Henry VII had asked James to
break the old league with France: all James was willing to concede
was that any such renewal would not be 'prejudicial' to England.

The Treaty of Perpetual peace was an imperfect document: for
one thing, the question of Berwick and the Debatable Land was

ignored; and for another the old claim of feudal superiority was passed over in silence. Neither of these were insurmountable problems. Scotland was never again to make a serious attempt to recover Berwick, and the problem of the Debatable Land was seen as one of law and order rather than of international relations. Feudal supremacy was a more troubling issue, but Henry VII never took this claim seriously; and it wasn't until the reign of his son that it emerged out of the political coffin. Undoubtedly the most serious weakness was the existence of the Auld Alliance. In other words, the peace was only 'perpetual' for as long as England and France enjoyed good relations, which they did during the latter part of the reign of Henry VII. However, if this tripartite relationship broke down Scotland would be forced to choose between one side or the other. Unbeknown to either Henry or James the grave of the new peace had already been dug some years before in Italy.

In 1494 Charles VIII had invaded Italy in pursuit of a long standing dynastic claim to the Kingdom of Naples, a fiefdom of the pope. This brought France into direct conflict not only with the papacy, but also with Spain, which also had interests in southern Italy. Charles' successor Louis XII deepened French involvement in the lands south of the Alps by laying claim to the Duchy of Milan, which helped to create a new division between France and the Empire under Maximilian Habsburg. This was a devil's cauldron which only needed a guiding hand to stir it up — finally provided by Pope Julius II, a warrior in the Vatican. It was Julius who was to form a new Holy League against France, destined to bring about the final crisis of James IV's reign. As if aware of the last act of the tragedy Dunbar wrote another poem after *The Thistle and the Rose* which he called *Lament for the Makaris*:

> Our plesance here is all vane glory,
> This fals warld is bot transitory,
> The flesh is brukle, the Feind is sle;
> Timor mortis, conturbat me.
>
> The stait of man dois change and vary,
> Now sound, now seik, now blith, now sary,
> Now dansand mery, now like to dee;
> Timor mortis, conturbat me.

Even before the death of Henry VII all was not well between England and Scotland. Days of truce, when wardens met to settle grievances, could, in themselves, become occasions for bloodshed. During one such day Sir Robert Ker of Ferniehurst, the Scottish warden of the middle march, was killed by John Heron, usually known as the Bastard Heron. This was a serious infringement of the treaty terms, but despite this Heron remained at liberty for some years. In 1505 Henry was alarmed by reports — false, as it proved — that the Scots were on the point of attacking Berwick. More seriously, he was concerned by the close links between James and Louis XII, who had succeeded Charles VIII in 1498. In 1508 he went so far as to arrest James Hamilton, the first Earl of Arran, on his return from a mission to Paris. Hamilton was eventually released, after a visit to the Scots court by Thomas Wolsey, Henry's chaplain; but the King went on to demonstrate his growing distrust of his son-in-law when fresh steps were taken to improve Berwick's defences in December. Most serious of all, from Henry's point of view, was the trouble and expense to which James had gone to build up a new Scottish Royal Navy.

Scotland had always been vulnerable to seaborne attacks. Even in times of peace English pirates, often operating with covert official approval, continued to be a problem. Before the end of the fifteenth century James began to spend money on ships; and in the period from 1511 to 1513 this expenditure had increased to £9,000 per annum. The first of his big ships, the *Margaret*, was launched at Leith in 1506. But Leith was too restricted a harbour for the kind of vessels James had in mind, so he ordered the construction of a 'New Haven' to the west of the port. It was from here in 1511 that the *Michael*, the largest of all the King's ships, was launched into the Forth. With a crew of 300 and 27 big guns she was one of the grandest vessels of the day, bigger even than the English *Great Harry,* launched the following year.

In April 1509 Henry VII died. He was followed to the throne by his second son, Henry VIII, who had taken the place and the wife of his elder brother, Arthur, who had died some years before. In one of his first acts the new King renewed the Treaty of Perpetual Peace. But Henry VIII was an entirely different kind of man from his cautious and parsimonious father. He was looking for adventure and glory, not safety and compromise. His father's careful accounting had left him with an ample treasury, which the new King was anxious to spend. In many ways he resembled the young James IV, and before long the two men were close to conflict.

It began simply enough. Henry showed his mettle when he refused to hand over some jewels to his sister Margaret, left to her in the will of her father. Old issues soon began to rankle, including the failure of the English government to detain the Bastard Heron. But by far the most serious incident to date was the fate of James' master sailor, Andrew Barton.

Some years before ships belonging to the Barton family were plundered by the Portuguese. Unable to obtain compensation from the King of Portugal, they were granted letters of reprisal by the Scottish King, which essentially allowed them to seek justice on their own terms. With his two ships, the *Lion* and the *Jenny Pirwen*, Andrew Barton sought out Portuguese merchantmen. It is also alleged that he attacked English ships engaged in trade with Portugal. Alarmed by the effects this would have on their profits the London merchants complained to Henry who ordered the Earl of Surrey's two eldest sons, Edward and Thomas Howard, to intercept Barton at sea. Their two men-of-war came across Barton's ships in the Downs on 2 August 1511. The ensuing fight was ferocious. Barton appeared on deck, Nelson style, in rich dress and bright armour to direct the contest; but he was mortally wounded by an English archer. An old ballad describes the outcome of the fight:

'Fight on, my men,' Sir Andrew sayes,
'A little I'm hurt, but not yet slaine,
I'le but lye doune and bleede awhile
And then I'le rise and fight againe.
Fight on, my men,' Sir Andrew sayes,
And never flinche before the foe;
And stand fast by St Andrew's cross,
Until you heare my whistle blow.'

They never heard his whistle blow,
Which made their hearts waxe sore adread,
Then Horseley sayd, 'Aboard, my lord,
For well I wott Sir Andrew's dead.'
They boarded then his noble shipp,
They boarded it with might and maine;
Eighteen score Scotts alive they found,
The rest were either maimd or slaine.

The *Lion* was taken back to port as a prize by the English. In response to James' protests Henry replied that kings ought not to concern themselves with the fate of pirates. It is certainly arguable that Barton had overstepped the bounds of his commission by attacking English shipping. But what angered James, aside from the death of his favourite seaman, was the arbitrary nature of the English action and Henry's failure to address the matter through the diplomatic channels set up under the treaty of 1502. His response to James' complaint was deliberately offensive. For James this was a clear breach of the spirit of the peace, and he expressed his feelings in a letter to Pope Julius II:

> Although in former years the King of England had caused him to make peace, ratified under apostolic censure, and given him his eldest daughter in marriage, yet, some time before he died, he neither regarded the treaty nor the relationship, allowing his subjects to make unprovoked attacks, which James could not retaliate. The present King of England, though he has ratified the treaty, pursues, slays and imprisons the Scots by land and sea, and takes no notice when James demands redress. Presumes, therefore that we are both absolved from our oaths.

Julius did not bother to reply; for Henry VIII was now his ally.

For a while Julius had been allied with France and other countries against the power of Venice. When the Venetian threat was effectively destroyed by Louis XII at the Battle of Agnadello, he began to have serious worries about the growth of French power in the Italian peninsula. A major dispute arose and Louis even tried to have Julius deposed as Pope.

In response Julius formed the Holy League with Venice and Ferdinand of Spain against France, although there was very little that was holy about this alliance. Henry VIII, seeing the prospect of resurrecting England's vanished empire in France, joined the League in November 1511. The following year the Emperor Maximilian joined.

For James these developments on the Continent were deeply worrying. The prospect of a new schism in the Catholic church was alarming enough, especially as the power of Islam was waxing under the leadership of the Ottoman Turks. Even more concerning was the prospect that France might be destroyed by the Holy League; for she was Scotland's principal bulwark against the present and future aggression of Henry VIII. James made his position plain in a letter to the King of Denmark in 1512 which shows he was still smarting from the Barton affair:

Nor is there any doubt that, if France were conquered, Scotland would by those folks, who now by the daily increase of injuries, heed not the breach of the peace, nor choose to make restitution.

He had good reason to be concerned by England's new aggressive diplomacy. Some of Henry's councillors, Edward Howard chief amongst them, were advocating that war with Scotland should be pursued as an alternative to war with France. Thomas Wolsey, an increasingly important figure in English politics, wrote to the Bishop of Durham, saying that Howard:

> ...mercielously incendyth the Kyng against the Scottis; by whose wantone meanys hys grace spendyth mych money, and ys more dysspoysyd to warre than paxe.

But, in fact, this was far from being the case. For James the Auld Alliance was essential for the security of Scotland; but he most definitely did not want war. Alone of all the western European heads of state he saw the divisions in Christendom as potentially disastrous. He tried to heal the breach between Louis and Julius and prevent a major conflict by directing the attention of his fellow monarchs to the danger from the east. He is often accused of a romantic lack of realism in advocating a crusade; and indeed, the time for such gestures was generally long past. For James, however, a crusade was the obvious way of preventing a catastrophe in the west, which threatened to drag Scotland down in its wake. But there is also, it has to be said, a certain failure on his part to see the whole political picture; a failure to see that the danger France was in was largely self imposed.

As 1512 progressed the room for compromise became ever more restricted. In January the English parliament, in awarding the King a fresh grant of money, revived the claim of overlordship, last used in 1482 by Edward IV. A month later James decided that the time had come to renew the Auld Alliance. On the way to Scotland the flotilla carrying the French ambassador, Charles de la Mothe, attacked some English merchant ships, sinking three and bringing seven with them to Leith. This did little to improve Anglo-Scottish relations. James was becoming ever more fatalistic, believing that war was now inevitable. The league between the two old allies was renewed in Edinburgh, on terms that were more direct than ever before:

> Whereas, formerly, the Kings of Scotland and France were only obliged to assist one another, in opposition to the English, or

131

such as others should offer to invert the hereditary right of
succession to their respective crowns, they become now bound to
aid and assist one another; and even in person, if occasion
should require it, against all who may live or die.

Even at this late stage, with France in open conflict with
England, James tried to avoid the inevitable final step, trying to
maintain a desperate balancing act between the Auld Alliance
and the Treaty of Perpetual Peace. The problem was that his
country was simply not ready for war in its contemporary form.
His experience of 1496–7 had shown him the limitations of the
antiquated Scottish host, which was especially weak when it
came to gunnery and the other aspects of modern military science.
Recognising this, he appealed to Louis for money, provisions,
artillery, munitions and trained soldiers of all types, especially
engineers. The French King ignored the appeal, repling that he
was too heavily committed elsewhere to offer assistance on the
scale requested. All that James eventually got were some captains
to train the Scots in the use of the new Continental pike.

The political and diplomatic manoeuvring between Scotland
and England in the period up to 1513 involve a large measure of
bluff and counter bluff. Henry signalled his readiness to go to
war with Scotland as early as December 1511 when he recalled
artillery that had been lent to the Low Countries 'on account of
my expedition against Scotland.' Even so, with his eyes firmly
set on the Continent, Henry did not really want war in the north,
but he was unwilling to make any real concessions. Thomas, Lord
Dacre, the warden of the marches and a personal friend of the
Scottish King, suggested that the political temperature might be
lowered if Henry made a small gesture of reconciliation, like
handing over Queen Margaret's jewels. Sadly, this moderate
proposal was simply ignored. All the King was prepared to do was
to send an embassy under Nicholas West, Bishop of Ely, to
remind James that any aggression against England would evoke
the penalty of excommunication in terms of the treaty of 1502.
James held only one card: that the implied threat of a Scottish
invasion would be enough to keep Henry at home. This also
formed an essential part of the strategic thinking of Louis XII.
But both men completely failed to appreciate the lesson of history:
that England had the capacity to fight both an offensive war
abroad and a defensive one at home.

When Maximilian joined the Holy League in November 1512 Louis was faced with a dilemma. To counter the threat of a combined English and Imperial invasion of Northern France he would have to withdraw his armies from Italy, a step he was not prepared to take. His troops would remain in the south for the campaigning season of 1513. The defence of the northern border would be entrusted to local forces; and as Maximilian was not strong enough to face the French on his own, James must play his part by preventing the departure of the English army for Europe. Scotland, in other words, must invade England to keep France in Italy. In place of the substantial military aid he requested, Louis encouraged James by promising to make him King of England and, when the war was over, to join with him in a campaign against the infidel. The King of Scotland had to be content with the distant prospect of crowns and crusades, both equally illusory.

A kind of war fever akin to that of 1914 began to grip western Europe in the summer of 1513. There were a few in Scotland, like William Elphinstone, the Bishop of Aberdeen, and Archibald Douglas, Earl of Angus, who spoke against war; but this went against the popular feeling in the country. Over the whole of the realm, the Highlands, the Lowlands and the Borders preparations were underway. In Edinburgh the master gunner, Robert Borthwick, worked day and night in making cannons. In East Lothian and Fife a regular watch was set up to warn of the approach of English ships; and at Aberdeen trenches were dug and guns mounted for '...resisting our auld ennemeys of Ingland.'

In June 1513 the English army sailed for Calais, to be joined at the end of the month by Henry in person, eager for his first taste of battle. Before leaving he had entrusted the defence of northern England to Thomas Howard, Earl of Surrey. Surrey had wanted to accompany the King to France, but was forced to remain at home to prepare for a likely Scottish attack. Frustrated by this he is said, according to the historian Edward Hall, to have vowed to make the Scottish King sorry that he was the cause of his remaining in England.

As part of his war preparations James promised to send his fleet to join in combined operations with the French. He also intended to use it to open up a third front for Henry. In the same month that the English King left for the Continent James received the Irish chieftain, Hugh O' Donnel of Tyrconnel, who was keen to begin a rising against the English. The exact details of what was agreed are unknown, although it seems to have involved a naval attack on English bases in the north of Ireland. Under the command of the Earl of Arran the *Michael* and the other ships of the fleet set sail towards the end of July, accompanied by the King as far as the Isle of May. From there Arran sailed around the north and down the west coast of Scotland. In fulfilment of the agreement with O' Donnel the chief English stronghold in Ulster, Carrickfergus Castle, was bombarded. Beyond that nothing was achieved. The fleet docked briefly at Ayr, before leaving finally for France, sailing into the mists of history. There is very little information on the fate of the Scottish navy after it left Ayr. It only seems to have arrived at its destination after the defeat at Flodden, to take part in some limited operations with the French. It's uncertain if any of the ships returned to Scotland. The grandest of them all, the *Michael,* was sold to the French.

With Henry in France James could delay no longer. Part of the army assembled on the Boroughmuir at Edinburgh, while the remainder was ordered to make for Ellem in Berwickshire, the muster point for the invasion of 1496. Men heeded the King's call from all parts of the realm: Highlanders from the north and west came with the Earls of Argyll, Huntly and Lennox; the Borderers on their light horses came with Alexander, the third Lord Hume; and Lowlanders with the Earls of Bothwell, Montrose, Crawford and Errol; Gaelic speakers and English speakers; town dwellers, fishermen and farmers. The exact number that gathered at Ellem will never be known; but at the very least it may have amounted to 30,000 men in all, the grandest army Scotland had ever seen.

As the army was assembling James sent his herald, Lyon King of Arms, to Henry's camp at Thérouanne in Picardy, where he delivered his message on 12 August 1513. All of James' grievances were mentioned, including the death of Barton, and the herald concluded by summoning Henry to return to England. In a fit of temper Henry replied:

> ...say to thy master that I am the very owner of Scotland and that he holdeth it of me by homage, and in so much as now contrary to his bounden duty he being my vassal doth rebel against me, with God's help I shall at my return expulse him from his realm...

Far to the north Lord Hume's Borderers, who had the shortest distance to travel to the muster point, grew weary of waiting for their fellow countrymen. To work off some of their aggressive energy Hume led them across the march at the beginning of August on a large scale raid in Northumberland. Many villages and farms were put to the torch and, in the age old fashion, much livestock was rustled from the countryside. Confident that the main enemy army was still far to the south Hume did not bother to take proper precautions, failing even to post pickets ahead of his main body.

From his base at Pontefract, Surrey sent ahead a body of 200 mounted archers under Sir William Bulmer. Bulmer summoned the local gentry to his aid, and on 13 August posted his force in ambush at Milfield, four miles to the north west of Wooler in Northumberland, just where Percy and Dunbar had waited to intercept Archibald the Tyneman in 1402. Totally unaware of the presence of the enemy, Hume rode strait into the trap. From under cover of bushes Bulmer's archers let loose a withering fire into the densely packed Borderers, weighed down with booty. Caught in a narrow pass between the lower slopes of the Cheviot Hills and the River Till Hume's men had little room to deploy. Soon many fell dead and wounded. Reeling from the arrow fire, the Scots were finished off by a sudden charge of the English cavalry. Unable to make a stand the Borderers broke and fled, leaving all their captured livestock behind. Hume managed to escape, leaving his banner behind; but 500 of his men were killed and 400 taken prisoner, including his brother, Sir George Hume. This episode, known as the 'Ill Raid', provided a gloomy foretaste of the coming disaster.

Hume's experience did not deflect James from his purpose. With his muster complete he crossed the Border at Coldstream on 22 August. Unbeknown to him censure had already been pronounced at Rome on the day that the Borderers met with disaster at Milfield; but, even if he had, it is likely to have made little difference to his purpose. Most of the soldiers who crossed with him were armed with the long eighteen foot Continental pike, some six feet longer than the traditional Scottish spear. In the hands of the Swiss and the German *landsknecht* these weapons had acquired a fearsome reputation; but they could only be used to effect in highly disciplined formations. James was accompanied by the French captain d'Aussi with some forty of his fellow countrymen, who had helped to train the Scots in the use of the weapon. It is open to question, though, if the Scots infantrymen had been given enough time to master the new techniques of battle, or, indeed, if the countryside into which they were now advancing would allow them to make best use of the training they had received.

Following in the wake of the army came Robert Borthwick with the artillery, seventeen guns in all, which required 400 oxen to drag them from Edinburgh. The majestic old lady, Mons Meg, who appears to have been more trouble than she was worth, was left behind. Even so, the whole Scots artillery train was too heavy for a field campaign, and only slowed down the progress of the army. Although the big guns could batter down castle walls, they were difficult to manoeuvre in battle conditions. Moreover, these weapons had to be handled with skill to make the maximum effect; unfortunately, James had already sent most of his best gunners off with the fleet.

What, then, were the aims of James' invasion? His ultimate intention was to take the pressure off France by bringing Henry back to England. The immediate tasks, though, seems to have been little different from those of his campaign in the valleys of the Till and the Tweed in 1496 and 1497. Norham Castle, which had defied the Scots in 1497, and, for that matter, throughout its recorded history, was the first serious target on the King's list.

The captain of Norham, John Ainslow, stood confident behind its strong walls, ready to defy James in the way that his predecessor, Thomas Garth, had sixteen years before. After six days bombardment James' heavy guns managed to make a breach in the outer walls. However, the inner defences remained intact, and an attempt to storm the castle was beaten back with heavy casualties. Yet Ainslow's defence had, if anything, been too vigorous; and towards the end of August he was forced to surrender, having exhausted all of his ammunition. The fall of Norham was an unexpected blow to Surrey, still too far away to send a relief force. It was an even greater blow to Thomas Ruthal, Bishop of Durham, who claimed that he would never recover from the grief.

From Norham the army moved westwards to take Wark Castle. Thereafter it advanced down the valley of the Till to the lesser strongpoints of Etal and Ford, which also fell to the Scots. These were important strategic objectives, commanding the only bridges across the Till between Twizel to the north and Doddington to the south. James was now able to move his army to either bank of the river at will. Pleased with his progress so far the King made his temporary headquarters at Ford Castle.

James' army was composed of many raw recruits who had little experience of war. Many had been demoralised by the fight for Norham. To make matters worse, the weather was deplorable, continuing wet and windy throughout the whole campaign. Disease began to spread and morale slumped still further. Gathering whatever spoils they could, many simply decided to make their way home. By early September men were arriving back in Edinburgh in such numbers that the town council was forced to issue the following proclamation:

> We charge straitlie and command in our Soverane Lord the
> Kingis name that all manner of persons that ar cummyng fra
> his army that thai address thame and returne againe thairto...

After leaving Henry, Surrey came north to Pontefract in early August to make his final preparations. As soon as he learned that James had crossed the Border he summoned all able bodied men to meet him at Newcastle on 1 September. He was also expecting his son Thomas, the Lord Admiral of England, who was sailing north with 1,000 men, the only part of the Continental army that returned to face the Scottish challenge. By 29 August Surrey was at Durham, where he learned of the fall of Norham. Depressed by this news he was also worried for the safety of the Lord Admiral, coming by sea in such foul weather. The following day he was joined at Newcastle by Lord Dacre, Sir William Bulmer, Sir Marmaduke Constable and the artillery train. Over the next few days more and more men started to arrive, the largest a contingent from Lancashire under Sir Edward Stanley. The camp at Newcastle was so crowded that Surrey moved his headquarters to Bolton-in-Glendale, close to Alnwick. Here, to his great relief, he was joined on 4 September by the Lord Admiral and his marines.

The muster was now complete and the old general had approximately 26,000 men under his command, made up chiefly of archers and other infantrymen armed with the bill, the English version of the Continental halberd, an eight foot long weapon with a fearsome, axe like head, which could be used for cutting and slashing. All were on foot, save for Dacre, who had some 1500 light Border horsemen. At Bolton a council of war was held and the battle dispositions agreed. Instead of the usual arrangement of vanguard, centre and rear, Surrey arranged his army into two large divisions each supported by smaller wings. The Lord Admiral was given command of the forward division, supported on his right by his younger brother Edmund Howard, and on the left by Marmaduke Constable. Surrey followed with the second division, with Dacre on his right and Sir Edward Stanley on his left.

Surrey was determined that James would not be allowed to slip away as he had in 1497. Speed was essential, especially as his supply situation was far from good. Amongst other things he was running short of beer, the essential fuel of medieval English armies. It was vital that the Scots army was located and destroyed as quickly as possible. To ensure that James would remain in England Surrey sent a herald, Rougecroix Pursuivant, to meet him at Ford and invite him to do battle on 9 September. To help him make up his mind the Lord Admiral sent his own message, reminding the King of his part in the defeat of Andrew Barton, saying that he had come to '...justifie the death of the said Andrewe, agaynste hym and all hys people...'These messages had the effect intended. James sent his own herald, Islay, announcing his intention to wait for the Howards until noon on Friday 9 September.

Why, we have to ask, did James accept such a challenge? Why, in other words, did he knowingly accept the risk of battle when most commanders since Robert Bruce had — unless the circumstances were exceptional — avoided large set piece encounters with the English? The traditional explanation is that he was blinded by outmoded notions of chivalry and honour. But the real answer to our questions is altogether far less nebulous.

First, it seems clear that James was confident in the sheer size of his army, which was at least as strong, if not stronger, than that of his enemy. He was proud of his guns and his pikemen, and anxious to let them prove themselves in battle. There was always, of course, the danger of the English longbow; but many of his troops were encased in the latest armour, or carried heavy wooden shields to parry the effect of arrow fire.

The second part of the explanation lies in the position he chose in which to meet Surrey. Just across the Till from Ford Castle lie the north eastern outriders of the Cheviots. The highest of these is Flodden Hill, in those days a treeless slope, rising to over 500 feet above sea level. From Flodden the ground falls away to the north west, before it rises again to Branxton Hill. To the west the approach is covered by Moneylaws Hill. The whole position resembles a huge irregular horseshoe shape, with the open end facing eastwards towards the Till. It was here, in a great natural fortress, that James placed his army. From the direct south Flodden was guarded by the heights of Housdean and Coldside Hills. The only approach is from the south east between Flodden Edge and the River Till, a dangerous, restricted route. It was at this open end of his 'fortress' that James arranged the guns, bearing directly on the bridge at Ford. Bannockburn had shown the importance of selecting a good position in battle; but the Flodden position was, if anything, too strong: any attempt to force it would have been military suicide. James was no Bruce, and Surrey was no Hotspur.

On 6 September the English army marched from Bolton-in-Glendale to Wooler Haugh, leaving the valley of the River Aln and entering that of the Till, where they remained for the next two days. From here they had a clear view of the Scots a few miles off. To Surrey the strength of the enemy position was immediately obvious. *The Trewe Encountre,* an account written soon after the Battle of Flodden, describes what he saw:

> The Kyng of Scottes did lye with his army in the egge of Cheviotte
> and was enclosed in thre parties, with three great mountaynes,
> soe that ther was noe passage nor entre unto hym but oon waye
> where was laied marvelous and great ordenance of gonnes.

For the second time Surrey's herald was sent to James to complain that he had taken a position 'more like a fortress' and to invite him to descend to do battle on the level plain at Milfield. Naturally enough, he refused. By now it was certain that James wanted a battle. Even so, it was to be a battle on his terms: Surrey must come to him; he would not go to Surrey. Ironically, from what we know of the coming battle, James may have fared better if he had indeed accepted Surrey's invitation, and allowed his pikemen the advantage of a 'level plain.'

Surrey was now faced with a simple choice: he had either to disband his army and retire south, leaving James in command of the field; or he could attempt to outmanoeuvre the Scots. The first was almost inconceivable, and would most likely have led to a charge of treason; but it was one that would have been forced on him in any case by his acute supply problems if the Scots continued to hold Flodden. The second involved a risky march to the north and west, which threatened to cut James' communications with Scotland. This would have the effect of forcing him out of his present position in a rapid march back towards the Border. The fact that James did not abandon Flodden, or was only able to do so when it was far too late, was to give England one of the most complete victories over Scotland in her history.

On the evening of 8 September the English army made its way back over the Till at Doddington marching on to camp at Barmoor Wood, where their position was concealed from the Scots by the hills beside Ford. From Watch Law the Lord Admiral observed that the weakest part of James' defences was Branxton Hill to the north. Here the ground rose far less dramatically than it did further to the south, and there was no danger from the Scots artillery. The following morning the vanguard under the Admiral set off at about 5 o' clock in the morning towards Twizel Bridge, which crosses the Till near to where it joins the Tweed. With him came the English artillery train. Surrey and the rearguard followed some time later.

We have no way of telling what James was thinking when he saw the enemy disappear off to the north east on 8 September. The threat to his communications must have been obvious; but it may be that he thought Surrey was abandoning the field and retreating towards Berwick. No attempt was made, however, to shadow the enemy's movements; so until late in the following day he had no idea of the true direction of Surrey's march. It seems likely that he was beginning to move north the following day. It would have taken some time to manhandle the heavy artillery out of the position covering the Till, and by the time this exercise was complete, the redeployment had become a race between James and Surrey for the possession of Branxton Hill.

Surrey's feint towards the Tweed succeeded more completely than he could ever have imagined. Some five miles to the north of James, too far away to be seen, even if the weather had permitted, the Admiral and the artillery made their slow progress across the narrow Twizel Bridge at 11 o' clock, while Surrey and the rear crossed further down the Till by the ford at Heaton Castle. Once the manoeuvre was complete James was cut off from Scotland. Surrey and his son then moved south towards Branxton, with the vanguard a mile or two further to the west. The first serious obstacle they encountered was the Palinsburn, a marshy stream which joins the Till at Sandyford. For the Admiral with the artillery the only crossing point was the little Branx Bridge. This was the critical point for the English army: the Scots with their artillery were now ranged on Branxton Hill, fully aware of the enemy below them. Howard was caught in a bottleneck at Branx Bridge, with his father and the rearguard some distance away to the east at Sandyford. He was in the range of the enemy guns. Luckily for him, they stayed silent.

It is not known exactly when James discovered that he had been outflanked: it was probably not until some time after mid day. Visibility was poor, and the weather continued to be wet and stormy. The only defensible position was now at Branxton, the northern wall of the fortress camp. Given the prevailing conditions, the redeployment of the army was painfully slow. It would have taken some time to pull the guns out of their existing positions for the move to the north, with men and oxen no doubt slipping and sliding in the mud. When the old camp was abandoned the King ordered it to be set alight, which sent up huge clouds of smoke into the turbulent sky. According to the author of *The Trewe Encountre*, this was a deliberate move to obscure the movement of his troops. But smoke does not fall or move along the ground, it rises; and unless the camp was situated away on the low ground to the south east below Flodden, and the wind was blowing hard towards the north west it's difficult to see how this fire could have provided the cover suggested. In any case, smoke is an unreliable ally: it is likely to have inconvenienced the Scots more than it hindered the English.

What now were the options open to James? He must have realised that he had been completely out generaled by the old English war-horse. Still, Branxton was a powerful position; and he got there first. It must be assumed that he had not changed his essential battle plan: the English, in other words, must come to him, not he to them. The best way of ensuring this would have been to hold the army just behind the ridge of Branxton, which would provide protection from English artillery fire. His own guns could be positioned on the ridge to cause maximum damage to the English on their approach, before their own guns were in position. James adopted neither of these moves. The army was arranged on, rather than behind, the ridge; and the artillery did not open fire until the English army passed beneath the effective sweep they could make from Branxton Hill.

The Scottish historian, Pittscottie, says that Robert Borthwick, the master gunner, pled with James to allow him to open fire as the English were crossing Twizel Bridge. This is an obvious mistake: Twizel could not be seen from Branxton or Flodden, and, at a distance of fife miles, was well beyond the range of even the biggest of the Scots guns. A better case can be made for Branx Bridge. Concentrated fire here would, indeed, have had seriously cut up the English vanguard. However, James' rejected Borthwick's advice, apparently intending to destroy his enemy as a whole, rather than in a piecemeal fashion.

Howard successfully negotiated the Palinsburn, after which the ground drops away slightly, before rising again to Piper's Hill, where the monument to the Battle of Flodden now stands. Out of the valley and on to this hill the vanguard emerged in full array. They were in no danger from the Scots artillery, which could not be depressed any further. Even so, Howard was now in a perilous position: there, less than half a mile to his front, was the whole of the Scottish army stretching far away to the left, leaving his flank completely uncovered. If James had changed his tactics and charged downhill at this point the vanguard might have been destroyed before Surrey brought the rearguard into position. The Admiral recognised his extreme peril and sent a message to his father, a mile and a half away to the east at Sandyford, to close as quickly as possible. Reacting quickly to this appeal Surrey came to meet his son, and then made his final arrangements for the battle.

On Branxton, James had arranged his army into four divisions. The left, under the joint command of Lord Hume and the Earl of Huntly, was made up of men from the Borders and the north east of Scotland. Next came the division under the Earls of Errol, Crawford and Montrose, with units from Fife, Angus, Perthshire, Clackmannan and Kinross. On their right was the most powerful and best equipped unit of all, commanded by the King in person, with the men of the western lowlands under the Earls of Cassillis and Glencairn, and the lords Herries and Maxwell. Here, also, were all the officers of the royal household, the Bishop of Caithness and the Archbishop of St Andrews, the King's own illegitimate son. On the Scottish right were the men from the Highlands and Islands under the Earls of Argyll and Lennox. A fifth division, commanded by the Earl of Bothwell, with the men from the Lothians, was held in reserve close to the King. There was a space of about 200 yards between each of the formations, with the artillery in between. All the infantrymen were armed with pikes, with long swords as a secondary weapon. There were obvious dangers in this arrangement: the centre was made up of the best equipped and best disciplined troops; but the wings were held by men, who, while they were excellent fighters, could not always be relied upon in battle conditions. Most serious of all, the King made ready to fight from the front.

Surrey made his own dispositions to mirror those of the enemy. On the far right, facing Huntley and Hume, was his youngest son, Edmund Howard, with a large contingent from Cheshire, including the men of Macclesfield, and other units from Lancashire and Yorkshire. Next came the Lord Admiral, with the marines and the men of the Bishopric of Durham, carrying the banner of St Cuthbert, a holy emblem that had accompanied many English armies, and units from Northumberland, Yorkshire and Lancashire. Marmaduke Constable's unit appears to have been merged with that of the Admiral. Close to the Admiral, possibly slightly to the rear, was the Border horsemen from Cumberland, Westmorland and Northumberland under Lord Dacre. This unit was destined to perform an important task as a mobile reserve. To their left was a large division, made up almost entirely of Yorkshiremen, under the Earl of Surrey and his headquarters staff. On the extreme left, Sir Edward Stanley, with the men of Lancashire and Cheshire, was some way to the rear, apparently still making his way across the ford at Sandyford. The royal artillery was stationed with the Admiral.

The contemporary and near contemporary accounts of the ensuing battle, all of them written from the point of view of the victor, make it very difficult to build up an accurate picture. It is not always possible to reconcile the contradictions within the narratives, and many of these have tended to make their way into the standard histories. Flodden is best seen as a series of smaller battles, which merged into a greater whole. Thus the English archers, which were of little account on one part of the field, had enormous impact in another. The role the artillery played may have been brief; but it was vital. The Borderers on both sides did not give up the fight, as some have argued — they simply held each other in check.

What is certain is that the Battle of Flodden began as an artillery duel at about 4 o' clock in the afternoon of Friday 9 September 1513. With the English occupying dead ground the heavy Scots guns roared to little effect, other than to frighten off a few men on the English right. Borthwick's men showed little skill in the use of their heavy weapons, which, in any case, were very badly situated. The English artillery, some twenty two guns directed by Sir Nicholas Appleby, was lighter and far easier to manipulate. It was also used with much greater accuracy. Soon all of the Scots guns fell silent. The English discharge was now concentrated in an uphill sweep, catching the Scottish divisions, silhouetted against the skyline, in a murderously accurate crossfire. This, in effect, was the beginning of the end for the Scots. James was now caught like the fourth Earl of Douglas at the Battle of Homildon Hill. His men could not be expected to withstand the English fire for long. But any attempt to redeploy out of artillery range behind the brow of Branxton Hill involved the risk of the army disintegrating in panic. We have no way of knowing what James was thinking at this point; but his mind was made up for him by the precipitate action of the men of Huntly and Hume on the left. In the words of *The Trewe Encountre:*

> ...our gonnes did so breake and constreyn the Scottishe great army, that some part of thaim wer enforsed to come doun towards our army.

That part of the field occupied by the Borderers and Gordons was a little less steep than the rest of the Scottish position, and the ground flattened out towards where Edmund Howard's men were situated. With levelled pikes the Scots made good progress towards their enemy. The wind and rain was blowing in the face of the longbow men, who loosed their weapons with only limited effect. Keeping up the momentum of their advance Hume and Huntly sliced into Howard's division, which disintegrated under the impact. Many were killed; many more fled from the field. Howard escaped with difficulty, falling back with the survivors in his command on the division commanded by his brother. At this critical point the advance of the Scots, now disorganised in victory, was checked by the charge of Dacre and the English Border horsemen. Hume and Huntly drew off, and, in some accounts, the Borderers began to pillage the English baggage. In this part of the field the battle was over.

Observing the success of the right the next two divisions began their own descent down the slope of Branxton, Errol and Crawford making for the Lord Admiral and the King making for Surrey. But in this part of the field conditions were altogether different from those on the left. The hill was steep, wet and slippery, forcing many to remove their shoes to obtain a grip on the ground. The ranks of pikemen, advancing in the style of the German *landsknecht,* were probably already beginning to lose formation before they reached the bottom of the hill. All momentum was lost when they reached a little burn, which had to be negotiated before the army began to ascend up the slope towards the English around Piper's Hill. Presumably they were also sorely harassed by continuing artillery fire. With the formations breaking up the billmen were able to penetrate the gaps to begin hacking and chopping, loping the heads off the pikes. Rather than long spears each man was left with a sixteen foot pole. Swords were drawn; but these could not match the range of the murderous swinging bills. Before long Crawford, Errol and Montrose were dead and their division all but destroyed, allowing the Admiral to turn on the exposed flank of the King's division.

Surrey's battle was particularly hard. Ranged against him were the best troops in the Scottish army; and despite the problems the pikes had in keeping formation, he was forced to give some ground. But James and his men were eventually brought to a standstill, allowing the bills to begin work. What happened to Bothwell's reserve is something of a mystery. All we know is that the Earl was slain in the fight, so it must be assumed that he advanced in support of the King shortly after the battle began, or after he saw his progress arrested by Surrey.

What of Argyll and Lennox on the right? Here the Scots looked out towards an empty front. Stanley was a considerable way behind Surrey and arrived late. His approach was completely unobserved by the Highlanders, transfixed by the bloody struggle in the centre. Stanley noted that Argyll and Lennox were in a strong position; but he could also see that the eastern part of the ridge where they stood, some 500 yards to the south of Mardon, was unoccupied. A dip in the ground here would allow him to approach the enemy flank under cover. His tactics were bold: part of his command was detached to begin a frontal attack, while he led the remainder round the side. The climb Stanley made was steep and the ground so slippery that, like the Scots in the centre, his men removed their shoes, even clambering up on hands and knees. To the front the less well armed Highland troops were already falling to English arrow fire; when arrows began to fall also on their flank from a totally unexpected direction it was simply too much. Argyll and Lennox were both killed, and their shattered brigade melted away to the west, across the central part of the battlefield, now thick with the dead and wounded. Stanley's men stopped their pursuit to begin the plunder of the dead.

We cannot be certain exactly when King James was cut down. As he was in the front rank it may have been fairly early in the fight. Nevertheless, his men fought on with Spartan heroism in a titanic struggle. Hume, still holding his ground to the left, is often criticised for not advancing to the aid of the King and his comrades in the centre. This charge is not altogether fair. Judging by the ease with which Dacre and the light cavalry had checked his advance, it seems likely that his pikemen were badly broken up. To have reorganised them and then turned in formation towards the centre would have been difficult: to have exposed his flank to Dacre would have been suicidal. Moreover, Hume held that part of the field over which the rest of the shattered Scottish army was allowed to retreat. It is thanks to him and Huntly that a disaster did not turn into a catastrophe. Pittscottie's story that he had left the King to get on with it, having done his own bit, is of later origin, composed long after Hume had been executed for treason during the reign of James V.

As for James himself, his judgement had been quite simply disastrous. He had, as in the past, gone into battle, not allowing for the proper direction and management of his army. He had been out-manoeuvred, out-generaled and out-fought; and, in the end, against this background, his bravery counted for nothing. The oft quoted remarks of the English historian, Edward Hall, deserve repeating:

> O what a noble and triumphant courage was thys for a kyng to fyghte in a battayall as a meane souldier: but what avayled hys strong harnes, the puyssaunce of hys myghtye champions with whom he descended the hyll, in whom he so much trusted that wyth his stronge people and great number of men, he was able as he thought to have vanquished that day the greatest prince of the world, if he had been there as the erle of Surrey was, or else he thought to do such a hygh enterprise hym selfe in his person, that should surmount the enterprises of all other princes; but how soever it happened God gave the stroke, and he was no more regarded than a poore souldier, for all went one way.

James' charge is said to have brought him to within a spear's length of Surrey, though this seems a little too much like the story of Richard III at Bosworth, added to illustrate the danger in which the elderly Earl had been placed. In fact, the King's body was discovered the following day, and only after some difficulty, stripped, as he was of his armour and mangled by several wounds.

The Battle of Flodden ended shortly after 6 o'clock, when the autumn darkness began to fall. There was no rout, no pursuit. The brave Scottish soldiers left the field with dignity and honour, their comrades on the left covering the retreat. Surrey, still uncertain of the outcome, held his men in check, a measure of the courageous determination with which the Scots had fought. It wasn't until the following morning that he realised how complete his victory had been. There before him around Piper's Hill lay a ghastly mountain of the dead. Some Scots horsemen appeared on Branxton Hill, but were quickly driven off, and Surrey's men took possession of Borthwick's silent guns. What was left of the Scots army then made its way in good order back over the Tweed.

Many had been left behind, to rest in England forever. James was joined in death by nine earls: Crawford, Montrose, Argyll, Lennox, Errol, Cassillis, Rothes, Bothwell and Glencairn, together with fourteen lords of parliament, as well as chiefs of the MacLeans, MacKenzies, MacDonalds and the Campbells of Glenorchy. His son Alexander, the Archbishop of St Andrews, had also been killed, as was the Dean of Glasgow, the abbots of Kilwinning and Inchaffry and the Bishop of Caithness and the Isles. In all, some 10,000 men of all ranks, a third or more of the Scottish army, had died. There were few prisoners. Most of the dead were buried in huge pits on the battlefield. The dead King, now officially excommunicated for breaching the peace of 1502, was taken first of all to Berwick. It was to be many years before he was finally buried. English casualties, amounting to some 1500 dead, were particularly heavy among the men of Cheshire, who had fought with Edmund Howard.

Flodden was essentially a victory of bill over pike. As a weapon the pike was only effective for as long as it was used in a battle of movement; but the hilly terrain of Northumberland did not suit its use. Indeed, the Scots may have fared better if they had kept to their more manageable traditional schiltron spears. Shortly after the battle Bishop Ruthal of Durham wrote to Thomas Wolsey:

...our billes qwite them veray welle and did more goode that
day thenne bowes for they shortely disappointed the Scotes of
their long speres wherin was their greatest truste, and whenne
they came to hande strokes though the Scotes faght sore and
valiauntley with their swerdes, yet they coulde not resiste the
billes that lighted so thicke and sore upon theym.

The infantrymen at Flodden, both Scots and English, had, in
most essentials, fought in a fashion that would have been
recognised by their ancestors for ages past. But this was the last
time that they were to come together as equals in battle. Two
years later King Francis I of France defeated the Swiss pikemen,
a crack infantry force, at the Battle of Margiano, using a
combination of heavy cavalry and guns, ushering in a new era in
the history of war.

# CHAPTER 9
# Stands Scotland Where it Did?

Let us die even as we rush into the midst of battle.
The only safe course for the defeated is to expect no safety.

*Virgil*

News of Flodden spread quickly throughout the realm. In Edinburgh the town council ordered all able bodied men to be ready to defend the city. Soon afterwards the construction of a new city wall was ordered, although its completion was to take far longer than is commonly assumed. Elsewhere the country made ready for the expected English invasion. Alexander, Lord Hume, was given responsibility for the defence of the marches. The royal council ordered that wappenschaws be held throughout the realm, and instructed all Scots serving in France to return as soon as possible with their arms and munitions. Fastcastle, Dunbar, and Edinburgh Castle were all strengthened. But the English never came. Surrey's victorious army was disbanded soon after the battle, much to the disgust of Bishop Ruthal, no doubt anxious to revenge the capture of Norham Castle, who lamented:

> ...if this victory mowzt be folowyd Scotlande were chastysid
> for ever, but such capitayns and souldioures as were at this
> business in mervoulous fowle wethyre, lachying mete and drynke,
> and whiche have also lost thayr horses and goodes, have lever
> dye than to comme thedyr again.

Although the Border remained tense over the winter and Lord Dacre was soon conducting major raids, the country at large was given peace to organise its affairs.

Once more Scotland faced the unhappy prospect of a long minority. The new King, James V, was only eighteen months old. As guardian of the young monarch his mother, Margaret Tudor, naturally expected to take a leading part in the government. But Margaret was volatile, self centred and untrustworthy; and, what is more, few had much confidence in the sister of an enemy King. Before long a party emerged which called for John, titular Duke of Albany, the son of James III's rebel brother, to come to Scotland and play a part in the direction of affairs. After James and his brother, the Duke of Ross, James IV's posthumous son, Albany was next in line to the throne. He had lived all of his life in France, and had no experience of Scotland or its affairs. Nevertheless, he was a living representative of the Auld Alliance, and could be expected to take a firm stand against England. When the General Council met at Perth in November 1513 it was decided both to renew the Auld Alliance and to invite Albany to Scotland to act as Governor.

Flodden had broken the military power that James IV had been at pains to build up, but, in the words of Sir Charles Oman, it left Scotland;

> ...just where Scotland had always been since the origin of the quarrel 200 years before, angry proud, and restive, and utterly impatient of English claims to interfere with her concerns.

The battle did, however, have a lasting effect on the attitude of Henry VIII, who believed that he could easily brush aside native resentments and dominate Scotland indirectly using whatever pro-English faction was available. He never understood the country and was to be constantly frustrated by the complexity of its politics, which was to undermine his schemes time and again. Throughout his life his ambitions were fixed firmly on France, with Scotland figuring as an important but peripheral consideration. The country, he believed, could be bent to his will by a slight application of military force and political pressure. He was wrong on both counts.

There was an understandable concern in Scotland that after the disaster in Northumberland it was only a matter of time before the English set about destroying the country's independence. The signs were not good. Henry made it known that he was the natural guardian of the infant James V, and instructed Lord Dacre to do nothing that would give the Scots a pretext for removing him to a more remote location where he would be 'more difficult for the King to attain.' He also wrote to the new Pope, Leo X, demanding the suppression of the metropolitan see of St Andrews, and expressed his intention of renewing the war as soon as possible. In July 1514 it was being reported in Venice that Pope Leo, keen to bring about a reconciliation between England and France, was proposing to let Henry 'have the rule of Scotland.' Now, perhaps more than ever, Scotland needed the support of France.

Flodden, it is sometimes suggested, marks the birth of a new cynicism towards the Auld Alliance on the part of Scotland. It would be truer to say that this attitude was created by the self interested politics and the blatant disregard for Scottish interests demonstrated by Louis XII and his successor Francis I in the years immediately after the battle. For paying such a high price in blood, Scotland demanded an unequivocal commitment from her ally. The message sent to Louis in November made the position perfectly clear:

> That sen the said king of Scotland togiddir witht mony of
> his noblis and lieges war slane and distroyit in batell now in
> northumbirland be the Inglish principaly in the quarell of France
> it wald pleis and lyke the said maist Cristian king to send the
> duke of Albany with his help and municions and all maner of
> necessrs for weir in the Realme of Scotland for the defence of the
> zoung king of Scotland the queyn his said Realm and noblis.

But, without consulting Scotland, Louis made peace with Henry in the summer of 1514. Although Scotland was included, it was on the most offensive terms imaginable: if the Scots raided England her inclusion would be void, although there was no compensating provision for English raids into Scotland. The new peace between the two countries was cemented by a marriage between Louis and Henry's second sister, Mary. Acting under English pressure, and despite promises to the contrary, Louis kept Albany in France. Considering the terrible sacrifice that Scotland had made to preserve France this was an astonishing betrayal. Cardinal Bernard Bibena said of the peace:

> ...that the king of France has not refrained from making a
> shameful agreement with the king of England, renouncing his
> protection for Scotland and leaving that realm to the government
> of the king of England.

In August, the same month that the Anglo-French peace treaty was signed, Queen Margaret married Archibald Douglas, the sixth Earl of Angus. Douglas was as unprincipled and ambitious as his grandfather, the fifth Earl, whom he had recently succeeded to the title. This was the beginning of a new pro-English alliance in Scotland. But most Scots had the measure of Margaret and

151

Angus and were not in any way disposed to submit to their government. Moreover, they had no particular desire to be included in Louis' peace.

After Flodden, Lord Dacre was given the task of undermining the authority of the Scottish government by a campaign of subversion, and of organising punitive raids into the south of the country. The first of these attacks came in October 1513. An even greater onslaught followed on the night of 10/11 November. This took the form of a two-pronged attack by Dacre from the east and his brother Christopher from the west march. The arms of the pincer were planned to close near Jedburgh. Before Christopher arrived Dacre was intercepted near Ruecastle by a large party of Scots and forced to retreat southwards to a place called Sclater Ford, where his pursuers were reinforced by three troops of Scots horsemen led by David Ker of Ferniehurst, the Laird of Bonjedworth and the Sheriff of Teviotdale. He was saved by the timely arrival of his brother and the party from Cumberland. Their joint force continued the retreat south towards Belling Hill. By now the whole countryside was alert to the English presence and another force of 2,000 horse under Lord Hume approached from the east. Rather than risk an all out fight the Dacres hurried back to the Border.

Elated by this success, Hume and his Borderers began a counter attack, signalling that the victory at Flodden was not as complete as the English had believed. Dacre was thrown on the defensive all along the march. Scots raiders crossed into England in December and again in March 1514. These were more than simple plundering forays. On 10 March Henry wrote in alarm to Dacre saying that he had heard that the Scots were planning an assault on Berwick and that the garrison was asking for urgent aid. Dacre was ordered to assist in the defence of the threatened town by bringing the guns taken at Flodden from Newcastle. Scots aggression began to place considerable pressure on the beleaguered Dacre, and soon the Royal Council was criticising his apparent inability to check their repeated onslaughts, forcing the warden to write, in a self pitying tone, in defence of his conduct:

> And as to the destruction of the King's bordoures and subgecttes...
> right harde and impossible it is for suche a poore Baron as I am
> to make resistance all along the east, middle and west marches
> against the Scotts without great help and assistance, where in
> times paste the Duke of Gloucester, being a King's broder, and

the earle of Northumberland, with there grete powers, could not
well keepe them...

Dacre's 'winter war' against Scotland had been a clear failure,
which considerably weakened the English party in the country.
In November 1514 the position was so bad that Margaret wrote
to her brother asking him to send an army as soon as possible
to help her against the opponents of her regency, of whom
Alexander Hume was one of the most important. Her greatest
concern, she continued, was that the remaining support she had
would vanish as soon as Albany arrived. Henry did not send an
army; but he did his best to keep Albany in France.

In January 1515 Louis died, and Francis I came to the throne.
Albany was finally allowed to sail for Scotland, arriving in May.
The Scots believed that he would come to prepare them for war:
much to their disappointment, he pressed for peace. On the
Borders the 'see saw' war was, for once, going their way. Many
were anxious to revenge the slaughter at Flodden. No attention
had been paid to Louis' shameful peace. But with Albany and
Francis both pressing for acceptance of the new Anglo-French
accord, concluded in April 1515, and with no prospect of French
military aid, they had to bow to the inevitable. With considerable
dignity the nobles and clergy wrote to Francis on 15 May confirming
their acceptance of the treaty:

> They take notice in this letter, of their late heavy misfortune
> known to all this world; but affirm, that their successful conflicts
> since that time with their enemies had taught them to entertain
> better hopes, and to repay the damages that they had sustained;
> adding, that at present, while the sense of their suffering was
> recent in their memories, and they had learned to dread less the
> strength of their foes, it would not have been wonderful, if they,
> who had not hitherto thought even of a truce with their enemies
> should have refused the peace that was now offered to them.

The Flodden war was over.

Over the next few years Albany proved himself to be a good
ruler. He restored order to the country, managing to negotiate
his way through the complex factional struggles. He did much to
preserve the liberty of the country despite the intrigues of Margaret
and Angus with Henry, whose position had been strengthened
when Lord Hume switched sides after Albany's arrival. But the

Governor was in a difficult position. The English saw him as a threat, even though he held to the Anglo-French peace treaty. Henry and his chief minister, Cardinal Thomas Wolsey, tried to cast Albany in the role of a Scottish Richard III, ready to murder his two young cousins, James V and the Duke of Ross, and seize the throne for himself, a propaganda offensive that was aided when Ross died of a childhood illness. Albany, however, was a good and faithful servant. His chief difficulty lay in trying to balance his duty to Francis I with his obligations to James V; and, on occasions, this was an almost impossible task. In 1517 he went so far as to warn Francis that if he did not agree to a new Franco-Scots marriage treaty then Scotland would look elsewhere for an ally against England. He then went to France in person to negotiate the Treaty of Rouen in August 1517, which held out the prospect of an eventual French marriage for James; but with relations between England and France continuing to be close he was not allowed to return to Scotland for four years.

In 1519 a new star began to shine in the European sky. The Emperor Maximilian died and was succeeded by his grandson, Charles V. Apart from the title of Holy Roman Emperor, Charles was also King of Spain, and ruled the Netherlands and southern Italy; beyond that he controlled the wealth of the New World. Francis was virtually surrounded by Habsburg power, and his struggle with the Emperor Charles was soon to be the dominant theme of his reign. For Henry, ever the jackal of the battlefield, the new contest in Europe opened afresh the paths of glory. In 1521 he entered into an alliance with Charles against Francis. It was now convenient for the French to dust off the Auld Alliance; and Albany was sent back to Scotland in November of the same year, charged with preparing the country for a new European war.

In the period of Albany's absence intense factional conflict had broken out once again. On one notorious occasion in 1520 the pro English Douglases had fought a bloody street battle in Edinburgh with the pro French Hamiltons, an affair known as 'Cleanse the Causeway.' Albany quickly established a fresh ascendancy over the Douglases and other rivals. Most were happy to see his return, and renewed attempts by Henry to have him replaced met with no success, even when he threatened the Scottish Estates with war.

Scotland made it clear that it would decide its own affairs, no matter what threats it faced from England. But fighting for its own government was one thing; fighting for France was quite another. By the time Albany returned the lessons of Flodden had been fully absorbed. France had clearly shown that its own interests came well before those of her Scottish ally; and there were now few in Scotland, even amongst the most ardent opponents of England, who were prepared to cross the fatal Border line in force when there was nothing to gain. Dacre, who had built up an effective network of spies in Scotland, reported to Henry that few of the nobles were keen to follow Albany to war. Events soon confirmed the accuracy of his intelligence.

Albany was certainly sensitive to the feelings of Scotland. As war came ever closer in the spring of 1522 he wrote to Francis saying, in effect, that the year 1513 would never come again; that Scotland could not be expected to take on the weight of England purely for the benefit of France. Unless the Scots received substantial military aid, he continued, they were most likely to make peace with England. But, like Louis in 1513, Francis claimed that he was too committed elsewhere to send help to Scotland.

When the summer came Europe went to war. Albany made his own final preparations. The host assembled at Roslin, and, equipped with artillery and the latest hand guns, began to move in the direction of Carlisle and the west march, less well defended than the east. Dacre's spies, the Queen-Mother chief amongst them, had kept him informed of Albany's plans. The army crossed the Sark and camped in the Debatable Land, a mere five miles from the Esk and England. With the Border approaching, many in Albany's camp began to have reservations about the wisdom of the campaign. Some of the senior nobility held a conference, in which the outcome of the last Scots invasion of England was recalled. It was not clear what the aims of the war were, and many were fearful that it was simply to serve France, regardless of the consequences. As a result the Earls of Argyll, Arran, Huntly and Glencairn all refused their further co-operation. Albany's appeals to honour made no impression. There was no alternative but to agree a short truce with Dacre and retire back to Edinburgh.

Albany was now convinced that he could not expect the Scots to act without French assistance. To obtain this he left Scotland in October to appeal to Francis in person. With Albany out of the way the English began a major peace drive. A three month truce was agreed in December as a preliminary to more comprehensive discussions. In return for a break with Albany and France the

English envoy in Edinburgh, Thomas Benolt, offered an attractive package: the return of Berwick, a marriage alliance between James V and Henry's daughter Mary, and a sixteen year truce. The Scots were tempted. In January the government expressed its willingness to consider these terms if a satisfactory Anglo-Scots treaty could be negotiated; but, in the end, mutual distrust was simply too strong, and the English proposal was no more successful than that of 1433. Besides, the French were now offering Scotland money, men and weapons in return for their adherence to the Auld Alliance.

As a sign of the new French commitment a small force of 500 men arrived in the spring. Shortly afterwards the Border war began anew. Earlier in the year the Earl of Surrey — the Lord Admiral of Flodden — had been appointed lieutenant general of the army against Scotland. English troops began to build up in force, and Surrey was joined by Thomas Gray, Marquis of Dorset, and Sir William Bulmer to begin a major campaign of raids, beginning in May 1523 In June Kelso was burned. Throughout the summer raids continued almost on a daily basis, the intention being to reduce the southern counties to a virtual desert.

On 24 September, as if to mark the dramatic conclusion of the summer campaign, Surrey crossed the Border in person with an army estimated at 10,000 men. The target was Jedburgh. To defend the town the Scots had only been able to muster 1500 soldiers; but these were the best the area could offer. As Surrey approached Jedburgh, the Borderers, under Dand Ker of Ferniehurst, manned the town's six defensive towers as well as the ancient abbey. Each of these positions was defended with desperate courage. Failing to make any progress, Surrey ordered Sir William Bulmer and Sir Thomas Tempest to set fire to the town. The soldiers in the towers and abbey continued to fight amidst the burning ruins until Jedburgh was completely destroyed. The following day Surrey ordered Lord Dacre to take Ferniehurst Castle, the stronghold of the Ker family, which was only accomplished with heavy loss. Surrey's men appear to have been unsettled by the unexpectedly tough Scots resistance. In camp that evening some of Dacre's horses broke loose, to be met with arrow and musket fire from the nervous soldiers, who believed themselves to be under attack. Some 800 horses were lost in the confusion. Dacre blamed the Devil, who, on this occasion, appears to have been on the side of Scotland. Surrey later reported to Henry:

I dare not write the wonder that my Lord Dacre and all his company doo saye they sawe that nyght six tymes of sperit and fereful sights. And unyversally all their company saye plainly the devil was that night among theym six tymes. I assure your grace that I fownd the Scottis at this tyme the boldest men and the hottest than ever I sawye any nation, and all the journey upon all parts of the armye kepte us with soo contynuall skyrmishe that I never saw the like.

With much of the Border country in flames Queen Margaret took the trouble to write to Surrey and Dorset asking them to spare the nunnery of Coldingham, on the grounds that the prioress, Isabella Hoppringill, was one of the best spies for England. Some time later Margaret wrote again to Surrey, complaining that the Border raids did little to harm the nobles, and recommending instead an advance on Edinburgh, which could be brought to its knees if he came on it suddenly. But Surrey's transport and supply problems prevented this. Besides, he believed that an advance on the capital would be less politically effective than Margaret supposed, and was intended by her as a convenient, if expensive, way of facilitating her exit from Scotland.

The same day that Jedburgh was put to the flames Albany returned to Scotland with the main part of the French expeditionary force — 4,000 footmen, many armed with the arquebus, a primitive musket, and 500 horse, with artillery, money and other supplies. Albany also brought with him Richard de la Pole, a nephew of Edward IV, and the last Yorkist pretender to the throne of England, sometimes known as 'The White Rose.' This was an impressive, well equipped force; but to a large extent Albany had sacrificed the advantage it gave him by arriving so late in the season. Francis was desperate for immediate action. In August Charles Brandon, Duke of Suffolk, had led some 16,000 troops to Calais to prepare for an attack on France. It was, therefore, vital for the Scots to begin a diversionary attack in the north.

Surrey made ready for the expected attack, and was kept advised at all stages by Margaret. On his orders Sir William Bulmer and Sir Richard Tempest destroyed all of the bridges over the streams near the Border, to delay the passage of Albany's Franco-Scots army. At the same time English raiders kept up the pressure in southern Scotland. Surrey was also aware that Scots morale was no better than it had been the previous year, hardly surprising, as few can have relished the prospect of a winter campaign. Indeed, the Earls of Huntly and Lennox tried to excuse themselves from the general muster of the Scottish army because, with winter coming on, they were unable to raise enough of their men. Constant delays meant that Albany was only able to begin his progress towards the eastern march in late October, a dangerously late time in the campaigning season.

Albany's march south was far from easy. The weather was wet, and the roads virtually impassable, especially for the artillery. Discontent began to grow alarmingly amongst the Scots troops, so much so that by the time they reached Melrose many simply refused to go any further south. With considerable difficulty Albany persuaded the army, like so many stubborn sheep, to accompany him along the north bank of the Tweed towards Wark Castle. Once in position the artillery began to bombard the fortress from the opposite side of the river. On 2 November, with the Scots still in a mutinous frame of mind, Albany sent a body of his French troops across the Tweed to take the castle by assault. Wark was defended at the time by Sir William Lisle with 100 troops under his command. George Buchanan, who was with the Scottish army, describes the attack on Wark in his *History of Scotland;*

> The French took the outward court by storm, but the English set fire to the barns, and the straw that was in them, which made such a smoke, that they drove them out again. For the next two days they battered the inner walls with their great guns; and after they had made a breach wide enough for entrance, the French again attempted the matter, and endeavoured to storm it, by means of the breach they had made; but those in the inner castle, which was yet entire, darted down all sorts of weapons upon them, and they lay exposed to every blow; so that, at last, having lost some few of their men, they were bid back to their army, and retreated across the river.

Some 300 Frenchmen died in the struggle for Wark.

While the attack was in progress Surrey, from his base on Holy Island, ordered his army to gather at Barmoor Wood, and from there began his march towards the Border. On hearing of his approach Albany retreated to Eccles. From here, with snow beginning to fall, the army was allowed to disband. Albany's winter campaign had been extremely ill advised; but, in the circumstances he was in, there was probably no other action he could have taken. Resentment against him began to grow, and the brave French soldiers were made to leave Scotland despite the stormy weather. For the English, the ignominious failure at Wark was an occasion for celebration. John Skelton, the poet laureate, recorded his own feelings in verse form:

False Scottes are ye:
Your hartes sore faynted
And so attaynted
Lyke cowardes starkke,
At the castel of Warke
By the water of Twede,
Ye had evill spede;
Lyke cankered curres,
Ye lost your spurres
For in that fraye
Ye ranne awaye,
With, hey, dog, hey!

Albany's credibility was destroyed. With the pro-English party growing in influence he decided to leave Scotland in May 1524, promising to return in September. He never came back. An able man, he had done his best in difficult circumstances; but in the end he had simply been unable to bridge the impossible gap between his duty to France and the needs of Scotland. He had come to Scotland in the period after Flodden when the country held firmly to a war policy with England and an unshakeable attachment to France. After a few years a numbness descended on the minds of the national community, a growing belief that Flodden had been a disaster brought on by the alliance, and an increased willingness to consider co-operation rather than conflict with England. If Blind Harry's *Wallace* had defined attitudes towards England in the late fifteenth century, then the new mood found expression in John Major's *Greater Britain*, published in 1521, which argued for a closer understanding between the two countries. This was an attitude born out of a profound loss of self confidence and a justified suspicion of the French alliance. It found practical expression in a new class of people, chiefly amongst the nobility, who were willing to enter into treasonable associations with the English. This had always been a feature of Scottish politics, but it became a positive epidemic in the course of the sixteenth century.

Taking advantage of Albany's absence Margaret resorted to a simple device to ensure he stayed in France. With the aid of James Hamilton, Earl of Arran, and John Stewart, Earl of Lennox, it was agreed that the regency was at an end, and the twelve year old James was elevated to rule in his own right. In practice, of course, he continued to be ruled by others; not, however, in the way that Margaret had envisaged. In 1525 her estranged husband, Angus, took custody of the King, and was to rule Scotland in his name, and in the interests of Henry, until 1528. James was held as a virtual prisoner, and his experience left him with an abiding hatred for the Douglases and the English connection.

The Douglas domination in Scotland had been assisted by the international situation. In February 1525 the army of the Emperor Charles had inflicted a catastrophic defeat on the French at the Battle of Pavia. For the next few years France sought good relations with England, and did nothing to upset her domination in Scotland.

At the age of sixteen James managed to throw off the control of his hated step father and rule in his own right. Douglas fled first to his castle of Tantallon, before seeking final refuge in England, where he was to remain for the remainder of James' reign. Henry was clearly disappointed by the loss of English influence in Scotland, but by this time he had other, more pressing matters on his mind, and made no more than a formal diplomatic protest. For, by one of the ironies of history, the deeply conservative and orthodox King Henry found himself caught up in a new storm blowing from Europe — the Reformation.

Although small Lutheran pockets had been established in both Scotland and England the official attitude of both governments was one of hostility. But in 1527, with no son to succeed him to the throne, Henry began divorce proceedings against his wife, Catherine of Aragon, the aunt of Charles V. Unable to obtain satisfaction from the Vatican, Henry began the break with Rome, largely complete by the mid 1530's. The Reformation added a new and complex dimension to the relations between England and Scotland. For Henry the continuing presence of a Catholic power on his northern march had an ever more important bearing on the question of national security, especially when the Pope threatened to launch a crusade against the English heretics.

For James the Auld Religion and the Auld Alliance was the axis around which his foreign policy was shaped. But arguably the

160

man who best personifies this link was David Beaton, Cardinal and Archbishop of St, Andrews, who was the last of the great churchmen representing a tradition that stretches back through James Kennedy to William Lamberton and Robert Wishart during the Wars of Independence. For these men the freedom of the Scottish Church from English ecclesiastic and political control had always been an issue. In Beaton's time the Reformation simply added a new piquancy to an age old struggle.

James' assumption of royal power did not immediately affect relations with England. Henry and Francis were still on good terms, so it was important for Scotland to keep the peace. In December 1528 a new five year truce was concluded at Berwick. By the beginning of the 1530's, with the struggle with Rome becoming ever more bitter, Henry had no desire for complications on his northern frontier. But in 1532 incidents on the Border began to get out of control, and the two countries drifted, once again, towards war. Henry ordered the Earl of Northumberland to place the local militia on a state of alert. At the same time he sought to make use of the exiled Angus, who agreed to recognise the King as the supreme overlord of Scotland and to serve in the conflict against his former countrymen. Even so, last minute efforts were made by both Henry and James to save the peace. But the mutual hostilities acquired their own momentum. In October English raiders burned Coldingham; and in November a force of 3,000 Scots entered Northumberland, destroying several villages. Dacre responded by entering south west Scotland in December, destroyed the town of Douglas and twelve other villages, before making off with 2,000 head of cattle and an even larger number of sheep. This raid, apparently the biggest mounted in winter for two hundred years, had been made on the suggestion of Angus.

Tired by these provocations James was anxious for revenge. He gathered his army and made ready to invade England early in the new year. But he was restrained by Francis. Keen, for his own reasons, to avoid an Anglo-Scots war the French King offered himself as a mediator. His determination to assist Henry went as far as advising him of James' preparations and urging him, as a precautionary measure, to send an army to the Border. Henry, busy with his marital problems, was happy to accept the offer of mediation, and representatives from all three countries came to Newcastle. The ownership of Edrington Castle, three miles to the west of Berwick, proved to be a sticking point; but

Henry agreed to leave it in the hands of the Scots, a measure of his anxiety to avoid a full scale war. This concession was confirmed in the final peace treaty of May 1534. The new truce was to last for as long as both monarchs lived, and for a year after the death of the first of them. In return for Henry's concession at Edrington James agreed not to act on any papal decree depriving the English King of his throne. A year later Henry, now supreme head of the Church of England, made his first attempt to persuade James to make his own break with Rome.

For the beleaguered King Henry the attitude of his nephew became ever more vital. In the autumn of 1536 he faced the greatest challenge of his reign, when much of northern England rose in revolt against his religious and social policies, an episode known as the Pilgrimage of Grace. Many of the northern gentry were implicated in this rising, including the Percies of Northumberland. Some calls were made for James to invade England in support of the old religion. Although James made no move to help the rebels, he later gave refuge to a number after the rising collapsed.

A cause of even greater concern to England was James' marriage to Francis' daughter Madeleine in January 1537, in long overdue fulfilment of the Treaty of Rouen. Henry was annoyed at this confirmation of the Auld Alliance; but with the principal Catholic powers, France and the Empire, once more at war it presented him with no particular danger at this time. However, the international situation moved dangerously against him the following year. By this time Madeleine had died and James had married another French noblewoman, Mary of Guise-Lorraine, the daughter of the Duke of Guise, destined to be one of the most formidable women in Scottish history. But far more serious, Pope Paul III had managed to bring about a reconciliation between Francis and Charles in June 1538, a month after James' second marriage. Soon after the Catholic League began to take shape; and in December Pope Paul published a papal bull excommunicating and deposing Henry VIII. The same month David Beaton, who had been instrumental in bringing about James' French marriages, was elevated to the office of cardinal on the recommendation of King Francis. Henry became increasingly fearful of the Scottish churchman, who was soon described as the worst enemy the King of England ever had.

For a time Henry's position was critical. Pope Paul was urging France and Spain to invade England to enforce his sentence against the King of England, and James was ready to take part in the Catholic crusade. Berwick, Carlisle and Calais were all strengthened as invasion fever gripped England. But the months passed and no armada came. Henry was more anxious than ever to improve his security by persuading James of the advantages of reform. In 1540 he sent Sir Ralph Sadler, an experienced diplomat, to meet James in Edinburgh to point out the financial benefits that would follow if he took Henry's example and dissolved the monastries. Sadler also took the opportunity to attempt to undermine Cardinal Beaton, who had succeeded his uncle as Archbishop of St Andrews, and had recently made a vigorous denunciation of the heretical English King. To bring about a new understanding Sadler suggested a meeting between the two monarchs. But James refused to be drawn. He was able to remain loyal to the 'Haly Kirk' and receive lucrative rewards for his loyalty without risking the political dangers of reformation. He was also confident of the Catholic alliance. However, in the end, political rivalry proved more enduring than religious agreement; and by 1541 Francis and Charles were once again at each others throats. With neither power anxious to antagonise England, Henry was free to put new diplomatic pressure on Scotland. Sadler came on a second embassy. This time James agreed to meet his uncle at York in September 1541.

With high expectations of the outcome of the meeting Henry arrived at York, the furthest north he was ever to come in the whole of his reign. A grand house was specially built for his nephew. He never came. Although Beaton was absent on a diplomatic mission in Paris, the other churchmen on James' council, fearful of the outcome of a meeting with the heretical English monarch, persuaded him not to attend. There were good reasons for this dangerous breach of protocol. James' two young sons had recently died, and it was feared that he might be forcibly detained in England, particularly risky when there was no heir to the Scottish throne. These fears were not entirely groundless, as from time to time the English had considered the possibility of kidnapping him.

Naturally enough, Henry was livid. His mood scarcely improved when he learned that a Scots raiding party had entered England on the west march, setting fire to John Musgrave's house and killing several people. He returned to London on 29 September, convinced that he had been made to look like a fool. Before he left York he ordered that all Scots should be expelled from Northumberland and that preparations should be made to defend the Borders. By the end of the year he was ready to enter a new alliance with Charles V against France. First matters with Scotland would have to be settled. Henry waited patiently for the right moment: it came in July 1542 when Francis declared war on Charles. Scotland stood alone.

Henry intended to bring Scotland to its knees by a combination of diplomatic and military pressure. In April the Archbishop of York was instructed to search for all documents bearing on the question of English feudal superiority over Scotland. Troops were mobilised on the frontier. In an attempt to settle the crisis James sent envoys to meet Henry at Windsor. Nothing came of these talks, and Henry ordered his forces on the Border to be ready to march against the Scots at an hour's notice. On 24 August, in retaliation for Scottish raids, Sir Robert Bowes, the captain of Norham Castle and warden of the east march, led a large force of 3,000 men in the direction of Kelso. He was accompanied by the Earl of Angus and his brother, Sir George Douglas. After ravaging the countryside they were ambushed on their return by a Scots force under George Gordon, Earl of Huntly, at Hadden Rigg, where the English received a sharp reverse. Hundreds were killed and hundreds more taken prisoner, including Bowes, his brother Richard and Sir William Mowbray. Angus and his brother escaped back across the Border.

Faced with this humiliation Henry became more intransigent. The Duke of Norfolk, formerly the Earl of Surrey, was ordered to assemble the army at Newcastle for an invasion of Scotland. Although James, aware of his dangerously isolated position, offered to reopen negotiations, Henry's terms amounted to an ultimatum: Bowes and his fellow captives were to be released without ransom; a new extradition treaty was to be agreed; the Scots were to give up all claim to the Debatable Land; and James was to come to London to agree the terms of a new alliance. James agreed to come to England, but no further than York. By now Henry wanted unconditional surrender, not negotiation. Soon after the talks broke down and the two countries prepared for war.

There were some in Scotland who welcomed the prospect of war. For Beaton and the churchmen, prominent members of James' Royal Council, war would have the advantage of ending any prospect of a political deal with England, which, they feared, would have a serious impact on the Catholic church. There were many others, though, who were considerably less enthusiastic, particularly amongst the gentry and nobility, some of whom were receptive to the teachings of the reformed faith, and almost all of whom distrusted the clergy. But undoubtedly the decisive factor in the war of 1542 was the distrust that many felt towards the King himself.

In many ways James V was one of the most tragic of the Stewart Kings. He had been deeply affected by the callous way he had been manipulated by his Douglas stepfather during his minority, which appears to have left him with an abiding suspicion of his magnates, bordering on paranoia. Even Huntly, the victor of Hadden Rigg, was accused of not pressing his advantage and was relieved of his military command. The King's personality and conduct — at times cruel and vindictive — was similar to James I and James III. The lack of mutual confidence between ruler and ruled was to create a crisis similar to those of 1436 and 1482. Most serious of all, it was indirectly responsible for the greatest military humiliation in Scottish history.

In October Henry declared war on Scotland, and Norfolk's army crossed the Border close to the end of the month, despite the lateness of the season. His operation was a complete failure. Short of supplies, including the all essential beer, he was forced to drag his heavy equipment over muddy Border tracks. Morale slumped and Norfolk fell ill. Nearby Scottish forces prevented his army fanning out, and he was confined to a fruitless march along the north bank of the Tweed towards Kelso, and then home again along the south.

Norfolk's humiliating withdrawal allowed the military initiative to pass to the Scots. It gave James an important tactical victory, which might have been followed up by limited operations along the Border. But the King overplayed his hand. Seemingly having learnt nothing from Albany's experience in 1523, he made ready to lead an army south into the same weather conditions that had frustrated Norfolk, and then to face an uncertain future in Northumberland. It was now November. The weather was cold and wet. Many came at the King's command; many did not. Almost at once the grumbling started. Some questioned the motives of the campaign; others the prominence of ecclesiastics in the King's council. At the camp of Fala Muir, a plateau near the western end of the Lammermuir Hills, the mule sat down and refused to move further. The national army of Scotland had changed little since the days of James I: it remained in almost all respects both feudal and tribal; the King did not have the resources to raise a contract army, like his English counterpart. Scottish soldiers, in other words, were tied in loyalty to their individual heads, be they Border laird or Highland chief, rather to the King as such. War, therefore, brought acute political perils for an unpopular monarch. A national army effectively put the King at the disposal of the nobility; and if the army refused to move, there was nothing he could do. James Stewart, the King's half brother, acted as a mouth piece for his fellow magnates, explaining that Scotland had gained the victory by Norfolk's retreat, and, while he and his fellow nobles were ready to defend Scotland, they were not prepared to cross the Border. There were even rumours of a Lauder style conspiracy against the King. James had no choice but to disband his mutinous army and return to Edinburgh. But this was not yet the end.

With the aid of Cardinal Beaton, James set about raising a second army, this time by 'privy letters' rather than a general muster. Two forces were raised. The first under Beaton and the Earl of Moray was based at Haddington to give the impression that an invasion of eastern England was intended. The second — some 18,000 men — marched with James towards Carlisle and the west march. It was now well past mid November, well past the normal campaigning season. What followed was to be one of the most curious encounters in all the Anglo-Scottish wars. Unfortunately, the records conceal more than they reveal, so any reconstruction of the events at Solway Moss must necessarily be of a tentative nature.

About November 20 the English began to receive reports that James was assembling a new army at Lauder. English spies accurately reported that the true direction of the King's march was Carlisle, giving the local forces plenty of time to prepare. Sir Thomas Wharton, the captain of Carlisle, with Lord Dacre and Sir William Musgrave summoned the horsemen of the west march to meet on 23 November. Beacons were lit to alert the whole of the north west Border that the Scots were approaching. James still had the advantage of numbers; he had, however, lost the advantage of surprise.

The King only made it as far as Lochmaben, where he took ill and was unable to proceed any further. Despite this bad omen the army was ordered to proceed across the Sark into the Debatable

Land, under what leadership and with what objective is not clear. The traditional tale, given by John Knox in his *History of the Reformation in Scotland,* is that once across the Sark the shadowy royal favourite, Oliver Sinclair, was proclaimed, on James' prior orders, to be the commander of the army. This is said to have been the cause of considerable resentment, as command was expected to go to Lord Maxwell, the warden of the west march. But why James did not organise the command structure of his army before it left Lochmaben is a mystery; and why Maxwell should have been expected to command a national army, generally given to more senior nobles like Huntly and Moray, is also a puzzle. It is certainly true that there was a complete failure in the leadership of the Scottish army; but the cause of the debacle at Solway Moss lies elsewhere.

The tidal tributaries of the Solway run through some dangerous, marshy ground, not a place to be caught unawares, as the English had found to their cost in 1448. The very size of the Scots army made the restricted ground even more of a problem, because there was little room to manoeuvre or deploy. Lack of discipline may have contributed to the disaster; but essentially the Scots were caught off balance by Wharton's brilliant counter stroke, which allowed him to make the most effective use of his light Border cavalry, most of whom were no doubt familiar with the terrain.

Wharton observed the Scots position at Solway Moss on 24 November from the vantage point of Hopesike Hill, between the River Lyne and Longtown. The dangers of their situation must have been immediately obvious to his experienced eye: their left wing lay close to a marsh, and the right flank lay exposed on open ground, with the River Esk to the front. Despite being heavily outnumbered he ordered an immediate attack. Musgrave's horsemen attacked, wheeled round and attacked again. Caught by surprise, and unable to form a battle line on the restricted and dangerous ground, the Scots began to panic. The whole force rolled up, back towards Arthuret Mill Dam, where it was caught between the marshes and the rising tide of the River Esk. Under the repeated English pressure the army simply disintegrated. The confusion was complete, as Calderwood vividly depicts in the *History of the Kirk of Scotland:*

> ...shouts were heard on everie side. Some Scottish men were
> stricken doun; some, not knowing the ground, were myred, and
> lost their horses. Some English horse, of purpose, were lett loose

to provoke greedie and imprudent men to presse at them, as manie did...the enemies, preceaving the disorder, increased in courage; before they shouted, but then they strooke. They shott speares and arrows where the companies were thickest. Some rancounter was made, but nothing availed. The souldiours cast from them their pikes, culverings, and other weapons; the horsemen left their speares; and so, without judgement, all men fled.

Such was Solway Moss, an encounter that one hesitates to dignify with the name of a battle. For the English the victory was more than complete — it was absolute. For the loss of seven men they had destroyed an entire army. Only twenty Scots were killed in the actual fighting, but many more were drowned in the swollen waterways, or were swallowed up by the morass. Bodies were still being caught in the fish nets on the Esk some days later. Most simply gave up, and the English took a rich booty in prisoners, including William Cunningham, third Earl of Glencairn, Gilbert Kennedy, third Earl of Cassillis, Lord Maxwell and his brother John, the lords Fleming, Sommerville, Oliphant and Grey together with many others of all ranks. The unfortunate Sinclair also fell prisoner, who even if he had been Napoleon could not have rescued the doomed army. God, so said John Knox, had fought against Scotland.

News of the disaster was carried to James, lying sick in Caerlaverock Castle. It had a profoundly depressing effect on his morale, which the birth of his daughter Mary in early December did nothing to lift. He died at Falkland on 14 December, leaving a week old girl as Queen of Scots. Three days later Sir George Douglas wrote '...Scotland ys doune, we may have yt for the takyng.' But she was to be saved by the most unlikely of heroes.

# CHAPTER 10
# The Year 1286 Has Come Again

He (Henry VIII) was like the giant in the fairy
tale, ever beguiled by the cunning little men.
*Andrew Lang*

Scotland had reached one of the lowest points in her history: the King was dead; the head of state was a tiny infant female, the youngest monarch ever. News of these dramatic events soon reached the Border, where the lord warden of the marches, John Dudley, Viscount Lisle, called a halt to all military operations because it was beneath the honour of his sovereign to make war '...upon a dedd bodye, or uppon a wydowe, or on a younge suckling...' But he seems to have concluded, on reflection, that Henry's honour was a much more elastic concept; for before the end of December he was writing to the King explaining that further action had been prevented by heavy snowfall, which had blocked all the Border passages.

For Henry the death of James and the accession of a female, his grand niece, to the Scottish throne opened up an entirely new set of possibilities: here was a way of breaking the French alliance for ever and tying Scotland to the interests of England. His own son and heir, Edward, was the right age to be a prospective bridegroom for the Scottish Queen. The victory at Solway Moss had put a number of important Scottish noblemen in his hands, some of whom had Protestant leanings and could be expected to support the proposed marriage as the price of their freedom; and there were others, like the Douglases, and Patrick Hepburn, third Earl of Bothwell, banished by James V in 1540, who were ready to return to Scotland to serve the English cause.

For a time it looked as if history had turned in a great circle: that, as J D Mackie once wrote, the year 1286 had returned. Scotland, for the second time, had a child Queen, and England another Prince Edward. England and Scotland would be united by marriage. There was, however, one critical difference: Henry Tudor was not a reincarnation of Edward I but of Henry V. With Francis I and Charles V now locked into the final act of a life long struggle, he began to dream again of lost empires. The last great military effort of his reign was a return to the war of his youth. Against this background, Scotland was a secondary consideration.

Still, the position was serious enough. Henry saw himself not just as Mary's guardian, and prospective father-in-law, but as her heir. Before the end of 1542 a great many of the Solway Moss prisoners were released after agreeing to work for the marriage of Mary and Edward. These men were the first of the 'assured' Scots, a group of people committed to working in the interests of England. But some of the most important prisoners — the Earls of Glencairn and Cassillis, and the lords Maxwell, Fleming, Sommerville and Grey — had also agreed to a further secret treaty, in which it was expressly stated:

> And whether the said daughter shall chance to come to his majesty's hands or not, or shall fortune to die hereafter...I think it shall be highly for the wealth of Scotland if it will please his Grace to take the whole rule, dominion, and government of the realm upon him...

With these men, and the Douglases, Henry was essentially returning to the politics of the 1520's, when he attempted to dominate the country indirectly using a pro-English party. As a measure of their good faith they were expected to work for the delivery into his hands of both the little Queen and Cardinal Beaton. In addition, they were to ensure that English garrisons were admitted to a number of strategically important castles in southern Scotland. Failure would almost inevitably have brought military intervention when the new season opened in 1543.

Faced with the dangers of an active English fifth column, and the possibility of a follow up to Solway Moss, the question of who was to control the Scottish government at this dangerous time was of particular importance. There was little doubt who the best man was — Cardinal David Beaton, an experienced diplomat, politician and administrator as well as a leading churchman. But Beaton was also known to be Henry's main enemy, and an effective advocate both for the Catholic faith and the French alliance. With Beaton in charge Henry would have taken much more forceful action against Scotland than he eventually did. Beaton appears to have tried to take control of the regency government in the early days after James' death; but the person who emerged in the dominant position, after a brief power struggle, was James

Hamilton, second Earl of Arran, and the heir presumptive to the Scottish throne.

History has been less than kind to James Hamilton, and often with good reason. As a soldier he was a disaster; as a politician he often allowed his personal ambitions to stand in the way of good policy. Yet despite his many and obvious weaknesses he was to perform an invaluable service. Scotland was in a far weaker position after Solway Moss than after Flodden: her army had been humiliated; a powerful section of the nobility had fallen into English hands, and was soon pledged to work for the political ends of Henry VIII; the growth of Protestantism threatened to give a new edge to the factional conflicts that inevitably followed from a royal minority. In these circumstances a strong governor, like Albany, would most likely have provoked a major English invasion. Arran was the man for the moment. He gave the appearance of malleability, and Henry was soon deluded into believing that he could be turned to his purpose. But Arran was his own man, driven by a deep personal ambition. He evaded, he temporised, he trimmed; and, like a chameleon, he was able to adjust quickly as the situation demanded. In his own way he probably did as much to preserve Scottish independence as Albany's firm government had in the 1520's.

Henry was initially distrustful of Arran, believing that he had the right to be the young Queen's protector. But the Governor made all the right moves: Beaton was arrested and held in the Douglas castle at Dalkeith; Angus and his brother were allowed to return to Scotland, and their estates were restored; Scotland began an experiment with the reformed religion; Bowes and the other English prisoners were released unconditionally; the refugees from the Pilgrimage of Grace were returned; and he agreed in principle to the marriage of Mary and Edward. All of this suited Henry; but it was quickly apparent that not all was going as planned.

When the Scots parliament met at Holyrood Abbey at Edinburgh in March 1543 Arran was confirmed in the post of Governor. However, while parliament also agreed to remove the forfeiture of the Douglases, it was made plain to the Governor that many were unhappy at the detention of Beaton. This made it extremely unlikely that Henry would ever be able to lay hands on the Cardinal, even though he was under the nominal control of Angus. More seriously, and before Henry had been able to make his precise demands known through official channels, the Estates set forth the terms upon which the English marriage was to be negotiated: Mary would not be delivered to the land of her prospective husband until she was ten; no fortresses were to be handed over to the English; Scotland's laws and liberties were to be preserved; even if the marriage was concluded Scotland was still to be governed by a native ruler; and if there were no heirs of the marriage then the crown would pass to the next lawful successor. By the time that Sir Ralph Sadler, Henry's official representative, arrived in Scotland the rules of the game had already been set; the first round of the diplomatic war had effectively been lost.

The problem was that Henry had considerably overestimated the influence, and even the motives, of his assured Scots. Glencairn and Cassillis certainly pushed Henry's case; but against a background of deep rooted suspicion of the English and their true motives, they could make little real progress. In the same month that the Scots parliament met, its English equivalent passed a new subsidy act in which the dead James was referred to as the 'pretensed King of Scottes being but a usurper of the Crowne.' Further reference was made to the 'crimes, treasones and rebellions' of his predecessors against their English lords, and that Henry was entitled to claim his 'right and title to the said Crowne and Realme.' Of course, this was little more than verbal dressing, and the King was hardly likely to push for the marriage of his only son to the daughter of a 'usurper.' Nevertheless, it did little to reassure wavering Scots opinion.

Even the Protestant card was one that could easily be overplayed. Although the Reformation had now taken root in Scotland, and there were especially strong Protestant pockets in Angus, Fife and parts of Ayrshire, in general it was still viewed with much suspicion. The more it was linked to the uncritical acceptance of the English marriage, the more unpatriotic it began to appear. In detaining Beaton Arran had placated Henry; but he also unleashed a national backlash against those who represented England, the marriage and Reform. Viscount Lisle reported:

> ...the ignorant and comen people grudgeth moche his (Beaton)
> keping in pryson and spekyth yt openly that the Governor was a
> good man, tyll he rounded with therle of Anguishe and his broder.

Angus and the English party were almost immediately checked by a national party headed by the Earls of Argyll, Moray and Huntly amongst others. These men generally had the support of public opinion, especially in Edinburgh, which remained firmly Catholic and pro French in outlook. Sadler's residence there was a far from comfortable experience.

Sadler arrived too late to influence the proceedings of the March parliament, so he immediately set about trying to obtain more favourable terms for the marriage discussions by some backdoor negotiations. Pressure was also put upon the assured lords to obtain better results than they had. But Sadler, like his royal master, was completely baffled by the complexity of Scottish politics, and the motives of those he dealt with. It was soon difficult for him to know whom he could trust. Even Glencairn and Cassillis, amongst the most reliable of the assured lords, told him that they would rather die than agree to end the Auld Alliance, still recognised by almost all Scots as the cornerstone of national policy. Others like Bothwell and Fleming abandoned their promises to Henry and went over to the national party. Sadler was most perplexed of all in his dealings with the Governor.

It was once said of Ian Smith, the former prime minister of Rhodesia, that dealing with him was like trying to nail a jellyfish to the wall. So it was with Arran. The man who understood him best was probably Sir George Douglas, who warned Sadler not to push the Governor too far. English demands upon him were more likely to have an effect directly opposite to the one intended. Henry demanded Beaton; Beaton was soon back home at St Andrews. The more the English pushed for custody of Mary, the less likely they were to get her. Douglas advised the ambassador to proceed with caution, for if Arran suspected that Henry planned to take control of the realm then he would immediately join the Cardinal's party:

> ...and in that querle, the hole realme wool stand fast with hym, and dye rather all in a daye, than they would be made thrall and subject to England.

Douglas also made plain the national mood when he said to Sadler that any attempt to remove Arran and subjugate Scotland to Henry's will would be met by fierce resistance, for:

> ...there is not so lytle a boy but he will hurle stones ayenst it, the wyves will come out with their distaffes, and the comons unyversally woll rather dye in it; yee and many noble men and all the clergie fully ayenst it...

173

Against this background of increasing doubt and mistrust, two people who were to have an important bearing of Arran's future conduct returned to Scotland from France. The first was his half brother John Hamilton, the Abbot of Paisley, and an ally of Cardinal Beaton. An astute and intelligent man, Hamilton had privileged access to the Governor, and was a persuasive advocate of the Cardinal's point of view. The second was even more important, albeit in a negative sense. Matthew Stewart, fifth Earl of Lennox, had, like Arran, links to the Scottish royal family, and was next in line to the throne after the Governor. Lennox was soon associated with the Cardinal's party; and as there were some doubts over Arran's legitimacy he represented a real danger to his authority. Arran was soon adopting a Janus-like appearance, presenting one face to Henry and Sadler and quite another to Beaton. But for as long as he looked as if he offered the best prospect of furthering English aims there would be no invasion in the summer of 1543, a time when Scotland would have been least able to cope with major aggression.

As the summer approached, Henry must have been increasingly aware that the gamble of 1542 had come close to being a complete failure. Angus and the other assured Scots had got virtually nowhere. Scots commissioners came to London to negotiate a marriage treaty, but not on the terms that the King had wished. Worst of all, it was clear that Beaton was in the ascendant.

Throughout the spring and summer the anti-English party grew steadily in power and influence. At St Andrews a convention of the clergy openly discussed the possibility of war, promising to raise funds by melting down church plate if necessary. It was a question not simply of defending the old religion but the political liberty of Scotland itself, a cause for which many of those present agreed to fight. Towards the end of July Beaton had assembled an impressive army with the power of four bishops, six abbots, six earls, eight lords and twenty-three lairds. He then advanced on Linlithgow, where Queen Mary had her nursery, with the intention of moving her to the safety of Stirling Castle, where she would be well out of Henry's reach. Unable to match the Cardinal's force, Arran had no choice but to comply.

Alarmed by these developments Henry offered to send Arran an army of 5,000 men. The Governor declined the offer, saying that the aid of 5,000 Englishmen would cause 20,000 Scots to desert him. Worried that Arran was about to give in to the anti-English party Henry made a proposal, which gives all the appearance of verging on desperation:

> Assuring the said governour that in case they ( the Cardinal's party) take awaye the person of the yong quene and dispose her mariage otherwise than by his highness consent, his majestie wyl by force of his title of superioritie, make him the king of the rest of Scotland beyond the Fyrth, ayding him with his power by see and land to recover the same.

Arran, showing greater courage and strength of purpose than many of his fellow noblemen, refused to take the bait, replying laconically that all his lands lay in the south of Scotland:

> ...which he would not gladly chaunge for any lyving beyonde the Frythe.

With a political earthquake underway in Scotland, the treaties of peace and marriage concluded at Greenwich on 1 July 1543, while outwardly representing an English diplomatic triumph, were little better than a masquerade. The Scots refused to renounce the league with France or to send Mary to England before her tenth birthday. The fruits of Solway Moss were withering away; as so often in the past, the English had won a battle only to lose the war. Soon the treaties of Greenwich were to be swallowed in quick sand.

Arran ratified the treaties on 25 August, although this was not binding until approved by parliament. But before this approval could be obtained Henry acted with almost inconceivable stupidity and arrogance. Some Scottish merchant ships were seized by the English on the grounds that they were trading with France, although this was a clear violation of the Greenwich treaty. Scotland was outraged. Even the commercial classes, some of whom were broadly Protestant in sympathy, were angered by this interference in their right to trade and lined up behind Beaton. In Edinburgh an attempt was made to assassinate Sadler. He fled for his life to the Douglas stronghold of Tantallon, before being escorted back to the Border by Sir George Douglas and a large armed band. Arran was so shaken by the reaction that he made his final peace with Beaton; and in December parliament both revoked the Greenwich agreements and renewed the Auld Alliance. Scotland's brief flirtation with the Reformation was also at an end, at least for the time being. A new war was now inevitable.

Greenwich failed not because of Henry's clumsy seizure of a few ships, but because there were too many people in Scotland worried by the implications of the English marriage. Above all, there almost none who were prepared to abandon France. Before he left Edinburgh Sadler wrote to the English Privy Council:

> Assuringe your lordships that as farre as I can se, the hole
> bodye of the realme is inclyned to Fraunce, for they do consider
> and saye that Fraunce requireth nothinge of them but frendeship...
> And Fraunce they saye hath alwayes ayeded theim with money
> and munytion...wheras on thother syde, Englonde they saye
> seketh nothinge els but to bringe theim to subjection, and to
> have superiorite and domynion over theim; while unoversally
> they doo so deteste and abhorre, as in my poore opinion they
> will never be brought unto it but by force.

Years later Sadler was also to report a conversation he had with the Scottish diplomat Sir Adam Otterburn, who said that the feeling in the country against Mary's marriage to Edward was so strong that even if the nobility consented 'yet our comen pepul, and the stones in the streets, wolde ryse and rebel agenst yt...' Henry had depended for the success of his schemes on a revolution of religion and political opinions strong enough to make England and Protestantism more attractive than France and Catholicism. But the time for such a revolution had not yet come.

Even before the December parliament revoked the treaties of Greenwich Henry was actively preparing for war. In September the Duke of Suffolk was instructed to advance with an army on Edinburgh to seize Beaton and Arran. But it was far too late in the season for England to mount a full scale military operation. Instead Henry authorised a fresh outbreak of Border raiding, which began in October and continued throughout the winter. By March 1544 a total of 124 villages and hamlets had been destroyed and huge quantities of livestock taken to England. In each place where the raiders struck Henry ordered that a notice should be pinned to the church doors saying 'You may thank your Cardinal for this.'

The defection of Arran had at least given Henry a new and important Scottish ally — Matthew, Earl of Lennox. Lennox was angry at the reconciliation between the Governor and Beaton, which was a major blow to his ambitions. Fighting not for honour or glory but office and position. Lennox determined to unseat

Arran by whatever means came to hand, the power of England included. Lennox was a useful addition to Henry's cause. He had a strong base of support in western Scotland centered on Dumbarton Castle, as well as many good contacts with the clan chiefs of the Highlands and Islands.

At the beginning of 1544 Lennox and the other pro English lords rose in revolt. A full scale civil war was avoided after Angus, Cassillis and Maxwell were all captured. They made peace with Arran and promised faithfully to serve their country in future, a pledge that was carried out with variable results. Lennox managed to hold Glasgow for a brief period, though with the general collapse of the rebellion he left for England, where he was joined by Glencairn. At Carlisle on 17 May both men entered into a private treaty with Henry VIII, in which a large pension was awarded to Glencairn's son Robert, Master of Kilmaurs, and Lennox was recognised as the rightful governor of Scotland and promised the hand in marriage of Lady Margaret Douglas, the daughter of Angus and Margaret Tudor. In return both men formally recognised Henry as the protector of the realm of Scotland and promised to deliver Mary into his hands. Lennox also promised to hand over Dumbarton Castle and the Isle of Bute, which would have given England a stranglehold on the main approach to western Scotland. Henry thus hoped to rescue the doomed marriage plan; but, by one of the many ironies in which history abounds, it was the child of the union between Matthew Stewart and Margaret Douglas — Henry, Lord Darnley — who was destined one day to be the second husband of Mary Queen of Scots.

To fulfil their side of the bargain Lennox and Glencairn returned to Scotland to begin a fresh rebellion. Lennox called his vassals to Dumbarton, while Glencairn collected some 500 of his tenants and advanced on Glasgow. But Arran, acting with some vigour, intercepted him with a larger force. Glencairn was beaten with heavy losses, including his second son, and fled, almost alone, to Dumbarton. Lennox, apparently unable to gather sufficient support to challenge Arran, and discouraged by the defeat of his ally, returned to England, leaving the castle under the charge of one of his retainers, Stirling of Glorat. He returned to the Firth of Clyde in August with a flotilla of eighteen English ships and 600 soldiers. The Isle of Arran — the property of the Governor — was ravaged, and Rothesay Castle on the nearby Isle of Bute was occupied. Lennox then proceeded to Dumbarton, expecting it to be handed over by Stirling; but, against all expectations, Stirling betrayed his master rather than his country. With the main aim of the campaign frustrated Lennox and his English auxiliaries returned to Bristol.

It was obvious that Henry was expecting too much from his Scottish adherents; but he did not have the force to back up their limited efforts. He was now allied to the Emperor, and as a consequence huge number of English troops were despatched to the Continent in early 1544 to begin a war against France. Angry at the rejection of the Greenwich agreement he was anxious for some form of action against his enemies. However, in view of his limited resources, this could only take the form of a large scale, punitive raid. Command of the operation was given to Edward Seymour, the Earl of Hertford, a skilful soldier who had accompanied Norfolk on his ill fated winter raid of 1542. To avoid past transport difficulties, and to carry him to the heart of the country, Hertford was to lead a seaborne operation. The instructions he was given were chillingly precise:

> ...Put all to fyre and swoorde, burne Edinborough towne, so rased and defaced when you have sacked and gotten what ye can of it, as there may remayn forever a perpetual memory of the vengeaunce of God lightened upon them for their faulsehode and disloyailtye. Do what ye can out of hande...to beate down and overthrowe the castle, sack Holyrood house, and as many townes and villages about Edinborough as ye may conveniently, sack Lythe and burne and subverte it and all the rest, putting man, woman and childe to fyre and sworde without exception, where any resistence shalbe made agaynst you, and this done passe over to the Fyfelande and extende like extremityes and destructions in all towns and villaiges whereunto ye may reach convenyently not forgetting among the rest so to spoyle and turne upset downe the Cardinalles town of St Andrews, as thupper stone may be the nether, and not one stick stande by another, sparing no creature alyve within the same, especially such as either in frendeship or blood be alyed to the Cardinal.

Henry's understanding of Scotland's geography was even weaker than his understanding of its politics. Hertford had to tell him that the scheme was too ambitious, and that operations were best limited to the area of the Forth estuary. He also tried to persuade Henry of the wisdom of fortifying and holding the important harbour of Leith, rather than destroying it, with no success; for the King was set on vengeance. Hertford set out from Tynemouth with 114 ships on 26 April. By early May 1544 he entered the Firth of Forth.

Arran had reacted with reasonable skill to the invasion of Lennox and Glencairn. This time, however, he appears to have completely lost his nerve. Despite having plenty of warning of Hertford's approach the Governor did nothing to oppose his landing at Wardie near Granton, a little to the west of Edinburgh. The host had been summoned to meet him at the Boroughmuir near Edinburgh by 5 May; but this was far too late. Hertford got the whole of his army and a few light field pieces ashore in three hours on 4 May, and then began his march on Leith. Arran attempted to block his passage at the mouth of the Water of Leith with a hastily assembled army. After a short artillery exchange the Scots were driven off, leaving their field guns behind. The next day the rest of Hertford's stores, and the big guns, were landed at New Haven. Leith was occupied the same day, after some Scots gunners were killed by arrow fire. Lord Sturton was left behind at the port with 1500 men, while Hertford took the rest of the army south to Edinburgh, along what is now Easter Road and then over Calton Hill.

When the army arrived towards the eastern end of the city Sir Adam Otterburn, provost as well as diplomat, offered to enter into discussions, which Hertford rejected. Faced with a demand for 'unconditional surrender' the town made ready to defend itself. Unable to force a passage through the Leith Wynd Port (gate) the army moved eastwards to Cannongate near Holyrood. At the Nether Bow Port the defenders fired on the English from the Flodden Wall, assisted by the big guns from the castle, which were positioned on the Royal Mile. Rather than wait for their own artillery the bowmen and arquebusiers — hand gunners — began a steady fire, forcing the defenders back. The guns were then drawn into place opposite the city gates, which were quickly destroyed. Fighting continued up the High Street. Some 300 to 400 of the citizen militia were killed defending their town, including David Halkerston who was cut down, sword in hand, guarding the entrance to a narrow wynd. While this fighting was going on the Scots artillery was withdrawn back inside the castle, and the captain, Hamilton of Stonehouse, kept up a steady fire on the invaders. Hertford had neither the time nor the equipment to lay siege to the castle, so he withdrew back to Leith after destroying much of the town. Before long the flames of Edinburgh were illuminating the night sky. There is no evidence that Hertford carried out Henry's order to massacre women and children; so he was either more merciful than his master, or Otterburn had taken the precaution of removing all civilians from the town prior to the battle.

At Leith Hertford was joined by a force of 4,000 Border horsemen. He used them to raid the countryside around Edinburgh, destroying all within a seven mile radius, including Craigmillar Castle. From Leith a seaborne force under Sir Nicholas Pointz crossed over to Fife, setting fire to Kinghorn and some adjacent towns, in token fulfilment of part of Henry's orders. Hertford returned to England by the overland rout on 15 May, after destroying Leith. The fleet also returned to base, taking as prizes the *Salamander* and the *Unicorn*, two of the best ships in the Scottish navy. Hertford's campaign of devastation continued all the way back to Berwick. Seton Castle, Musselburgh, Preston and Haddington were put to the flames. The worst atrocity was committed at Dunbar, after, as Hertford relates, the town was taken by surprise:

> And by reason that we took them in the morning — who, having watched all night for our coming, and perceiving our army to dislodge and depart, thought themselves safe of us, were newly gone to their beds; and in their first sleep closed in with fire — the men, women and children were suffocated and burnt.

The following day the army entered Berwick, having lost under forty men in the whole operation.

This was only the beginning. In the two years from June 1544 something like 159 different raids were mounted across the Border. Most were fairly small scale and major forays like Hertford's were not typical. England was carrying out a war by degrees designed to make normal life in southern Scotland virtually impossible. Accurate accounts were kept by the English of their campaign of economic warfare which make for depressing reading. In the period up to December 1544 alone 192 'towns, towers, stedes, barmkyns, parish churches and castell houses' were taken and burnt. Livestock rustled in the same period amounted to 10,386 cattle, 12,429 sheep, 1296 horses and 200 goats. Every tactic was employed, including extending the concept of 'assurance' to whole groups of people, who were then expected to attack their neighbours. The Armstrongs of Liddesdale were the first of the Border clans to accept English assurance. Many others became collaborators, either out of fear or out of greed. Bad as it was none of this brought the marriage of Queen Mary and Prince Edward one step closer.

Arran's failure to mount an effective challenge to Hertford showed him to be a poor soldier, a judgement confirmed in December, when he tried to retake Coldingham, captured and fortified the previous month by Sir Ralph Evers, the lord warden of the middle marches. Although he was well equipped with artillery the strength of the English resistance unsettled him, and his attacks were not pressed with any real vigour. At the approach of a relief force he drew off in some haste, leaving his artillery behind. Reacting quickly to the emergency Angus and his men managed to rescue the guns, carrying them off to Dunbar. Despite this the Earl continued to play a double game, keeping open his contacts with the English while fighting in the army of Scotland. Rumours of treason had the effect of lowering morale and generally weakening the Scots capacity to resist.

Evers and his colleague, Sir Brian Layton, the captain of Norham Castle, kept up the pressure over the winter. On one occasion they burnt the tower of Broomhouse around the ears of an elderly lady and her family, to the horror of the local country people. But what was worse for them they also burnt the abbey of Melrose, desecrating the ancient tombs of the Earls of Douglas, including that of the victor of Otterburn. Angus could not ignore this insult to his family's honour. He waited for the right occasion. It came in February 1545 when Evers and Layton advanced in the direction of Jedburgh with an army estimated at 5,000 men, a mixed force of English Borderers, foreign mercenaries and assured Scots, including many Armstrongs. As a badge of identification, all wore a red cross outside their armour.

On learning of Ever's approach Angus and Arran came to Melrose. They were able to muster no more than 300 men. Keeping to the high ground the Scots shadowed the enemy army until it set up camp in the valley of the River Teviot between Monteviot and the village of Ancrum. They were observed by the Scots from the vantage point of Peniel Heugh Hill overlooking Ancrum Moor. Unable to face the English with such a small troop Angus sent pleas for assistance out across the devastated countryside. In response the two commanders were joined on 27 February by

181

Norman Leslie, the Master of Rothes, with a troop of 1200 lances, and soon after by another cavalry force under the command of Sir Walter Scott of Buccleuch, an old veteran, skilled in all aspects of Border warfare. The Scots now had in excess of 2000 men, still much weaker than the enemy, but enough for a surprise attack. Angus was in favour of an immediate onslaught; but, on the advice of Buccleuch, the army was repositioned on the low ground between Peniel Heugh and Lillard's Edge, where it was totally concealed from the English in the valley below. To their front was a treacherous marsh, parts of which still survive, over which ran an old Roman road. This road offered the only line of advance for the English. Here the Scots dug pits, which they covered with branches and turf. Still acting on Buccleuch's advice the whole army dismounted and drew up in line of battle, while the horses were led by the camp followers to some high ground to the rear, where they could be seen by the English. The trap was set.

From the valley the English commanders had a clear view of what appeared to be an army in disorderly retreat. This was an opportunity that could not be allowed to pass. The casual destruction with which Evers and Layton had been associated was a tedious affair with little chance of glory. Here, at last, was an opportunity of a second Solway Moss. The whole army set off in rapid pursuit, not pausing to arrange a proper order of advance. The mounted vanguard under Layton and Sir Robert Bowes was followed at some distance by Evers and the infantry. It was late in the afternoon; the Sun was setting and a strong wind was blowing into the face of the charging army. They moved so rapidly that the exhausted men and horses were in some confusion when they reached the marshy ground at the top of the hill. There, only a short distance to their front, stood the Scots in line of battle. The surprise was complete.

For Evers this was a critical moment. His army was strung out and disordered. To halt and regroup would have been dangerous; to retreat downhill would have been catastrophic. Relying on force of numbers the English commander ordered Layton and Bowes on an immediate charge. With the wind coming from the north east the smoke from the harquebuses, both Scots and English, blew into the faces of the cavalry, generally adding to their confusion. Without full infantry support the horsemen were soon cut to pieces. The vanguard was thrown back on the centre, which in turn fell back on the rear as the Scots pressed forward.

Seeing the way the battle was going the assured Scots, some 700 men, tore off their red crosses and attacked their former allies. Before long the English army collapsed, with men fleeing in every direction. Seeing a chance for revenge the local people, including the women, grabbed whatever weapon came to hand and joined the pursuit, with calls of 'Remember Broomhouse.' Over 600 of the English force were slain, including Evers and Layton, and 1000 were taken prisoner. Scottish casualties were light. According to local legend they included a country girl by the name of Maiden Lillard, whose lover had been killed by the English on one of their raids. She died fighting with a sword in hand, and a monument stands to her near the battlefield with the following inscription:

> Fair maiden Lillard lies under this stane,
> Little was he stature, but muckle was her fame;
> Upon the English loons she laid mony thumps,
> And, when her legs were cuttit off,
> She fought upon her stumps.

The Battle of Ancrum Moor may not have been one of the great engagements of the Anglo-Scots wars; but it was certainly the most serious military reverse suffered by England during the reign of Henry VIII. The news of the victory soon spread, and was received with some jubilation in Paris and Rome. Francis, who had been at war with Henry since the previous year, celebrated the occasion by mounting a seaborne attack on Portsmouth and the Isle of Wight. Panic spread across the whole of the English Border. To restore the situation Henry appointed Hertford, who since the Edinburgh raid had been with the King in France, as captain-general in the north with orders to repair Norham and the other Border fortresses as quickly as possible. For a time, England was on the defensive. For Angus the victory at Ancrum did much to restore a reputation badly tarnished by some fairly sordid double dealing. It was written of him:

> The Earle of Angus did so gallantly and valiantly behave himselve
> in this batell, that all suspitione of hes favouring the Englische
> was quyte extingusshed.

Sadly, it was not long before these suspicions were brought back to life.

For Francis the unexpectedly tough Scottish resistance to England opened up the prospect of a war on two fronts. In

September 1544 the English army had captured the port of Boulogne, much to the fury of the French King. Francis was eager for revenge; and, to this end, he decided to send a French auxiliary force to Scotland, the first since the ill-fated campaign of 1523. The intention was to help the Scots take the offensive against northern England. Command of the expedition was given to Jacques de Montgomery, Seigneur de Lorges, one of the captains of the King's Scots guards. Arran was pleased to receive the promise of French military aid. Although Coldingham and other places were recovered from the English after Ancrum Moor, Scotland was too weak in specialist troops and artillery to follow the success up with an advance into England.

Before the French arrived the English attempted to reopen negotiations in April on the basis of the Greenwich treaties. A convention of the nobility was held at Edinburgh to discuss the proposal. Cassillis, speaking on behalf of Henry, said that if the treaties were accepted the King would overlook the injuries he had received in the past, a quite astonishing assertion, considering that a good part of southern Scotland lay in ruins. Not surprisingly, the convention declared the treaties of peace and marriage to be at an end. Cassillis informed Henry on April 20 of the failure of his offer, and recommended that he organise an immediate invasion of Scotland. Henry was in no doubt that Beaton was responsible for the failure of the peace proposal, and encouraged Cassillis to begin plotting the Cardinal's assassination. Shortly afterwards, Hertford began to concentrate troops on the Border, including German, Spanish and Italian mercenaries.

Montgomery landed at Dumbarton at the beginning of June with an impressive force of 3500 professional soldiers. In response the Privy Council decided to hold a national muster at Roslin Moor on 28 July to join with the French on a cross Border invasion. But a good proportion of the pro-English nobles, including Angus, had slipped back into their old treasonable practices. Arran's expedition was effectively undermined by a widespread conspiracy even before it set out, so it is no surprise that the invasion of England was a disappointing failure. By the middle of August the army, with the vanguard under the command of Angus and his associates, was on the retreat, having done no more than burn a few Northumbrian towns. Angus, Cassillis and others were soon urging Hertford to launch a fresh invasion to 'further the peace and marriage.' With the government unable to protect them many

Scots on the Border rushed to accept assurance. Once again, the military initiative passed to the English.

For the beleaguered Arran a new danger began to take shape in the west in the course of 1545. Donald Dubh, a grandson of the last Lord of the Isles, had been held as a state prisoner for most of his life. But he managed to escape from Edinburgh in the confusion of 1544, making his way back to the Isles. He was warmly welcomed by his kinsmen and before long an old dream came to life for the last time in history. In October 1544 word had reached Mary of Guise that 'the lord of the Ilis is broken forth.' Soon after it was reported in England that a new king had emerged from amongst the 'Scottish Iyrsshe.' Here was an ideal opportunity for Henry to revive an old friendship, and create a major embarrassment for Arran in the west, which would help to support English pressure in the south. The man to cement a new alliance with the Lord of the Isles was none other than Matthew of Lennox.

Donald took up residence with his Irish kinsmen at Knockfergus, where he gathered a fleet of 180 galleys and an army of 4,000 men. He wrote to Henry VIII, declaring:

> Your lordship shall consider we have been old enemies to the realm of Scotland, and when they had peace with the King's Highness (Henry VIII) they hanged, beheaded, imprisoned and destroyed many of our kin, friends, and forbears, as testified by our Master the Earl of Ross, now the King's Grace subject...and many other cruel slaughter, burning and hereschip that has been betwixt us and the said Scots...

Lennox came to meet the Islemen in Ireland on 28 July 1545 to agree the terms of the alliance. A further meeting was held with Donald's envoys in London in early September, in which the agreement took its final shape. In return for English support in restoring him to the Lordship of the Isles and Earldom of Ross, Donald acknowledged Henry as his liege lord, and agreed to support his views in regard to the marriage and in all other affairs, under the direction of the Earl of Lennox. He also agreed to mount an attack on Dumbarton Castle, and to leave a force behind in the Isles to pin down the Earls of Huntly and Argyll. This was a good plan; but, luckily for Arran, it was appallingly mismanaged. Lennox, who was vital to its success, was sent to aid Hertford on the Scottish march. By the time he returned to

Ireland Donald's army had largely dispersed. Soon after Donald Dubh died. With no generally acceptable successor both the rebellion and the lordship of the Isles followed him to the grave.

The operation that Lennox was sent to assist was to be the last major attack on Scotland during Henry's reign. Soon after Arran and the Franco-Scots army left the Border, Hertford laid his own plans. He waited until the harvest was gathered to deliver his planned counter stroke, at a time when he could do the most damage. His army advanced towards Kelso in early September. At his approach one hundred people including twelve monks barricaded themselves in the Abbey, which could only be taken by assault. In the confusion a few of the defenders managed to escape, though most were slaughtered by the Spanish mercenaries. Kelso Abbey was systematically destroyed, as were the other great Border abbeys at Melrose, Jedburgh and Dryburgh. They were never restored. What is left stands today as a reminder of Hertford and the 'Rough Wooing.' The destruction continued throughout the surrounding countryside until Hertford returned to England on 23 September. Shortly afterwards he wrote to Henry, saying that he had:

> ...done such hurt as has not been in any raid this hundred
> years, except at the last journey to Edinburgh.

Ugly as it was Hertford's second raid was as politically barren as the first; for it brought the aims of Henry's punitive war not a bit closer. The whole campaign of terror destroyed any possibility of Scotland accepting the marriage treaty, and for many the English party, such as it was, was the party of treason. Only a handful of self seeking nobles and some religious reformers continued to support the marriage. Numbered amongst them was a preacher named George Wishart, an agent of the English, who was a particular inspiration for John Knox. It is possible that Wishart was part of the plot to murder Beaton, but the evidence is circumstantial. All that is certain is that he was burned as a heretic on 1 March 1546 in the Cardinal's town of St Andrews. Soon after the plot to murder the Cardinal took its final form.

On 29 May a group of Fife lairds under the leadership of Norman Leslie, son of the Earl of Rothes, and William Kirkaldy of Grange broke into the castle and murdered Beaton. This was a political act, a success for Henry VIII, which has sometimes be draped in a garb of religious revenge; for Beaton was killed not

186

primarily as a persecutor of Protestants — surprisingly few died at his hands — but as an enemy of England. Almost none of the men who entered the castle that day were motivated by religious principles; and even Knox, who hated Beaton, was to describe some of his murderers as 'men without God.' The morality of the act seems to have escaped most contemporaries; even the Catholic Charles V congratulated Henry on disposing of a great enemy. His assassins, soon to be known collectively as the Castilians, blockaded themselves in St Andrews Castle, holding it as an English outpost for over a year.

The following month France and England signed the Treaty of Camp, bringing Henry's last war to an end. Rather than the great empire of Henry V he was left with Boulogne, which was to be returned to France in 1554. The war had been ruinously expensive. Even had she wanted to, England was in no position to attack Scotland in 1546. Scotland accepted inclusion in this treaty in August, although conditions on the Border remained far from easy. On January 28 1547 Henry VIII died, having achieved none of his main aims in Scotland or France. In his place came a sickly boy, Edward VI. Hertford, the new King's uncle, was created Duke of Somerset and named as Protector of England. Uppermost in his mind was the marriage of his royal nephew. To Scotland's cost he set about pursuing this with a greater determination than the late King. The Rough Wooing was now to enter its deadliest phase.

# CHAPTER 11
# Black Saturday

Quhat cummer haue ye had, in Scotland,
Be our auld enemies of Ingland?
Had nocht bene the support of France
We had been brocht to great mischance.

*Sir David Lindsay of the Mount*

Protector Somerset was in many ways a remarkable man. As a
soldier he had made his reputation in the brutally efficient Scottish
raids of 1544 and 1545. But he had also fought in France, and
was one of the first to realise that Henry's political and military
strategy had failed because no clear priorities had been set;
because, in other words, the King had tried to deal with two sets
of problems at the same time, often using the wrong methods.
Who was better placed than Somerset to conclude that the
campaign of violence and terror in Scotland had been a complete
failure? The Scots were remarkably resilient. Not just in the
recent past but throughout history they had shown a capacity to
recover quickly from invasion as soon as their enemy withdrew.
For centuries of military effort all England had to show was
Berwick; and in the recent wars, despite extensive collaboration
in the south of the country, they had only managed to retain a
precarious hold on the castle at Langholm. Something more
decisive was required if the marriage of Edward and Mary was to
be achieved: not just temporary raids and quick victories, but a
permanent English presence in Scotland. There were to be no
more adventures in France; Scotland and the marriage question
was to have England's complete attention.

But Somerset was not to be allowed a free hand in Scotland. A
few weeks after his death Henry VIII was followed to the grave by
Francis I. His son, Henry II, began a major change in French
foreign policy. He had been deeply affected by the humiliating
loss of Boulogne, and was determined to regain the town at the
earliest opportunity. The Scottish Queen Mother's Guise relatives
acquired a prominence in the new King's councils, which ensured
that he also developed a lasting interest in Scottish affairs. To

assist in this change of emphasis he shifted away from French involvement in Italy, which had caused such trouble for his predecessors, and ensured that there were no further entanglements with the Emperor Charles. Before long the fate of the infant Scottish Queen was to be of much interest to King Henry as it was to Protector Somerset.

With England preparing for a new war against Scotland the position of St Andrews was a matter of some embarrassment to Arran. Soon after the Cardinal's murder he had assembled men and guns to lay siege to the castle, although his operations were carried out with no particular vigour. His son had been in St Andrews when it had been captured by Leslie and the others, providing them with a politically useful hostage, which may account for some of the Governor's diffidence; but in general the poorly conducted siege demonstrated the Scotland had not kept pace with the developments in modern warfare. It wasn't simply that the artillery was badly sited, or the mining operations carried out with no great skill, bad as this was. What made it worse was that St Andrews, despite improvements carried out by Beaton, was largely a medieval castle, and as such was especially vulnerable to gunfire. If the Scottish army could not cope with this obstacle, then it would have no chance against the new style of fortification which had developed in Europe. Somerset learned much from Arran's failure.

Failing to make any progress against the Castilians, Arran arranged a truce towards the end of 1546. In return for a complete withdrawal of all of Arran's forces the Castilians agreed to surrender the castle on receipt of a papal absolution for the murder of Beaton. They had no intention of carrying out their side of the bargain. Rather, they deliberately played for time, hoping for early English assistance. During this welcome breathing space they terrorised the local countryside, as Pittscottie describes in his history:

> They wald ryde and wshe out athort the countrie quhair they
> pleisait and quhillis burnand and raissand fyre in the countrie
> and slay and shed bloode as they plessit, quhillis wssit thair
> bodyis in leichorie witht fair memen, sevand thair appetyte as
> they thecht goode.

Clearly these were men in need of moral guidance, and John Knox arrived at the gates on 10 April ready to provide some. All were confident of English support. An agreement was concluded during the previous month with Andrew Dudley, Somerset's representative, in which the Castilians agreed to hold St Andrews against the Scottish government, and, in time, to surrender both it and Arran's son to the English. Sadly for them, the French got there first.

Concerned by his failure at St Andrews, Arran had sent a message to France appealing for money, arms and artillery. More particularly, in view of the weaknesses of Scottish engineers, he asked for men skilled in the attack and defence of fortifications, and who understood the 'ordering of battles.' In response he was sent a fleet of galleys under the command of Leo Strozzi, a tough and experienced soldier. Strozzi arrived at St Andrews towards the end of July, sending word to the Governor to meet him there. It was immediately apparent to the French commander that if the Scots had shown no great skill in pressing their attack, neither had the Castilians in ensuring their defence. Although both the steeple of the abbey church and the roof of St Salvator's college overlooked the castle, the defenders had allowed them to remain intact; and it was in these places that Strozzi placed his ordnance, a position that enabled his gunners to fire right inside the castle. Some additional support was provided by a battery of mortars, drawn up near the castle gates. Unable to withstand the ensuing barrage, the Castilians surrendered on 31 July, only a few hours after the opening shots. All, including Knox, were sent off to serve a term as slaves on the French galleys. Encouraged by this quick success Arran set off for the west march and Langholm was soon back under Scottish control.

Strangely, Somerset seems not to have appreciated the importance of St Andrews until it was too late. It would seem that he wished to avoid any direct clash with the French, which could have had a serious effect on his preparations for invasion, almost complete by the time Strozzi took St Andrews. In August the Scots diplomat Adam Otterburn was able to report that:

> I saw afoir my eis verray gret preparation of weir and actualle
> the gret hors the harnes the hagbutaris and all gorgious reparrale
> set forward towart our realme.

Since March the Scots had been busy with their own preparations: warning beacons were set up on the march and along the east coast; troops of horsemen kept a look out for the English; various castles were strengthened; artillery was gathered and a fleet sent to patrol the west coast. Finally, on 1 July, all Scots were ordered to be ready for war. But these preparations were partially undermined by fresh evidence of widespread treason.

After the fall of St Andrews a number of documents had been captured. Amongst these was a list of two hundred Scots nobles and gentlemen who had bound themselves to serve the English. It was no surprise that the list was headed by some of the usual suspects: the Earls of Bothwell, Cassillis, Glencairn, Marshal with the lords Kilmaurs and Grey. Bothwell had agreed to surrender the strategically important castle of Hermitage in Liddesdale in return for a promised marriage to the Duchess of Suffolk. It also appeared that Lord Grey was attempting to subvert the Earls of Errol, Sutherland, Atholl and Crawford. This put the Governor in a virtually impossible position. With Scotland facing a major invasion he could not afford the political risk of taking action against those of uncertain loyalty, which might destroy his own military preparations and undermine national morale. The only action he took was to put Bothwell in prison, which only served to put the other conspirators on their guard.

By the end of August Somerset was ready. His army, which was mobilised at Newcastle, amounted to about 17,000 fighting men, supported by pioneers and other specialists. Most of the ordinary English infantrymen were armed, as usual, with bows and bills, although some came with hand guns and the long Continental pike. The army was also well supplied with artillery. But the important difference was that about a quarter of the force — over 4,000 men — comprised of mounted troops, a large proportion of which was made up of heavy cavalry as well as the lighter Border horse.

For many centuries English soldiers had ridden into battle, but they dismounted and fought on foot, almost as an article of faith. Somerset's army was the first since the days of Edward II to be spearheaded by a major body of horsemen, who were intended to fight as cavalry. This reflected the latest military thinking on the Continent, where, since the French victory over the Swiss at Margiano, cavalry used in conjunction with artillery had acquired a new domination. Many of the horsemen were specialist troops, including a body of Spanish harquebusiers led by Pedro de Gamba. Other formations included a crack English unit raised for the defence of Boulogne, and know in consequence as the

'Bulleners,' as well as the Gentlemen Pensioners, a bodyguard raised by Henry VIII. For the details of the campaign historians are indebted to William Patten, who accompanied the English army, and shortly afterwards published his account entitled *The Expedicion into Scotland of Edward, Duke of Somerset.*

Before Somerset left Newcastle he was joined by a small group of forty renegade Scots under the Laird of Mangerston, probably a disappointment after such widespread reports of treason. By 31 August 1547 the army was at Berwick, crossing the Border the following day. It was followed up the east coast by a supply fleet of some eighty ships under Admiral Edward Clinton. On the evening of the first day Somerset reached Eyemouth on the Berwickshire coast. At this important point on the main road between Berwick and Edinburgh he introduced Scotland to another innovation in contemporary warfare — a style of fortification know as *Trace Italienne* — the Italian design — so called because they had been developed in Italy some years before as a defensive response to French artillery. These new forts with their low, thick walls, and huge pointed angle bastions, all masked from view by broad, deep ditches and earthen counterscarps presented a low profile to attacking artillery, but a perfect platform for defensive fire. They had been used extensively by both the French and English during the Boulogne campaign, but the new fort at Eyemouth was the first in the British Isles, and a model for many others.

From Eyemouth, Somerset continued north to Cockburnspath. Here the Lammermuir Hills extend right down almost to the coast. The only way through is over a long, narrow glen known as the Pease; and it was at this good defensive position that the English expected the Scots to make a stand. But Arran had other plans and the army was allowed time to negotiate the obstacle. Once across Somerset took the small castles of Dunglas, Innerwick and Thornton, ignoring the powerful fortresses of Tantallon and Dunbar, which he passed on his right flank. On 5 September the first contact was made with the Scots, when a body of light cavalry tried to ambush the Earl of Warwick, Somerset's second in command. They were quickly driven off. As Somerset passed Hailes Castle the garrison gallantly opened fire, but to no effect. Longniddry was reached on the evening of 8 September, and the army made camp to the west near Salt Preston, now Prestonpans. Admiral Clinton had, in the meantime, sailed on towards Leith and was the first to catch sight of the main Scottish army, lying to the west of the River Esk at Musselburgh. He came ashore and reported the news to Somerset, who ordered him to anchor the fleet near the mouth of the Esk, as close as possible to the shore.

Arran had reacted quickly to the news that the English were approaching the Border. Afraid that the country might be suffering from war weariness he decided to demonstrate the gravity of the situation by sending the fiery cross throughout the kingdom. This extraordinary procedure, of ancient Celtic origin, was more commonly used to summon Highland clans. But it certainly had the desired effect. Soon over 20,000 men had answered the call, almost certainly the largest Scots army since Flodden. Too late to block the Pease he had, nevertheless, taken a strong natural position over the west bank of the River Esk at Edmonstone Edge. His southern flank was protected by a bog known as the Shire Moss, and the north by the sea.

Arran was strong both in numbers and position; yet his host was essentially an anachronism, a hang over from a feudal past. Apart from a few hackbutters he had none of the specialist troops that Somerset had gathered at considerable expense. The only cavalry he had was a force of light Border horse. Most of the troops were armed with the Swiss pike, the same weapon they had carried at Flodden. The pikemen were protected by a light iron jacket and a conical helmet with 'a great kercher wrapped twice or thrice about his neck; not for cold but for (against) cutting.' A group of Highland archers were stationed on the northern flank near to the sea, as brave but as volatile as ever. Conspiracy and treason had done much to weaken morale, with important noblemen like Glencairn and Cassillis absent from the muster. Increasing religious divisions made the position worse, and the growing number of Protestants would have been suspicious of the large number of Catholic priests in the army, who carried a great banner depicting the church kneeling before Christ with the legend 'Forget not thy afflicted Bride, O Lord.' The force was, however, well deployed above the Esk on Edmonstone Edge, and could be expected to give a good account of itself in a defensive battle.

From the camp at Salt Preston Somerset had a good view of the enemy, some three miles to the west. A short distance to his own left the ground began to rise in long ridges from the coastal plain towards Fawside — now Falside — Hill. It was here on Friday 9 September, the thirty fourth anniversary to the day of the Battle of Flodden, that the Scottish cavalry appeared, attempting to provoke the English into a rash attack. Part of the force was deployed along the hillside, with a reserve hidden just behind the slope. Somerset, realising that this was a trap, refused to allow his men to break ranks, but part of the heavy cavalry under Lord Grey was detached from the main force and given permission to charge the enemy. Although the first English assault was beaten back with some loss, the main Scots force and the reserve were soon enveloped in flanking movements to the right and left, and were driven off with heavy casualties. Lord Hume, the commander, was severely wounded, dying later in Edinburgh Castle, and his son was captured with many other gentlemen. The part of the Scottish cavalry wing which managed to escape was to play no further part in the battle, with serious consequences for the main action on the following day.

From Salt Preston the English army deployed along Fawside Hill towards Carberry, two miles to the south west. From the vantage point of Carberry Hill Somerset could see the strength of Arran's position, described in Patten's account as follows:

> The plot where they lay was so chosen for strength, as in all
> their country, some thought there was not a better. Safe to the
> south by a giant marsh; and to the north by the Firth; which
> side also they fenced with two field pieces and certain hackbuts
> a crock, lying under a turf wall. Edinburgh, on the west, at their
> backs; and eastwards, between us and them, they were strongly
> defended by the course of a river, called the Esk, running north
> to the Firth; which, as (though) it was not very deep of water, so
> (yet) were the banks of it so high and steep...as a small sort
> (company) of resistance might be able to keep down a great
> number of comers up.

Any attempt to outflank the Scots to the left would have meant sending the army far to the south over the rugged ground towards Dalkeith, a dangerous move which would have broken communications with both the fleet and the base at Berwick. The Protector decided that his only option was a frontal attack. Before making his final plans he sent a message to Arran, promising that if the marriage of Mary and Edward was allowed to go ahead Scotland would still keep its laws, parliament and institutions. The Governor refused to listen.

Towards the northern part of Arran's position the river cut in a deep bend round the low hill of Pinkie Cleuch on the east bank, where the small village and church of Inveresk were situated. There were no Scottish troops here even though the hill stood close to the only bridge across the Esk at Musselburgh. Immediately perceiving this as the weak point in Arran's defence Somerset decided to place his artillery at Inveresk. With Clinton's ships close to shore this would allow him to catch the Scots in a crossfire from the north and east, thus providing cover for the right wing of the army as it forced its way across the bridge, followed in echelon by the centre and left. The success of this plan hinged on English occupation of Pinkie Cleuch before the Scots realised what their intentions were. On Somerset's order the whole army began to leave Fawside and move to the north west. It was now Saturday 10 September.

Arran's pikemen were arranged in three divisions: he commanded the centre, the Earl of Huntly the left close to the coast at Fisherrow, and the Earl of Angus the right. On his northern flank Huntly was covered by the Highland archers commanded by the Earl of Argyll, while what was left of the cavalry stood to the south of Angus, close to the Shire Moss. The artillery was divided between the right and left, and was apparently drawn by men rather than horses or oxen. Unfortunately, as with Flodden, there is no contemporary Scottish account of the Battle of Pinkie, so we have to guess the reasons for Arran's actions. All we know with any certainty is that when he saw Somerset on the move he ordered the whole army across the Esk. It may be that he thought that the enemy was about to retreat on the high road back to England, and this was an opportunity to trap and destroy them by a rapid charge of pikemen. Whatever the reason, it was a disaster. In astonishment Angus initially refused to obey Arran's command. He was only forced to advance on pain of treason. As soon as the Esk was crossed the Scottish army was delivered into the hands of the Duke of Somerset.

With Angus and Arran fording the river Huntly and Argyll's divisions began to pour over the bridge at Musselburgh. For the English it was an astonishing sight. Somerset was presented with an unexpected opportunity, which he was quick to exploit, as was Admiral Clinton. Seeing the enemy emerge from the protection of the turf wall at Fisherrow Clinton ordered his warships to open fire. Their salvos fell amongst the lightly clad Highland archers, who panicked and fled back along the shore. Huntly's left flank was now completely exposed to Clinton's fire. The Master of Grey and many others fell dead, forcing Huntly further inland, converging on the left of Arran's division in an attempt to get out of range. Soon after they were joined by Angus, and the whole army became one huge mass of pikes. The Scottish cavalry, now too weak to take part in the battle, remained in position on the west bank of the Esk.

On seeing Arran's unexpected advance Somerset ordered his army to stop and take up position on the slope of Fawside. The pike and billmen were drawn up in two formations in the centre, with hackbutters and archers on the flanks. The guns were placed at intervals between the infantry and the cavalry on the northern and southern wings. On the plain below, the Scots poured over Pinkie Cleuch and moved towards the English with considerable speed. To allow his gunners to get into position it was vital for Somerset that their progress was halted. There was only one way to do this. Lord Grey and Sir Ralph Vane with the veteran heavy cavalry, together with Lord Fitzwalters and the demi-lances, were ordered to charge the flank of the leading Scots division commanded by Angus. As the horsemen thundered towards them the Scots halted and lowered their pikes. For a time it looked as if the Battle of Bannockburn was about to be repeated. Patten takes up the story:

> The Scots stood at defence, shoulders right together, the foreranks stooping low before, their followers behind holding their pikes in both hands, the one end of the pike against the right foot, the other against the enemy's breast, so nigh as place and space might suffer. So thick were they that a bare finger should as easily pierce through the bristles of a hedge-hog, as any man encounter the front of the pikes.

Angus was assisted in his defence by a broad, muddy ditch which lay between him and the charging cavalry: still they came on with commendable courage. Faced with a wall of steel the outcome was inevitable: horses were ripped open, and men lifted out of their saddles. Those who fell on the ground were dispatched with the short double edged daggers that the Scots carried at their waist. Elated by their success the pikemen were gleeful, shouting 'Come here loons! Come here heretics.' Lord Fitzwalter was killed, along with many others. Grey drew off, mustered the Bulleners and renewed the attack, with no better results than before. Shelly, the commander of the Bulleners was killed, and

Grey himself was seriously wounded when a pike was thrust through his mouth. With some difficulty the shattered heavy cavalry was drawn off back up the hill. But their objective had been attained: the Scots had been halted. Somerset's artillery was now ready to fire.

From a distance of no more than 200 yards the guns opened up. The dense mass of static pikemen was a perfect target; soon long alleys had been cut into their ranks. While the barrage was underway the archers and hackbuters advanced forward and discharged their weapons. To add to the misery Pedro de Gamba and the horse arquebusiers rode the edge of the ditch in front of Angus' division, firing into the faces of the pikemen as they passed. The only chance Angus had was to continue the advance; but this was made almost impossible by the dead horses and cavalrymen that lay before him. In any case, Grey's charges had locked the pikes together, and it would take time to disentangle them. Time was the one thing that Angus did not have. The battle was destined to repeat not Bannockburn, but Falkirk.

It was clear that the vanguard could not take this murderous onslaught for long. Angus decided to fall backwards, a difficult movement in the midst of a battle, although not impossible with a cavalry screen. No such screen could be provided. Angus's men fell back as best they could in the face of the uninterrupted English fire; but they did not pause to regroup at the foot of the hill. In individuals and groups men began to drop their weapons and run. Panic spread to Arran and Huntly's divisions, as each man began to think only of his own safety. The Governor's shouts of 'treason' added to the general sense of fear and despair. Somerset's cavalry had now regrouped and began to charge, as Warwick and the infantry also marched towards the disintegrating Scots army. To make their flight easier the Scots abandoned both weapons and armour. They scattered in all directions, some making for Edinburgh, others for the Shire Moss near Dalkeith. All were desperate to avoid the vengeful English cavalry, who had advanced into action with shouts of 'Remember Peniel Heugh', the scene of the Scots victory two years before. The ground on both sides of the Esk was so thick with abandoned pikes that Patten likens the scene to a woodyard. Many had died in the battle; many more were cut down in the relentless pursuit. The mood was now one of complete desperation, as men tried to escape death. Patten vividly captures the spectacle that followed:

Some others lay flat in a furrow, as though they were dead, and thereby were passed by our men untouched...some, to stay in the river, covering down his body, his head under the root of a willow tree, with scant his nose above the water for breath. A shift, but no succour, it was to many that had their skulls (helmets) on, at the stroke of the follower, to shrink their heads into the shoulders, like a tortoise into its shell. Others again, for their more lightness, cast away shoes and doublets; and ran in their shirts. And some were seen in this race, to fall flat down all breathless, and to have run themselves to death.

Thousands of men lay dead. They included Lord Cathcart, who in the early morning before the battle drew up his will with an obvious sense of impending doom, requesting that a mass be said for his soul at 'the Blackfriars at Ayr, where my forebears lyis.' He was joined in death by Lord Elphinstone and Lord Fleming; the chief of the MacFarlanes and Gordon of Lochinvar; as well as eldest sons of a number of peers — the masters of Buchan, Livingstone, Methven, Ogilvy, Erskine, Graham and Ross. All seven of the sons of Sir Thomas Urquhart of Cromarty fell at Pinkie. In Edinburgh alone the battle had created 360 widows. One old veteran, John MacKenzie of Killin, was lucky to survive both Flodden and Pinkie. The scene from Fawside Hill was one of complete horror:

Some, with their legs off; some but hought (ham strung) and left lying half dead; others, with the arms cut off; divers, their necks half asunder; many, their heads cloven; of sundry, the brains pasht (smashed) out; some others again, their heads quite off: with a thousand other kinds of killing.

The people of Musselburgh, Inveresk and the surrounding villages were ordered to bury the slain in great pits in the battlefield.

The English also took a number of prisoners, of whom the Earl of Huntly was the most important. When asked by his captors what he now thought of the marriage of Edward and Mary he replied 'I...haud weil with the marriage, but I like not this wooing', thus bequeathing to history the name by which this whole period was to be known. From the Scottish camp on Edmonstone Edge Somerset and his men celebrated the triumph by sending up a great cheer, heard in the streets of Edinburgh, no doubt with a shudder. By 17 September news of the victory had reached London, where huge bonfires were lit in celebration. John Knox declared the defeat to be the judgement of God on the perjured Governor and all who assisted him in the 'unjust quarrel.' But for most Scots it was remembered simply as Black Saturday.

The Battle of Pinkie was the last great fight between England and Scotland as independent nations; it was also the last outing in history for both the Scottish schiltron and the English longbow. The character of war had changed dramatically: now artillery and cavalry were the undisputed masters of the battlefield. Scotland was not able to deal with the new realities on its own. For the last time she called on France. Once again the English had proved they could win a battle: they had not yet won the war.

News of the defeat was carried by Arran to the Queen Mother at Stirling. Mary acted with calm resolution. Expecting Somerset to advance into central Scotland she sent her daughter closer to the Highlands to take refuge at Inchmahome Priory on the Lake of Mentieth, while sending word of the disaster to King Henry and her French kinsmen. Although Arran was to hold on to power for another seven years, the defeat at Pinkie considerably weakened his credibility. He was so unpopular that it was soon reported that the women of Edinburgh were ready to stone him to death. As for his military ability Lord Grey reported to Somerset that the general view was that:

> If Scotland again 'had to do' with England, the Governor for his greatness must not dismount, but if he should remain mounted, the rest might fly: therefore he must appoint a lieutenant, and himself not come to the field.

Mary of Guise, on the other hand, was to grow steadily in stature, especially following the arrival of the French army in 1548.

After Pinkie Somerset occupied Leith without opposition, though he did not have the time or resources to take Edinburgh, let alone advance to Stirling. He was content to re-open negotiations for the marriage and to continue his policy of establishing fortified bases throughout the south east. Rather surprisingly, he did not trouble himself to fortify and hold the important port of Leith, despite having suggested this some time before to Henry VIII. This was a serious oversight. Although the town had been partially destroyed by an accidental fire, it could easily have been restored. Based at Leith, and supplied by sea, the English would have been able to dominate the Firth and a good part of central Scotland. Haddington was to be chosen the following year as the headquarters of the English occupation of south east Scotland. In time, this proved to be a major strategic error.

When the Protector crossed back into England before the end of September 1547 the new occupation policy had taken root, with garrisons at Eyemouth, Broughty Craig at the mouth of the Firth of Tay, Hume Castle, the island of Inchcolm in the Forth, and at Roxburgh, where a new fort had been created out of the ruins of the old castle destroyed by the Scots in 1460. While Somerset was marching to Pinkie,Thomas Wharton, warden of the west marches, had led an invasion into south west Scotland with the Earl of Lennox and established garrisons at Castlemilk, Moffat and Dumfries. Haddington was fortified early in the new year, and its mighty angle bastions, built in the new Italian style, projected out over the local countryside. Dundee was taken by the English garrison at Broughty Craig, as were various other places in the course of 1548 and 1549, although an attempt to capture Dunbar was successfully beaten off by the Scots garrison. Many Scots bowed to the new realities and accepted collaboration as the only safe course of action. Active steps were also taken to advance Protestantism as another aid to English control. By the summer of 1548 Somerset's strategy was bearing fruit, and an English pale of occupation was firmly established in much of the south east and parts of the south west of Scotland.

Somerset used every means to make the marriage acceptable to the Scots, including a major propaganda offensive, amongst the first of its kind in history. In 1547, just before the English invasion, James Henderson published *An Exhortacion to the Scottes,* saying the Treaty of Greenwich had been rejected because of the influence of 'Priests and Frogges.' Henderson appealed to a common sense of Britishness, describing the French as 'auncient enemies rather than auncient frendes.' He advocated that the two kingdoms should be merged into one and that the terms Scot and English should be abolished in favour of Briton. Further publications followed advocating the creation of an 'Empire of Grete Britayn.' But neither hard blows nor soft words made the marriage or Britishness any more acceptable to most Scots, who continued to resist this attempted sixteenth century *Anschluss* with vigour. Somerset's whole campaign was to have an outcome entirely different from the one intended.

The defeat at Pinkie and Mary of Guise' appeal for French aid opened up a new prospect for Henry II. He would not in any circumstances allow the country to go under, which would have been a serious blow to French prestige. But ever since Flodden, Scotland had been an awkward and often bloody minded ally. What if she could be tied more directly to the French interest? What, in other words, if Queen Mary were to be betrothed to the Dauphin Francis, born in 1544, rather than to Edward of England? This new marriage proposal was to be the price of major French aid for Scotland. Arran, who had ambitions for Mary to marry his own son, was persuaded to accept this proposal by the bribe of the rich French duchy of Châtelherault.

Even before the French troops arrived, Scotland showed that the spark of native resistance had not yet been extinguished. In February 1548 the English launched a two-pronged offensive into southern Scotland in the west and the east. In the west Lord Wharton together with the Earl of Lennox advanced to link up in the Nith valley with John Maxwell, eldest son of Lord Maxwell, for a joint attack on James Douglas of Drumlanrig, the only important unassured Scot left in the area. But the English were defeated by Angus and Douglas aided by Maxwell, who had agreed to change sides. Wharton escaped to Dumfries and then back to Carlisle with some difficulty. Soon after Maxwell took Dumfries and by the summer the Scots held the military initiative in the west.

In the east, Grey of Wilton had been more successful, reaching Haddington and setting up garrisons at Hailes Castle, Nunraw, Yester, Hermanston, Waughton, Saltoun, Ormiston and Brunstane. No sooner had he gone, however, than the Scots resumed the offensive and captured the last three minor strongholds. Constant Scots pressure also compelled the English to abandon the fort on Inchcolm in March.

In June 1548 the French army arrived at Leith under the command of Andre de Montalembert, Sieur de Essé. Bases were established at Dunbar, Blackness and, the most important of all, Leith. The army, in excess of 5,000 men, was made up of professional soldiers of many nationalities, German, Swiss and Dutch as well as French. They brought with them all the latest equipment, including hand guns and artillery. Montalembert's force was the most recent in a long line stretching back to Jean de Vienne in 1385. But there was an important difference from the past: this time the French had come to stay.

Shortly after his arrival Montalembert was joined by Arran with 5,000 Scots troops. It was now clear that the base at Haddington was the key to the English occupation in the east of Scotland, so the combined Franco-Scots army quickly invested the town. As the guns and mortars began their work parliament met at a nunnery near to the town on 7 July. Here the price for the French aid was finally settled: it was agreed that Mary should be sent to France to become the prospective wife of Francis. Shortly afterwards the six year old Queen sailed from Dumbarton. She was not to return to Scotland for thirteen years.

The departure of Mary was a fatal blow for Somerset. Victory in battle, occupation, propaganda and collaboration had all failed to achieve his fundamental political goal. In desperation he revived the old claim of suzerainty and threatened France with war if the marriage of Mary and Francis went ahead. In Scotland the conflict acquired an ugly and bitter character. Arran refused quarter to any Scot taken in arms for the English; and Somerset responded by a threat to treat all Scots as rebels against the English crown. It is said that the Scots bought English prisoners from the French with the intention of torturing them to death.

Haddington was a good place to defend, standing, as it did, on a low plain with no surrounding hills. With its new fortifications, modelled on the Italian style, it was virtually impregnable; and this is surely why the site appealed to Somerset. Yet in looking at it from the point of view of a military engineer the Protector had failed to take into consideration wider logistical problems. In the end the whole strategy hinged not on the strength of the forts, or the courage of English soldiers, but on the problem of supply. Jean de Beauge, the French historian of the campaigns of 1548 and 1549, captured the essence of Somerset's problem:

> But I know not, if they considered, that these otherwise great
> conveniences, were attached with a notable disadvantage, that
> the place was not to be succoured with men or munitions,
> without a prevailing army.

Somerset's whole garrison policy was a failure. It had been conceived as a less expensive and more effective alternative to periodic invasions; but it proved to be a massive drain on resources. The siege of Haddington was temporarily raised only after the Earl of Shrewsbury entered Scotland in August 1548 with an army of 15,000 men, almost as many as had taken part in the Pinkie campaign; yet no sooner had he left than the town was once more under attack. To solve the insuperable problem of supply, one

English commander, the Earl of Rutland, introduced a policy of compulsory requisition from local farmers. This only had the effect of alienating the Scots, even those who had accepted assurance, still further. In the end Somerset was reduced to hanging on in Scotland, hoping that Henry would be the first to tire of the effort. In the race of will and resources England was the loser, not France.

In August 1549, with Somerset facing military ruin in Scotland and growing political problems at home, Henry added to the pressure by beginning a war for the recovery of Boulogne. Faced with this new threat it was no longer possible to keep up the increasingly frantic effort in Scotland. The following month the Earl of Rutland was sent into Scotland with 6,000 men to bring out the garrison of Haddington, undefeated in battle but weakened by hunger and disease. Somerset's domestic, military and foreign policy had now completely unravelled. Not long after the evacuation of Haddington he was replaced as head of government by John Dudley, Earl of Warwick, soon to be created Duke of Northumberland.

Under Dudley's guidance there was no new initiative in Scotland. It was now little more than a case of trying to save as much as possible from the wreckage. In February 1550 the castle of Broughty Craig, long a source of trouble in the region of the Firth of Tay, was retaken by storm. The war was now forced back towards the Border, where the English still held on with some determination to the forts at Eyemouth and Roxburgh. It was by now obvious that there was little possibility of recovering Mary from the French or of retaining the vulnerable outpost of Boulogne. Warwick accepted the inevitable and opened peace negotiations with Henry II.

The position of Scotland was an important part of the negotiations leading up to the Treaty of Boulogne. Warwick was prepared to hand over all castles and forts in Scotland with the exception of Roxburgh and Eyemouth, which he saw as an essential part of a buffer zone on the east march. This was a major barrier to progress in the negotiations. It was eventually agreed that they would be evacuated and demolished. In return the French and Scots agreed not to build new fortifications on the sites. English troops did, however, continue to hold on to both fortresses until the Treaty of Boulogne was confirmed by the Anglo-Scots Treaty of Norham in June 1551. As part of the new peace the old question of the Debatable Land was finally settled in September 1552, when the parish of Canonbie went to Scotland and Kirkandrews to England. The new frontier was marked by a shallow ditch known as the 'Scots dyke.'

The final part of our story takes us through a period rich in paradox and irony; a period where enemies became friends and friends became enemies. Scotland had survived its last major struggle against England with the help of France; but only a few years after the war ended it was France, and not England, that was seen as a threat to the nation's independence.

The wars of Henry VIII and Protector Somerset had left many deep wounds. Even with the return of peace many Scots wanted the French to remain as an insurance against future English aggression. Within a few years all this was to change. Once English military pressure was lifted Scotland was able to consider her position more clearly than she had been at any time since before the disaster at Flodden. The French had always been the dominant partners in the alliance. For the most part, though, they had been kept at a distance. Now they were the dominant partners in Scotland itself. In freeing itself from one prospective master Scotland had acquired another. In 1554 Arran — or Châtelherault, as we should now refer to him — was replaced as regent by Mary of Guise, a competent woman who did her best to address the needs of Scotland; but, like Albany in the early 1520's, she realised how much Scotland owed to France, and this was a reckoning that could not be put off for ever.

In 1553 the boy King Edward VI died, having reigned but never ruled. Northumberland tried to preserve Protestant England, and his own power, by having his daughter-in-law, Lady Jane Grey, declared Queen. She was soon thrust aside in favour of the rightful claimant, the Catholic Mary Tudor, a bitter, unhappy woman destined to pass into history as Bloody Mary. She married Philip II of Spain, the son of Charles V, who, apart from his Spanish inheritance, controlled the Habsburg Netherlands and large parts of Italy. In 1557 Philip and Henry went to war. Inevitably, Queen Mary was drawn into the conflict on the side of her husband. Henry wrote to the Scottish regent in the autumn urging her to attack England. The last war between England and Scotland was about to begin.

Perhaps for the first time in history there were few people in either kingdom who welcomed war with the old enemy. When the Scottish and English commissioners met in June 1557 in an attempt to preserve the peace the Earl of Cassillis is reported to have said to the Earl of Westmorland:

By the mass, I am no more French than you are a Spaniard. I
told you once, in my lord your father's house, in King Henry VIII
his time, that we would die, every mother's son of us, rather
than be subjects unto England. Even the like shall you find us to
keep with France.

Mary of Guise was aware of the dangers of pushing a reluctant
Scotland into war. She was also aware that Scotland could not
expect continuing French support if she were not prepared to
fulfil her side of the bargain. On her orders the fort at Eyemouth
was repaired, although this was contrary to the Treaty of Boulogne.
She also recalled the Scots commissioners from Carlisle. Despite
the obvious reluctance of the nobility, the antique Scottish host
was duly summoned for the last time and trundled towards the
Border under the command of Châtelherault. When it reached
Kelso the mood was so bad that the Regent addressed the army
in an attempt to raise morale. She warned of the dangers of an
English invasion and urged an immediate attack on Wark Castle;
but no sooner had they left her at Hume Castle than disputes
errupted between the French and Scottish commanders. Mutiny
broke out and, as in 1523 and 1542, most of the Scots simply
refused to cross the Border in what was perceived to be solely in
the interest of France. A few of the troops, in the company of the
French, went on to attack Wark. Making no progress, the whole
force soon retired back across the Tweed.

Although there was to be no major engagement, the desultory
Border war continued for most of the following year. Berwick, for
the last time in its history, was the flashpoint of the struggle. In
January 1558 Calais fell to the French, leaving Berwick as the
last outpost of England's medieval empire. With the new French
fort at Eyemouth presenting a serious threat to the town's security,
Mary ordered the defences to be completely rebuilt in the latest
Continental style. A little to the west of the town a party of French
soldiers dislodged the English from the castle of Edrington, thus
increasing the pressure. During the summer a minor battle took
place on Halidon Hill, which overlooks Berwick from the north west,
and was the scene of a disastrous Scottish defeat in 1333. A party
of soldiers from the garrison had been stationed there to protect
the townspeople going about their business in the local countryside. Unaware of an enemy presence in the area they dropped
their guard and were surprised by a party of Scots and French
from Eyemouth, who beat them off the hill. Three unsuccessful

attempts were made to retake the position until the Scots and French were forced to make a quick retreat after the arrival of Sir James Crofts with reinforcements from Berwick.

However, the year 1558 was more notable for important developments elsewhere. In April Mary Queen of Scots married the Dauphin Francis at Notre Dame Cathedral in Paris. In November the Scots Estates agreed to offer Francis the crown matrimonial, effectively making him King of Scotland. This was the first Union of the Crowns, and for many it looked as if Scotland was destined to become a province of France, in much the same way as the ancient duchy of Brittany. The Scots had, of course, built the same safeguards for national liberty into the marriage treaty that had accompanied the negotiations with the English in 1543; but in Paris, Mary signed a secret agreement with Henry II which effectively nullified these guarantees:

> Mary, Queen of Scots...has said and declared that, in the event of her decease without heirs begotten of her body...she has given and by these presents gives, by pure and free gift, to take effect on her death, to the King of France who is or shall be, the kingdom of Scotland according to what it consists and comprises, beside all such rights to the kingdom of England as can or shall belong and pertain to her now and in time to come...

This last clause was to have important short term implications. In the same month that Francis became King of Scotland Mary Tudor died, to be succeeded by her half sister Elizabeth, who soon returned England to the Protestant camp. In the eyes of Catholic Europe Elizabeth, the daughter of Anne Boleyn, was illegitimate, and therefore the rightful Queen of England was now Mary Stewart, the great granddaughter of Henry VII. Acting on the advisce of her father-in-law, Henry II, she and her husband quartered their arms with the arms of England, which in time was to prove to be a grave political miscalculation.

In the spring of 1559 the war between Philip and Henry finally came to an end. Not long after, Henry died. Francis II and Mary were now the King and Queen of France, as well as Scotland; and, in some eyes, they were also King and Queen of England. In Scotland the end of the war left the French more dominant than ever. As a consequence a new kind of Protestant nationalism began to emerge, headed by a group of noblemen known as the Lords of the Congregation. For these men it was France and not

England that now presented the chief threat to the liberty of Scotland. In May John Knox returned to Scotland from the Calvinist stronghold of Geneva. Before long the Scottish Reformation was underway as an attack on the auld religion, on the one hand, and the auld alliance, on the other. The identification of the Catholic church with the French alliance had the effect of linking Protestantism with patriotism, an interesting reversal of the situation in the 1540's. But against the modern French army, secure in impressive fortifications of Leith and elsewhere, the rag taggle force of the Congregation could make little progress. With the Reformation in danger of being strangled at birth the Protestant lords called for the assistance of the ancient enemy. History was about to stand on its head.

Elizabeth I was a deeply conservative monarch. Nothing was more repellent to her than subjects who rebelled against their lawful prince. Even so, she could not ignore a direct challenge to her own authority. It was not the struggles of the Congregation that ended French rule in Scotland, but the pretence of Francis and Mary to the English royal title. The defeat of the Protestant lords in Scotland would have been a serious blow to English security. Egged on by William Cecil, her chief minister, she entered into an alliance with the Scots Protestants at Berwick in February 1560. The object of this treaty, it was expressly stated, was not to undermine the authority of Mary and Francis, but to safeguard Scotland's independence against the French, or 'the defence of the just freedom of the Crown of Scotland from conquest.'

With the English navy under Admiral Winter blocking the Forth an army under Arthur Grey, fourteenth Baron of Wilton, crossed the Border on 29 March, rode to meet the Congregation army at Prestonpans, and soon after began the siege of Leith. While the attack was underway Mary of Guise, the last great defender of the Auld Alliance, died in Edinburgh Castle. The French at Leith fought bravely; but running short of supplies they entered into negotiations with the English. In July the Treaty of Edinburgh was concluded in which both the French and English agreed to leave Scotland. With no defence left, the Catholic church in Scotland was finished as a national force. The ancient alliance between France and Scotland limped on for a few months, finally passing into history with the sudden death of Francis II in December 1560. Rather than a satellite of France, Scotland was to become, in time, the satellite of England.

# CHAPTER 12
## The Fruits of War

Saying, Peace, peace; when there is no peace

*Jeremiah*

After 1560 there was to be no more war between England and Scotland. This did not mean the end of trouble on the Border. Over two hundred years of conflict had created a tough, self reliant people. War, and the threat of war, arrested the development of the Border region, both in a political and economic sense. There was simply no point in sowing crops which could be easily destroyed either by invading armies, or, more commonly, in the casual frontier raiding, which continued regardless of the formal relations between the two countries. Wealth was measured, rather, in livestock, especially cattle, which could be moved to a place of safety as the occasion demanded. In these conditions people inevitably grouped together for mutual safety, leading to the emergence of warrior clans. In Scotland the Maxwells, Johnstones, Armstrongs, Elliots, Scotts, Kerrs and Humes, were matched in northern England by the Grahams, Hetheringtons, Carletons, Fenwicks and Forsters. There were also numerous smaller groupings; and some, the Armstrongs and Grahams most notably, could be found on both sides of the frontier.

In time of war the Border clans formed the first line of each nation's defence; and even in peacetime they continued to rob and murder one another. For all that, they tended to have more in common with each other than they had with the more settled communities to the north and south. Governments in both Edinburgh and London tended to distrust the Borderers, believing them capable of collusion and treason. Allegations about the conduct of the lords Hume and Dacre at Flodden is the most noted example of this; but there were others. In September 1545 the English Borderers refused to carry out the systematic destruction ordered by Hertford, forcing him to call on the services of his foreign mercenaries; and the allegiance of the Scottish Armstrongs was notoriously fickle.

The problem with using the frontier clans in defensive system was that more often than not national politics tended to get caught up in local disputes. In the early days powerful chieftains like the Percies and Douglases used war as a means to build up their power on the marches, to the point where they represented a real danger to the national government. The English tried to solve this problem by appointing outsiders as march wardens, with variable results. For the rulers of Scotland, always short of cash, this tended not to be an option. With the fall of the house of Douglas in 1455, power on the marches fragmented, making conditions, if anything, even more difficult. Attempts to impose outsiders on the warring Border clans were generally disastrous. In one notorious case in 1516 Anthony Darcy, the Sieur de la Bastie, a colleague of John Duke of Albany and appointed by him as warden of the east marches, was murdered and had his head cut off by the Humes, who resented interference in what they considered to be their own territory.

Even when the two countries were at peace Edinburgh and London had neither the will nor the resources to control lawlessness on the marches. Solutions to this endemic problem tended to be dramatic, but with only short term results, like the infamous arbitrary execution of Johnnie Armstrong, Laird of Gilnockie, by James V in 1530. For the most part the governments tended to ignore the problem, so that even during the reigns of Elizabeth I and James VI, when the two countries were at peace, conditions on the Border tended to get steadily worse, to the point where reiving became a daily — or, rather, nightly — occurrence. This is hardly surprising, considering the experience to which the Borderers had been subject to earlier in the century. There were times during the reigns of Henry VIII and Edward VI when the English Borderers were encouraged to attack their Scottish counterparts on any pretext whatsoever. It was at this time, especially in the 1520's that the reiving brotherhoods began to acquire their final shape, and a new savagery entered Border life. One author described the process as follows:

> Now under the influence of this brutal treatment Border life began to slip away from its connections with civilisation. The Borderers ceased to regard themselves as bound by any laws and degenerated into gangs of brigands, whose hand was against every man, and who made little distinction between friend and foe. The English government soon found that it was easy to create this state of affairs, but difficult to end it. It was a result

of a few years of infamous policies, but it took half a century to bring things back again even to the rude condition which existed before deliberate barbarity intensified its worst features.

The legacy of this period which climaxed in the Rough Wooing can still be seen all along the Border in the ruins of the peel towers that the wealthier Borderers built for their own protection. Today these provide an evocative reminder of a strange and violent past, captured by Sir Walter Scott in his poem *Marmion:*

> And still I thought that shatter'd tower
> The mightiest work of human power;
> And marvell'd as the aged hind
> With some strange tale bewitch'd my mind,
> Of forayers, who, with headlong force,
> Down from that strength had spurr'd their horse,
> Their southern rapine to renew,
> Far in the distant Cheviot blue
> And, home returning, fill'd the hall
> With revel, wassel rout, and brawl.
> Methought that still with trump and clang,
> The gateway's broken arches rang;
> Methought grim features, seam'd with scars,
> Glared through the window's rusty bars,
> And ever, by the winter hearth,
> Old tales I heard of woe or mirth,
> Of lovers' slights, of ladies charms,
> Of witches' spells, of warriors arms.

For those lower down the social scale, the fortified farmhouse — known as a bastel — offered some protection from robber gangs; but most people simply took to their heels, carrying with them whatever meagre possessions they had. The houses they left behind were no more than huts of clay, often with the floor scooped out of the earth, covered by a thatched roof. The easiest way to destroy these primitive structures was to set fire to the roof, which caused the clay walls to crumble. To prevent this, if they were given adequate warning, many of the country people removed their roofs in time of danger, and replaced them when they were able to return.

If violence was an essential part of Border life, so too was reiving. To ensure that their frontiers were well defended both governments had actively encouraged settlement on the Borders, offering land at low rents. This had the effect of increasing the population beyond the capacity of the area's economy to support it, making the raid an important way of supplementing limited incomes. Both governments had tried to control robbery and rustling by an elaborate system of Border laws, warden courts and truce days; but it was often impossible to implement this system, even when the will was present. All too often the wardens themselves were active participants in the whole system of blackmail — a word invented in the Borders — and plunder, generally adding to the sense of insecurity in the region; and in some places — the Debatable Land, most notoriously of all — the only law that operated was the law of arms.

Local officials were often so starved of resources by central government that they had no chance of dealing effectively with the problems in their areas. On one occasion Sir William Eure, the English warden of the east march towards the end of the sixteenth century, was reduced to writing in frustration:

> ...wishing to God, I had never lived to serve where neither her
> Majesty nor her officer is obeyed; fearing unless assisted by her
> Majesty's forces, Tyndale will be laid waste as other parts of the
> March are.

It is easy to understand the feelings of officials like Sir William when we consider the sheer scale of the problem. Wardens had to deal not simply with outlaws and robber barons, but with little private armies. The Armstrongs of Liddesdale, to take only one example, were able to assemble some 3,000 horsemen in the 1520's. Such was their strength that they were able to engage in an unofficial war in 1528 with Lord Dacre, the march warden of the time, over the Debatable Land. Since the beginning of the century the Armstrongs, under pressure of population, had begun to expand from Liddesdale into the Debatable ground. By 1528 they had even constructed some peel towers, although this was contrary to the rules governing the use of this no-mans-land. Dacre had advanced against them with 2,000 men; but the Armstrongs were forewarned by some of the English Borderers, and defeated the warden in battle. This humiliation could not be allowed to pass, so Dacre returned with reinforcements, including some artillery sent to him by the other English march wardens, and set about destroying the Armstrong settlements.

With the whole countryside in arms private quarrels often grew into huge public feuds, which took generations to die down. When it came to avenging family honour nationality was quite irrelevant. One of the bloodiest, and longest lasting, of these clan quarrels was between the Scottish Maxwells and Johnstones on the west march. The exact cause of the dispute is unknown, though it appears to have been a contest over power and influence in the south west of Scotland. As early as the 1520's Lord Dacre was reporting to Cardinal Wolsey that the feud was turning the Debatable Land into a desert. It continued to burn throughout the sixteenth century, finally coming to a murderous climax on 6 December 1593. Fighting for their very existence, and using all the skills of Border warfare, 400 Johnstones managed to defeat 2000 Maxwells, Scotts and Elliots at the Battle of Dryfe Sands, close to Lockerbie. Some 700 Maxwells are said to have been killed, including their chief. Many were cut down retreating through the streets of Lockerbie, leading to the expression 'A Lockerbie Lick', which for many years after was used in Annandale to denote a severe wound. As a measure of the desperation with which the Johnstones fought their ranks included Robert Johnstone of Raecluech — he was only eleven years old. Dryfie Sands was the last of the Border battles, and was possibly the most savage neighbour dispute in British history.

Despite many mutual provocations on the marches there was neither the will nor the desire in Edinburgh and London for a full scale war. For Elizabeth, the Catholic Mary Queen of Scots was an awkward political problem, especially after she returned to Scotland from France in 1561; but Mary was too tied up in domestic difficulties to be a serious threat to the English Queen. After Mary was deposed in 1567 Scotland was left in the care of a series of pro-English regents during the minority of James VI — including the Earl of Lennox for a time — all of them dependent on the good will of Elizabeth. When James came to manhood he was generally recognised — although never officially — as the likely heir of the unmarried English Queen. An unwarlike and timid man, he was anxious to avoid anything which would upset the political balance. Even the execution of his mother in 1587, after almost twenty years as a prisoner of the English, occasioned no more than a superficial protest. It's hardly surprising, therefore, that against this background even fairly major Border incidents, which in the past would almost certainly have led to war, were quickly brushed aside. We need only mention two of the most important — the Raid of Reidswire in 1575 and the rescue of Kinmont Willie from Carlisle Castle in 1596.

From time to time English wardens met with their Scottish counterparts on prearranged days of truce to settle disputes. One such meeting was held at Reidswire on the Border at Carter Bar on July 7 1575 between Sir John Forster, the English warden, and Sir John Carmichael, the keeper of Liddesdale. Each man was accompanied by a large retinue of armed Borderers. A quarrel broke out between the wardens, and to the cry of 'To it, Tyndale' the English began to fire their longbows — still the favoured weapon in this part of the country until the 1580's. The Scots were driven back, but managed to get the better of the English when a body of citizens arrived from Jedburgh carrying firearms. Several Englishmen were killed in the murderous brawl known as the 'Raid of Reidswire', the most notable of whom was the deputy warden, Sir George Heron. Forster and several other men of note were taken prisoner. For a brief period the situation on the Border became very tense, with many seizing the opportunity to recommence raiding; but there was no war. London seems to have accepted that part of the blame for the scuffle lay with Forster; and the Scottish regent, the Earl of Morton, did his best to ensure that the matter was quickly forgotten. He sent Forster home with some falcons as a present, which, in the grim humour of the Borders, led to the observation that the Regent had got the worst of the bargain, giving live owls for dead herons.

The second incident concerned a particularly notorious reiver by the name of William Armstrong of Kinmont, a descendent of Johnnie Armstrong of Gilnockie, more widely known simply as Kinmont Willie. He had attended a truce day on the west march near Kershopefoot in March 1596, and by well established Border practice he should have been immune from arrest until the following day. But on his way home he was spotted by a group of Englishmen, who, unable to let this opportunity pass, took him prisoner, presenting their prize to Lord Scrope, the march warden, at Carlisle Castle. Angered by this clear breach of the Border law Walter Scott of Buccleuch, the keeper of Liddesdale, tried to obtain redress through the usual international channels. When his protests were ignored he decided to take more direct action. Gathering 80 of his followers — or 500 in Lord Scrope's account — and sure of the co-operation of the English Grahams, he rode through the night of 12/13 April in the direction of Carlisle, with scaling ladders, crowbars, hand-picks and axes. He then broke into the castle by the postern gate, rescued Willie and hurried back to Scotland, leaving the humiliated Lord Scrope blind with fury. This incident became the basis of one of the most famous of the Scottish Border poems, *The Ballad of Kinmont Willie*, which concludes in a triumphalist tone:

> Buccleuch has turn'd to Eden Water,
> Even where it flowed frae bank to brim,
> And he has plunged in wi' a' his band
> And safely swam them through the stream.
>
> He turn'd him on the other side,
> And at lord Scroope his glove flung he-
> 'If ye like na my visit in merry England,
> In fair Scotland come visit me!'
>
> All sore astonish'd stood lord Scroope,
> He stood as still as rock of stane;
> He scarcely dared to trew his eyes,
> When through the water he had gane.
>
> 'He is either himsell a devil frae hell,
> Or else his mother a witch maun be;
> I wadna have ridden that wan water
> For a' the gowd in Christentie.'

Scrope had been made to look like a fool in his own country. With his pride badly dented he wrote to the Privy Council, greatly exaggerating the size of Buccleuch's force, and promising revenge for this insult to the Queen's dignity. But in the end it proved to be a matter of no great international importance: Scrope led a reprisal raid into Liddesdale and Elizabeth put pressure on James to arrest Buccleuch. Once again James was reluctant to do anything that might endanger the succession. Buccleuch, a personal favourite of the King, was handed over to the English government, and imprisoned for a time at Berwick. He was soon returned unharmed. Neither Scrope's injured honour nor Buccleuch's boldness were allowed to be the occasion for war.

The death of Elizabeth in early 1603 provided the opportunity for a last great frenzied outbreak of Scots raiding into England known as the 'Ill Week.' With their King now on his way south to claim the throne of England as James I it may be that many saw this as a final opportunity, the last act of a dying way of life. Before long James began to direct his attention to the last traces of the old Anglo-Scottish wars. Even the term 'the Borders', too redolent of ancient wars, was to be legislated out of existence, and replaced with the more innocuous 'Middle Shires.' James failed in this attempt to eliminate the past by a semantic conjuring trick. His campaign against the Border clans was altogether more successful. The Borderers, once the forefront of national defence, were now a political embarrassment, whether they be Scots or English. One by one the old robber clans were destroyed; some by transportation, others by hanging. Old battles became no more than a memory, as Scotland sank into the long sleep of union. The greater, as Henry VII once remarked, drew the lesser; an ancient nation became little more than the province of a new empire.

# Select Bibliography

**Documentary and Narrative Source**

The Auchinleck Chronicle, edited by T. Thomson, 1829.

Balfour, Sir James, Historical Works, 1824.

Beaugue, Jean de, The History of the Campagnes of 1548 and 1549, translated by P. Abercromby, 1707.

Boece, Hector, The Chronicles of Scotland, edited by E. C. Batho and H. W. Husbands, 1941.

Bower, Walter, Scotichronicon, volume eight, edited by D. E. R. Watt, 1987.

Buchanan, G., The History of Scotland, 1821.

Calderwood, D., History of the Kirk of Scotland, 1842.

Calender of Border Papers, 2 vols, edited by J. Bain, 1894–6.

Calender of Close Rolls., 1914–1963.

Calender of Documents Relating to Scotland, vol IV, 1357–1509, edited by J. Bain, 1888.

Calender of Documents Relating to Scotland, vol V, 1108–1516, edited by G. G. Simpson and J. D. Galbraith. Undated.

Calender of Patent Rolls, 1895–1982.

Calender of Scottish Papers, 1547–1563, edited by J. Bain, 1898.

Calender of State Papers. Edward VI, 1547–1553, edited by C. S. Knighton, 1992.

Calender of State Papers and Manuscripts. Milan, edited A. B. Hinds, 1912.

Calender of State Papers and Manuscripts.. Venice, edited by R. Brown, 1867.

Capgrave, John, The Chronicle of England, edited by F. C. Hingeston, 1858.

The Days of James IV. Exracts from Royal Letters etc, Arranged and edited by G. Gregory Smith, 1900.

A Diurnal of Occurances within Scotland, 1513–1575, anonymous, 1833.

Edward VI, The Chronicles and Political Papers of Edward VI, edited by W. K. Jordan, 1966.

An English Chronicle of the Reigns of Richard II, Henry IV, Henry V and Henry VI, edited by J. S. Davies, 1856.

English History from Original Sources, edited by F. H. Durham, 1902.

Flodden Papers. Diplomatic Correspondence between the Courts of France and Scotland, 1507–1517, edited by M. Wood, 1933.

Fordun, John of, Chronicle of the Scottish Nation, edited by W, F. Skene, 1872.

Froissart, Jean, Chronicle of Froissart, translated by Sir John Bourchier, Lord Berners, 1901–1903 edition.

Grafton, Richard, Chronicle; or, History of England, 1809.

Hall, Edward, Chronicle of England, 1809.

216

# Select Bibliography

*The Hamilton Papers*, 2 vols, edited by J. Bain, 1890–2.

Hardyng, John, *Chronicles*, 1812.

Herries, Lord, *Historical Memoirs of the Reign of Mary Queen of Scots*, 1836.

Higden, Raphael, *Polychronicon*, Peter Traveris edition, 1527.

*The Historical Collection of a Citizen of London in the Fifteenth Century*, edited by J. Gairdner, 1860.

Holinshead, Raphael, *The Scottish Chronicle*, 1805.

Knox, John, *History of the Reformation*, 2 vols, edited by W. Croft Dickinson, 1949.

*The Late Expedition in Scotland sent to the Right Honourable Lord Russell*, anonymous, in 'An English Garner', edited by E. Arber, 1877–1896.

Lesley, John, *The History of Scotland from the death of James I in 1437 to 1541*, 1830.

*Letters of the Kings of England*, edited by J. O. Halliwell, 1846.

*The Letters of King Henry VIII*, edited by M. St Clare Byrne, 1968.

*The Letters of James V*, edited by R. K. Hanny and D. Hay, 1954.

*Letters and Papers, Foreign and Domestic of the Reign of Henry VIII*, catalogued by J. S. Brewer; revised by R. H. Brodie, vols 1–21, 1965 reprint.

*Letters and Papers Illustrative of the Wars of the English in France*, edited by J. Stevenson, 1861–1864.

Major, John, *A History of Greater Britain*, translated and edited by A. Constable, 1892.

*Materials Illustrative of the Reign of Henry VII*, 2 vols, edited by W. Campbell, 1873–7.

Monstrelet, Enguerrand de, *The Chronicles of England, France and Spain*, translated by T. Johannes, 1840.

*Original Letters Illustrative of English History*, 11 vols, edited by H. Ellis, 1824–1846.

*The Paston Letters, 1422–1509*, edited by J. Gairdner, 1872–1875.

Patten, William, *The Expedicion into Scotland of Edward, Duke of Somerset*, 1548.

Pinkerton, John, *The History of Scotland*, 1797.

Pitscottie, Robert Lindesay of, *The History and Chronicles of Scotland*, 1899.

*Pluscarden, the Book of*, edited by F. H. Skene, 1880.

*Proceedings and Ordinances of the Privy Council of England*, vols 1–7, edited by H. Nicols, 1834.

*Royal and Historical Letters During the Reign of Henry IV*, edited by F. C. Hingeston, 1860.

Sadler, Sir Ralph, *The State Papers and Letters of Sir Ralph Sadler*, edited by A. Clifford, 1809.

*The Scottish Correspondence of Mary of Lorraine*, edited by A. I. Cameron, 1927.

Skelton, John, *The Poetical Works of John Skelton*, edited by A. Dyce, 1843.

*A Source Book of Scottish History*, edited by W. Croft Dickinson, G. Donaldson, and I. A. Milne, 1958.

Stow, John, *The Annales, or General Chronicle of England*, 1614.
*Syllabus of Rymer's Foedera*, edited by T. D. Hardy, 1873.
*Three Fifteenth Century Chronicles*, edited by J. Gairdner, 1860.
*The Trewe Encountre or Batayle Lately Don Between England and Scotland etc*, annonymous, in 'Proceedings of the Society of Antiquaries of Scotland', vol 7, pp 143–152, 1867–1868.
Vergil, Polydore, *The Angliaca Historia of Polydore Vergil, 1485–1537*, edited and translated by D. Hay, 1950.
*The Westminster Chronicle, 1381–1394*, edited and translated by L. C. Hector and B. F. Harvey, 1982.
Wyntoun, Andrew of, *The Original Chronicle of Andrew of Wyntoun*, edited by F. J. Amours, 1908.

**Secondary Works.**

Anderson, W, *The Scottish Nation etc*, biographical history, 3 vols, 1863.
Armitage Smith, S., *John of Gaunt*, 1904.
Armstrong, R. B., *The History of Liddesdale, Eskdale, Ewesdale, Wauchopedale and the Debatable Land*, vol 1, 1883.
Armstrong, W. A. *The Armstrong Borderland*, 1960.
Arthurson, I., 'The King's Voyage into Scotland: The War that Never Was', in *England in the 15th Century: Proceedings of the 1986 Harlaxton Symposium*, edited by D. Williams, 1987.
Arthurson, I., *The Perkin Warbeck Conspiracy, 1491–1499*, 1994.
Balfour Melville, E. W. M., *James I, King of Scots, 1406–1437*, 1936.
Balfour Melville, E. W. M., 'The Captivity of James I'. in the *Scottish Historical Review*, vol XXI, pp 45–53, 1924.
Balfour Melville, E. W. M., 'The Later Captivity and Release of James I', in the *Scottish Historical Review*, vol XXI, pp 89–100, 1924.
Balfour Paul, J., 'Edinburgh in 1544 and Hertford's Invasion', in the *Scottish Historical Review*, vol VIII, pp 113–131, 1911.
Barbé, L. A., *Margaret of Scotland and the Dauphin Louis*, 1917.
Barrett, C. R. B., *Battles and Battlefields in England*, 1896.
Bates, C. J., *The Border Holds of Northumberland*, 1891.
Bates, C. J., *The History of Northumberland*, 1895.
Bean, J. M. W., 'Henry IV and the Percies', in *History*, vol 44, pp 212–227, 1959.
Bingham, C., *James V*, 1971.
Bingham, C., 'Flodden and its Aftermath', in *The Scottish Nation*, edited by G. Menzies, 1972.
Black, J. B., *The Reign of Elizabeth, 1558–1603*, 1964.
Boardman, S., 'The Man who would be King: the Lieutenancy and Death of David Duke of Rothesay, 1378–1402', in *People and Power in Scotland: Essays in Honour of T. C. Smout*, edited R. Mason and N. Macdougall, 1992.
Boardman, S., *The Early Stewart Kings, 1371–1406*, 1996.

# Select Bibliography

Borland, R. *Border Raids and Reivers*, 1910.

Bradley, P. J., 'Social Banditry on the Anglo-Scottish Borders in the Late Middle Ages', in *Scotia*, vol XII, pp 27–43, 1988.

Bradley, P. J., 'Henry V's Scottish Policy: a Study in Realpolitik', in *Documenting the Past*, edited by J. S. Hamilton and P. J. Bradley, 1989.

Brown, A. L., 'The English Campaign in Scotland, 1400' in British Government and Administration, edited by H Hearder and H. R. Lyon, 1974.

Brown, M, *James I*, 1994.

Burne, A. H., *The Battlefields of England*, 1950.

Burne, A. H., *More Battlefields of England*, 1952.

Burne, A. H., *The Agincourt War. A Military History of the latter part of the Hundred Years War from 1369 to 1453*, 1956.

Burns, J. H., 'The Political Background of the Reformation' in the *Innes Review*, 10, pp 199–233, 1959.

Bush, M. L., *The Government Policy of Protector Somerset*, 1975.

Caldwell, D. H. 'The Battle of Pinkie', in *Scotland and War. AD 79–1918*, edited by N. MacDougall, 1991.

Campbell, J., 'England, Scotland and the Hundred Years War' in *Europe in the late Middle Ages*, edited by J. Hale, R. Highfield and B.Smalley, 1970.

Carre, W. R., *Border Memories*, 1876.

Cassavetti, E, *The Lion and the Lillies*, 1977.

Chalmers, G., *Caledonia*, 1888.

Charlesworth, D., 'Northumberland in the early years of Edward IV', in *Archaeologia Aeliana*, vol XXI, pp 69–81, 1953.

Chrimes, S. B. 'Some Letters of John of Lancaster as Warden of the East Marches Towards Scotland', in *Speculum*, 14, pp 3–27, 1939.

Chrimes, S. B., *Henry VII*, 1972.

Conway, A., *Henry VII's Relations with Scotland and Ireland*, 1932.

Craig Brown, T., *The History of Selkirkshire*, 1886.

Creighton, M., *Carlisle*, 1889.

Croft Dickinson, W., *Scotland from the Earliest Times to 1603*, revised by A. A. M. Duncan, 1977.

Davies, C. S. L., 'Provision for Armies, 1509–50; a study in the Effectiveness of Early Tudor Government', in the *Economic History Review*, 17, 1964–1965.

Dickinson, G., 'Some Notes on the Scottish Army in the first half of the Sixteenth Century', in the *Scottish Historical Review*, vol 28–29, pp 133–145, 1949–50.

Dodds, G. L., *Battles in Britain*, 1996.

Donaldson, G., *Scotland: James V to James VII*, 1965.

Donaldson, G., *The Auld Alliance*, 1985.

Doran, S., *England and Europe, 1485–1603*, 1986.

Douglas, G., *A History of the Border Counties — Roxburgh, Selkirk and Peebles*, 1894.

Douglas Simpson, W., 'Hailes Castle', in the *Transactions of the East Lothian Antiquarian and Field Naturalists Club*, 1948.

Dunlop, A. I., *The Life and Times of James Kennedy*, 1950.

Dunlop, D., 'The Masked Comedian: Perkin Warbeck's Adventures in Scotland and England in 1495 and 1497', in the *Scottish History Review*, vol LXX, pp 97–128, 1991.

Eaves, R. G., *Henry VIII's Scottish Policy, 1513–1524*, 1971.

Elliot, G. F. S., *The Border Elliots and the Family of Minto*, 1897.

Elliot, W. F., *The Battle of Flodden and the Raids of 1513*, 1911.

Fergusson, J., '1547: The Rough Wooing', in *Blackwood's Magazine*, vol CCLXII, pp 183–194, 1947.

Fergusson, J., *The White Hind and other Discoveries*, 1963.

Fisher, H. A. L., *The History of England from the Accession of Henry VII to the Death of Henry VIII, 1485–1547*, 1906.

Fleming, D. H. *Mary Queen of Scots*, 1897.

Fonblanque, E. B. de, *The Annals of the House of Percy*, 1887.

Forbes Leith, W., *The Scots Men-at-Arms and Life Guards in France*, 1882.

Ford, C. J., 'Piracy or Policy: the Crisis in the Channel, 1400–1403', in *Transactions of the Royal Historical Society*, vol 29, pp 63–77, 1979.

Franklin, D., *The Scottish Regency of the Earl of Arran. A Study in Failure*, 1995.

Fraser, W., *The Book of Caerlaverock*, 1873.

Fraser, W., *The Scotts of Buccleuch*, 1878.

Fraser, W., *The Red Book of Mentieth*, 1880.

Fraser, W., *The Douglas Book*, 1885.

Gairdner, J., *Richard the Third*, 1898.

Goodman, A., *The Wars of the Roses: Military Activety and English Society, 1452–1497*, 1981.

Goodman, A., 'The Anglo-Scottish Marches in the Fifteenth Century: a Frontier Society?', in *Scotland and England, 1286–1815*, edited by R. A. Mason, 1987.

Goodman, A, and Tuck, J. A. editors, *War and Border Societies in the Middle Ages*. 1992.

Gransden, A., *Historical Writing in England, 1307 to the early Sixteenth Century*, 1982.

Grant, A., *Independence and Nationhood: Scotland, 1306–1469*, 1984

Grant, A., 'Scotland's 'Celtic Fringe' in the Late Middle Ages: The Macdonald Lords of the Isles and the Kingdom of Scotland', in *The British Isles, 1100–1500*, edited by R. R. Davies, 1988.

Grant, A., 'The Otterburn War from a Scottish Point of View', in *War and Border Societies in the Middle Ages*, edited by Goodman, A. and Tuck, A., 1992.

Grant, A., 'Scottish Foundations: late Medieval Contributions', in *Uniting a Kingdom? The Making of British History*, edited by A. Grant and K. J. Stringer, 1995.

Gregory, D., *History of the Western Highlands and Isles of Scotland*, reprint 1975.

Griffiths, R. A., *The Reign of Henry VI*, 1981.

## Select Bibliography

Harris, G. L., *Cardinal Beaufort*, 1988.

Hay, D., 'Booty in Border Warfare', in *Transactions of the Dumfriesshire and Galloway Natural History and Antiquarian Society*, vol 31, pp 145–166, 1954.

Head, D. M., 'Henry VIII's Scottish Policy: a Reassessment' in the *Scottish Historical Review*, vol LXI, pp 1–24, 1981–82.

Herkless, J. and Hannay, R. K., *The Archbishops of St Andrews*, 1913.

Hodgkin, T, 'The Battle of Flodden', in *Archaeologia Aeliana*, vol 16, pp 1–46, 1894.

Hodgkin, T., *The Warden of the Northern Marches*, 1908.

Hume, David, of Godscroft., *The History of the House and Race of Douglas and Angus*, 1820 edition.

Hutchison, H. F. *The Hollow Crown: A life of Richard II*, 1961.

Jacob, E. F., *The Fifteenth Century, 1399–1485*, 1985.

Jeffrey, A., *History and Antiquities of Roxburghshire and Adjacent Districts*, 4 vols, 1855–1864.

Jermingham, H. E. H., 'An Affray at Norham Castle, and its Influence on Scottish and English History', in *The Scottish Antiquary or Northern Notes and Queries*, vol XV, pp 179–188, 1901.

Jordan, W. K., *Edward VI: the Young King*, 1968.

Jordan, W. K., *Edward VI: the Threshold of Power*, 1970.

Keith, R., *An Historical Catologue of the Scottish Bishops*, 1824.

Keith, R., *The History of the Affairs of Church and State in Scotland*, 1844.

Kendall, P. M., *Richard the Third*, 1955.

Kennaway, M., *Fast Castle: the Early Years*, 1992.

Kermack, W. R., *The Scottish Borders to 1603*, 1967.

Kightly, C., *Flodden. The Anglo-Scots War of 1513*, 1975.

Kirby, J. L., *Henry IV of England*, 1970.

Lang, A, *A History of Scotland*, vols 1 and 2, 1907 edition.

Lawrie, J., *The History of the Scottish Wars*, 1825.

Leather, G. F. T., 'The Battle of Flodden' in *History of the Berwickshire Naturalists Club*, vol XXIX, pp 236–269, 1937.

Lewis, N. B., 'The Last Medieval Summons of the English Feudal Levy, 13 June 1385', in the *English Historical Review*, vol 73, pp 1–26, 1958.

Lloyd, J. E., *Owen Glendower*, 1931.

Logan Hume, G. J., 'The Battle of Ancrum Moor', in the *History of the Berwickshire Naturalists Club*, vol XXV, pp 159–165, 1933.

Lomas, R., 'The Impact of Border Warfare: The Scots and South Tweedside, c 1290–1520', in the *Scottish Historical Review*, vol LXXV, pp 143–167, 1996.

McDairmid, M. P., 'The Date of the Wallace', in the *Scottish Historical Review*, vol XXXIV, pp 26–31, 1955.

MacDonald Fraser, G., *The Steel Bonnets*, 1995.

MacDougall, N., 'Scotland's Foreign Relations — England and France', in *Scottish Society in the Fifteenth Century*, edited by J. M. Brown, 1977.

MacDougall, N., *James III*, 1982.

MacDougall, N., 'Bishop Kennedy of St, Andrews: a reassessment of his political career', in *Church, Politics and Society: Scotland 1408–1929*, edited by N. MacDougall, 1983.

MacDougall, N., 'Richard III and James III, Contemporary Monarchs, Parallel Mythologies', in *Richard III: Loyalty, Lordship and Law*, edited by P. W. Hammond, 1986.

MacDougall, N., *James IV*, 1989.

Macfarlane, L. J., *William Elphinstone and the Kingdom of Scotland, 1431–1514*, 1985.

McGladdery, C., *James II*, 1990.

Macinnes, A. I., 'Scotland and the Manx Connection: Relationships of Intermittant Violence, 1266–1603', in the *Isle of Man Natural History and Antiquarian Society*, vol VIII.

MacIvor, I., 'Artillery and the Major Places of Strength in the Lothians and the East Border, 1513–1542', in *Scottish Weapons and Fortifications, 1100–1800*, edited by D. H. Caldwell, 1981.

Mackay Mackenzie, W., *The Secret of Flodden*, 1931.

Mackenzie, A, *History of the MacDonalds and Lords of the Isles*, 1881.

Mackenzie, A. M., *The Rise of the Stewarts*, 1957.

Mackenzie, W. M., 'The Debatable Land', in the *Scottish Historical Review*, vol XXX, pp 109–125, 1951.

Mackie, J. D., 'The English Army at Flodden', in *Miscellany of the Scottish History Society*, third series, vol VIII, 1951.

Mackie, J. D., 'The Auld Alliance and the Battle of Flodden', in *Transactions of the Franco-Scottish Society*, vol VIII, pp 35–56, 1935.

Mackie, J. D., 'Henry VIII and Scotland', in *Transactions of the Royal Historical Society*, fourth series, vol 29, pp 93–114, 1947.

Mackie, J. D., *The Earlier Tudors*, 1966.

Mackie, R. L., *James IV of Scotland*, 1958.

McLaren, M., *If Freedom Fail*, 1964.

McNiven, P., 'The Scottish Policy of the Percies and the Strategy of the Rebellion of 1403', in the *Bulletin of the John Rylands Library*, 62, pp 498–530, 1979–8.

Macrae, C., 'The English Council and Scotland in 1430', in the *English Historical Review*, vol 54, pp 415–426, 1939.

Mack, J. L., *The Border Line*, 1926.

Makinson, A., 'Solway Moss and the Death of James V', in *History Today*, vol 10, pp 106–115, 1960.

Marshall, R. K., *Mary of Guise*, 1977.

Maxwell, H., *A History of Dumfries and Galloway*, 1896.

Megaw, B. R. S., 'The Scottish Invasion of Man in 1456', in the *Journal of the Manx Museum*, vol 6, pp 23–4, 1957.

Merriman, M., 'The Platte of Castlemilk', in *Transactions of the Dumfries-shire and Galloway Natural History and Antiquarian Society*, vol XLIV, pp 175–181, 1967.

# Select Bibliography

Merriman, M., 'The Assured Scots: Scottish Collaboration with England during the Rough Wooing', in the *Scottish Historical Review*, vol 47, pp 10–34, 1968.

Merriman, M., 'War and Propaganda during the Rough Wooing', in *Scottish Tradition*, vol 9/10, pp 20–30, 1979–80.

Merriman, M., 'The Forts of Eyemouth: Anvils of British Union?', in the *Scottish Historical Review*, vol 67, pp 142–155, 1988.

Miller, E., *War in the North*, 1960.

Neilson, G., 'The Battle of Sark', in *Transactions of the Dumfriesshire and Galloway Natural History and Antiquarian Society*, vol 13, pp 122–131, 1898.

Nicholson, R., *Scotland. The Later Middle Ages*, 1974.

Oman, C. W., *Warwick the Kingmaker*, 1891.

Oman, C. W., 'The Art of War' in *Social England*, edited by H. D. Traill and J. S, Mann, vol III, pp 90–101, 1902.

Oman, C. W., 'The Development of the Art of War', in *Social England*, III, pp 288–296, 1902.

Oman, C. W., *The History of England from the Accession of Richard II to the death of Richard III*, 1906.

Oman, C. W., 'The Battle of Pinkie', in *The Archaeological Journal*, vol XC, pp 1–25, including an appendix 'A further note on the Battle of Pinkie' by C. de W. Crookshank, 1933.

Oman, C. W., *A History of the Art of War in the Sixteenth Century*, 1937.

Palmer, J. J. N., *England, France and Christendom*, 1972.

Paul, J. B., 'Ancient Artillery. With some notes on Mons Meg', in *Proceedings of the Society of Antiquaries of Scotland*, vol 50, pp 191–201, 1915–16.

Pease, H., *The Lord Warden of the Marches of England and Scotland*, 1913.

Pollard, A. F., 'The Protector Somerset and Scotland', in the *English Historical Review*, vol 13, pp 464–472, 1898.

Pollard, A. F., *England Under Protector Somerset*, 1900.

Pollard, A. J., *North-Eastern England During the Wars of the Roses*, 1990.

Potter, D. L., 'The Treaty of Boulogne and European Dipolomacy', in the *Bulletin of the Institute of Historical Research*, vol 55–6, pp 50–65, 1982–3.

Prebble, J., *The Lion in the North*, 1971.

Rae, T. I., *The Administration of the Scottish Frontier, 1513–1603*, 1966.

Raine, J., *The History and Antiquties of North Durham*, 1852.

Rait, R. S., *Relations between England and Scotland*, 1901.

Ramsay, J. H., *Lancaster and York*, 2 vols, 1892.

Ramsay, J. H., *The Genesis of Lancaster*, 2 vols, 1913.

Richmond, C. F., 'English Naval Power in the Fifteenth Century', in *History*, vol 52, pp 1–15, 1967.

Ridley, J., *John Knox*, 1968.

Ridley, J., *Henry VIII*, 1985.

Ridley, J., *Elizabeth I*, 1987.

Ridpath, G., *The Border History of England and Scotland*, 1810 edition.
Robson, J., *Border Battles and Battlefields*, 1897.
Ross, C., *Edward IV*, 1975.
Sadler, J., *Battle for Northumbria*, 1988.
Sanderson, M. H. B., *Cardinal of Scotland. David Beaton, c 1494–1546*, 1986.
Scofield, C. L., *The Life and Reign of Edward the Fourth*, 2 vols, 1923.
Scott, W., *Minstrelsey of the Scottish Borders*, 1932.
Stewart Black, C., *Scottish Battles*, 1936.
Seward, D., *The Hundred Years War*, 1978.
Seward, D., *Henry V as Warlord*, 1987.
Seymour, W., *Battles in Britain, 1066–1547*, 1975.
Simpson, M. A., 'The Campaign of Verneuil', in the *English Historical Review*, vol 49, pp 93–100, 1934.
Sinclair, G. A., 'The Scots at Solway Moss', in the *Scottish Historical Review*, vol II, pp 372–377, 1905.
Slavin, A. J., *Politics and Profit. A Study of Sir Ralph Sadler, 1507–1547*, 1966.
Steel, A., *Richard II*, 1962.
Stephen, L. and Lee, S eds., *The Dictionary of National Biography*, 1908–09.
Steuart, A. F., 'Inchkeith and the French Occupation', in *Transactions of the Franco-Scottish Society*, part 1 vol VII, pp 36–96, 1920.
Storey, R. L., 'The Wardens of the March Towards Scotland, 1377–1489', in the *English Historical Review*, vol 72, pp 593–615, 1957.
Storey, R. L., *Thomas Langley and the Bishopric of Durham, 1406–1437*, 1961.
Stuart, M. W., *The Scot who was a Frenchman*, 1940.
Swinton, G. S. C., 'John of Swinton: A Border Fighter of the Middle Ages', in the *Scottish Historical Review*, vol XVI. pp 261–279, 1919.
Taylor, J., *The Great Historic Families of Scotland*, 2 vols, 1889.
Tuck, J. A., 'Richard II and the Border Magnates', in *Northern History*, vol III, pp 27–52, 1968.
Tuck, J. A., 'The Emergence of the Northern Nobility', in *Northern History*, vol XXII, pp 1–17, 1968.
Tuck, J. A., *Richard II and the English Nobility*, 1973.
Tucker, M. J., *The Life of Thomas Howard, Earl of Surrey and Second Duke of Norfolk, 1443–1524*, 1964.
Tyson, C., 'The Battle of Otterburn: When and Where was it Fought?', in *War and Border Societies*, edited by Goodman, A. and Tuck, A., 1992.
Tytler, P. F., *History of Scotland*, vols III, IV, V and VI, 1841.
Veitch, J., *History and Poetry of the Scottish Border*, 2 vols 1893.
Walton, R. H., 'The Otterburn Story', in the *History of Berwickshire Naturalists Club*, vol 35, pp 217–255, 1961.
Weir, A., *Lancaster and York: the Wars of The Roses*, 1995.
Werham, R. B., *Before the Armada. The Growth of English Foreign Policy, 1485–1588*, 1966.
Wesencraft, C. F., *The Battle of Otterburn*, 1988.
White, R. H., *The History of the Battle of Otterburn*, 1857.

# Select Bibliography

White, R. H., 'The Battle of Flodden', in *Archaeologia Aeliania*, vol III, pp 197–236, 1859.

Williams, R., *The Lords of the Isles*, 1984.

Wolffe, B., *Henry VI*, 1981.

Wormald, J., *Mary Queen of Scots. A Study in Failure*, 1988.

Wylie, J, H., *History of England under Henry the Fourth*, 4 vols, 1884–1898.

Wylie, J. II., *The Reign of Henry V*, three vols, vol III with N. T. Waugh, 1914–1929.

## Unpublished PhD Theses

Cardew, A. A., *A Study of Society in the Anglo-Scottish Border, 1455–1502*, St Andrews University, 1974.

Ditcham, B. G. H., *The Employment of Foreign Mercenary Troops in the French Royal Armies, 1415–1470*, Edinburgh University 1979.

MacRae, C., *Scotland and the Wars of the Roses*, D. Phil, Oxford University, 1939.

Merriman, M., *The Struggle for the Marriage of Mary Queen of Scots: English and French Intervention in Scotland, 1543–1550*, University of London, 1974.

# Index

# Index

Bannockburn, the Battle of (1314) 32, 42, 83, 139, 196, 197
Bardolph, Lord 37, 39
Barmoor near Lowick 50, 140, 158
Barnet, the Battle of (1471) 99, 124
Barton, Andrew 129, 130, 134, 138
Bass, Rock, castle on 38
Bauge, the Battle of (1421) 58, 59, 60, 61, 63, 75
Beaton, David, Cardinal and Archbishop of St. Andrews 161, 162, 163, 164, 166, 170, 171, 172, 173, 174, 175, 176, 184, 186, 187, 189
Beaufort, Edmund, Earl of Mortain, subsequently Duke of Somerset 74, 83
Beaufort, Cardinal Henry 53, 54, 72, 74
Beaufort, Joan, Queen of Scots 53, 54
Beaufort, John, Earl of Somerset 59, 60
Beaufort, Thomas, Duke of Exeter 50
Beaufort, Margaret 99
Beaumont, John 18
Beaumont-le-Cletif
Bedford, John of Lancaster, Duke of 40, 41, 46, 47, 50, 56, 62, 63, 64, 65, 66, 68, 70, 77
Belling Hill 152
Benolt, Thomas 156
Berwick-upon-Tweed, town and castle 1, 2, 5, 6, 7, 8, 10, 18, 23, 26, 36, 37, 41, 46, 48, 50, 73, 74, 75, 78, 85, 86, 88, 89, 90, 91, 92, 93, 95, 101, 103, 104, 105, 106, 107, 108, 109, 111, 113, 114, 116, 119, 120, 122, 125, 126, 127, 128, 140, 147, 152, 156, 161, 163, 180, 188, 192, 194, 205, 206, 214
the Treaty of (1560) 207
Berwickshire 1, 29, 134, 192
Blackfriars, Ayr 198
Blackfriars, Perth 74
Blackheath, the Battle of (1497) 123
Blackness 42, 104, 201
Blind Harry, author of *The Wallace* 101, 159
Bohemia 72
Bois-de-Vincennes 62
Boisrufin 61
Boleyn, Anne 206
Bolingbroke, Henry, see Henry IV
Bolton-in-Glendale 137, 139
Booth, William, Archbishop of York 95
Boroughmuir, Edinburgh 134, 179
Borthwick, Robert 133, 136, 141, 142, 143, 147

Bosworth Field, the Battle of (1485) 113, 124, 147
Bothwell, Patrick Hepburn, 3d Lord Hailes, 1st Earl of 107, 108, 116
Bothwell, Adam Hepburn, 2nd Earl of 134, 142, 145, 147
Bothwell, Patrick Hepburn, 3d Earl of 160, 173, 101
Boulogne 184, 187, 188, 191, 192, 203
the Treaty of ( 1550) 203, 205
Bourbon, Charles de, Comte de Clermont 68
Bourges in Berry 57, 63, 64
Bower, Walter, Abbot of Inchcolm 74, 75
Bowes, Sir Robert 164, 171, 182
Bowes, Richard 164
Bowet, Henry, Archbishop of York 50
Bramham Moor, the Battle of (1408) 39
Brandon, Charles, Duke of Suffolk 157, 176
Branspeth 12, 92
Branx Bridge 140, 141, 142
Branxton Hill 138, 140, 141, 142, 144, 147
Branxton Tower 121
Bristol 178
Brézé, Pierre de 94, 95
Britanny, the Duchy of 115, 116, 206
Brodick Castle 37
Broke, Lord Willoughby de 63
Broke, Lord Willoughby de 112
Broomhouse Tower 181, 183
Broughty Craig, fortress at 200, 203
Bruges, Louis de, Seigneur de le Gruthuyse 90
Brunstane 201
Brunton, Alexander, of Earlshall 131
Buchan, the Master of 198
Buckingham, the Duke of 111
Bull, Stephen 115
Bulleners, the 192, 196
Bulmer, Sir William 135, 137, 156, 157
Burgundy, Charles the Bold, 4th Duke of 102
Burgundy, John the Fearless, 2nd Duke of 55, 56, 57
Burgundy, Margaret of York, dowger Duchess of 118
Burgundy, Philip the Good, 3d Duke of 57, 77, 78, 80, 87, 89, 90, 99
Burnt Candelmas, the (1356) 5
Bute, the Isle of 177
Butler, Catherine 117

227

# Index

# Index

# Index